INNOVATION IN PUBLIC TRANSPORT FINANCE

Transport and Mobility Series

Series Editors: Richard Knowles, University of Salford, UK and Markus Hesse, Université du Luxembourg and on behalf of the Royal Geographical Society (with the Institute of British Geographers) Transport Geography Research Group (TGRG).

The inception of this series marks a major resurgence of geographical research into transport and mobility. Reflecting the dynamic relationships between socio-spatial behaviour and change, it acts as a forum for cutting-edge research into transport and mobility, and for innovative and decisive debates on the formulation and repercussions of transport policy making.

Also in the series

Hub Cities in the Knowledge Economy
Seaports, Airports, Brainports
Edited by Sven Conventz, Ben Derudder, Alain Thierstein and Frank Witlox
ISBN 978 1 4094 4591 3

Institutional Barriers to Sustainable Transport
Carey Curtis and Nicholas Low
ISBN 978 0 7546 7692 8

Daily Spatial Mobilities
Physical and Virtual
Aharon Kellerman
ISBN 978 1 4094 2362 1

Territorial Implications of High Speed Rail
A Spanish Perspective
Edited by José M. de Ureña
ISBN 978 1 4094 3052 0

Sustainable Transport, Mobility Management and Travel Plans
Marcus Enoch
ISBN 978 0 7546 7939 4

Innovation in Public Transport Finance

Property Value Capture

SHISHIR MATHUR
San Jose State University, USA

Routledge
Taylor & Francis Group

LONDON AND NEW YORK

First published 2014 by Ashgate Publishing

Published 2016 by Routledge
2 Park Square, Milton Park, Abingdon, Oxfordshire OX14 4RN
711 Third Avenue, New York, NY 10017, USA

First issued in paperback 2016

Routledge is an imprint of the Taylor & Francis Group, an informa business

British Library Cataloguing in Publication Data
A catalogue record for this book is available from the British Library

The Library of Congress has cataloged the printed edition as follows:
Mathur, Shishir.
  Innovation in public transport finance : property value capture / by Shishir Mathur.
    pages cm -- (Transport and mobility)
  Summary: "The vast majority of funding for public transportation comes from local and national governments. With all levels of governments currently, and for the foreseeable future, under significant fiscal stress, any new transit funding mechanism is to be welcomed. Value capture (VC) is one such mechanism, which involves the identification and capture of a public infrastructure-led increase in property value"--Provided by publisher.
  Includes bibliographical references and index.
  ISBN 978-1-4094-6260-6 (hardback)
1. Local transit--United States--Finance. 2. Urban transportation--United States--Finance. 3. Real property--Valuation. 4. Impact fees. I. Title. II. Series: Transport and mobility series.
  HE4461.M433 2014
  388.4'042--dc23

                                                                  2014000195

ISBN 13: 978-1-138-25013-0 (pbk)
ISBN 13: 978-1-4094-6260-6 (hbk)

Contents

To my parents,
Hemendra Shanker Mathur and Mridula Mathur

my wife,
Richa

and my sons,
Tanmay and Anay

List of Figures

List of Tables

List of Abbreviations

ABAG	Association of Bay Area Governments
ACS	American Community Survey
AGI	Adjusted Gross Income
APTA	American Public Transportation Association
ATF	Bureau of Alcohol, Tobacco, Firearms and Explosives
ATP	Ability-to-Pay
BAAQMD	Bay Area Air Quality Management District
BAD	Benefit Assessment District
BART	Bay Area Rapid Transit District
BCDC	Bay Conservation and Development Commission
BCT	Broward County Transit
BMCLP	Bethesda Metro Center Limited Partnership
BMJD	Bethesda Metro Joint Development
BRT	Bus Rapid-Transit
BTP	Beneficiary-To-Pay
CALTRANS	California Department of Transportation
CARB	California Air Resource Board
CSAC	California State Association of Counties
CBD	Central Business District
CCC	Contra Costa Centre
CDFA	Council of Development Finance Agencies
CFD	Community Facilities District
CIP	Capital Improvement Plan
CMAP	Chicago Metropolitan Agency for Planning
CMAQ	Congestion Mitigation and Air Quality Improvement Program
CPI	Consumer Price Index
CRA	California Redevelopment Association
CTA	Chicago Transit Authority
CTIDF	Comprehensive Transportation Impact Development Fee
DCST	DC Surface Transit, Inc.
DCTA	Dade County Transportation Administration
DDA	Disposition and Development Agreement
DOT	Department of Transportation
DP	Development Plan
EPA	United States Environmental Protection Agency
ET	Equivalent Tenement
FAR	Floor Area Ratio

FHWA	Federal Highway Administration
FTA	Federal Transit Administration
FTCBB	Foothill Transportation Corridor Backbone
FY	Fiscal Year
GAO	United States Government Accountability Office
GDP	Gross Domestic Product
GHG	Green House Gas
GLA	Gross Leasable Area
GTPUDA	Gujarat Town Planning and Urban Development Act
HKSAR	Hong Kong Special Administrative Region
HTF	Highway Trust Fund
HUD	United States Department of Housing and Urban Development
IBGE	Instituto Brasileiro de Geografia e Estatística
ICU	Infrastructure Contribution Unit
ISTEA	Intermodal Surface Transportation Efficiency Act
ITIA	Illinois Tax Increment Association
JDA	Joint Development Agreement
JPA	Joint Powers Authority
KCRC	Kowloon–Canton Railway Corporation
LACMTA	Los Angeles County Metropolitan Transit Authority
LACTC	Los Angeles County Transportation Commission
LED	Light-Emitting Diode
LID	Local Improvement District
LPR	Land Pooling and Readjustment
LVT	Land Value Taxation
MARTA	Metropolitan Atlanta Rapid Transit Authority
MDT	Miami-Dade Transit
MFI	Median Family Income
MOU	Memorandum of Understanding
MPO	Metropolitan Planning Organization
MTA	Metropolitan Transportation Authority
MTC	Metropolitan Transportation Commission
MTRC	Mass Transit Railway Corporation
MTRCL	Mass Transit Railway Corporation Limited
NoI	Notification of Intention
NoMa	North of Massachusetts Area
NPS	National Park Service
PBOT	Portland Bureau of Transportation
PDA	Priority Development Area
PDC	Portland Development Commission
PMSA	Primary Metropolitan Statistical Area
PPP	Public-Private Partnership
PRC	People's Republic of China
PSP	Planning Scheme Policies

RCW	Revised Code of Washington
RDA	Redevelopment Agency
RFD	Rural Free Delivery
RFP	Request for Proposal
RFQ	Request for Qualifications
RSQI	Rail Service Quality Index
RTZ	Rapid-Transit Zone
SAD	Special Assessment District
SADD	Station Area Design and Development
SAF	Special Assessment Factor
SAFETEA-LU	Safe, Affordable, Flexible, Efficient Transportation Equity Act-A Legacy For Users
SCRTD	Southern California Rapid Transit District
SDC	System-Development Charges
SFCTA	San Francisco County Transportation Authority
SFMTA	San Francisco Municipal Transportation Agency
SJHTC	San Joaquin Hills Transportation Corridor
STP	Surface Transportation Program
TCEA	Transportation Concurrency Exception Area
TDR	Transfer of Development Rights
TEA-21	Transportation Equity Act for the 21st Century
TIDF	Transit Impact Development Fee
TIF	Tax Increment Financing
TOD	Transit-Oriented Development
TPO	Town Planning Officer
TRID	Transit Revitalization Investment District
TSDC	Transportation System Development Charge
UCA	Urbanization Control Area
UITP	International Association of Public Transportation
UMTA	Urban Mass Transportation Assistance Act
UO	Urban Operations
UPA	Urbanization Promotion Area
URA	Urban Renewal Area
USDOT	United States Department of Transportation
VC	Value Capture
VMT	Vehicles Miles Travelled
VTA	Santa Clara Valley Transportation Authority
WMATA	Washington Metropolitan Area Transit Authority

Preface

Four key factors that have impacted the transit funding landscape in the US prompted me to write this book. First, maintaining urban transit systems that are financially self-sustaining through fare-box revenue alone is extremely difficult. In fact, none of the major transit systems in the US are able to fully cover transit system operating expenses, let alone capital expenditures. Internationally, except for perhaps Hong Kong's Metro system, none of the major transit systems are financially self-sustaining. Even Hong Kong's transit system often depends upon revenues from real estate development and capital grants from the Hong Kong government.

Second, while at the federal level there is an increasing realization of the many benefits of providing transit in urban areas, this realization is not matched by financial assistance. Federal transit funds as a percentage of total transit expenditures have hovered around 15–20 percent for more than a decade.

Third, over the last two to three decades, the general disposition of the taxpayers in the US lies in moving away from a cross-subsidization principle to a beneficiary-to-pay principle. Therefore, local residents who do not see a direct benefit from transit frequently oppose the use of their tax dollars to fund transit systems. In the face of such headwinds, the local agencies that are often in charge of developing and running transit systems find themselves in a tremendous fiscal bind. These local agencies are desperate to find new funding sources that yield significant revenues that are administratively not very complicated, and that are legally and politically feasible.

Finally, an increasing number of empirical studies show that several types of public infrastructure and services, including the mobility and accessibility provided by transit systems, increase property values. This finding, given constrained transit funding, has piqued the interest of policy makers, practitioners and researchers and has encouraged them to explore ways in which transit-system-led increases in property value can be identified and captured to fund transit that has led to such increases in the first place. In short, how do we use "value capture" or "property value capture" to fund transit?

I am not suggesting that value capture is a brand new financing tool. In fact its variants have been used in the US since the seventeenth century and from much earlier around the world. However, relatively recent is the desire to systematically investigate ways in which we can use this mechanism to fund public transit. This book, through several US-wide case studies and a few international case studies, reviews the use of various property value capture mechanisms to fund transit. These mechanisms include special assessment districts, tax increment financing, transit impact fee, and joint development projects. I have tried to balance the theory and practice of property value capture so that the book could be useful to a wide range of audience.

This book would not have been possible without the help of several individuals who provided key project-specific information. They are: Lisa Abouf, Froilan Baez, Martin Berger, Joanne Carr, Karla Damian, Brad DeBrower, Vicky Diede, Albert Hernandez, James Kennedy, Kathryn Levine, Ethan Malone, Jay Reyes, Charles Rivasplata, Rick Rybeck, Mark Segun, Ted Tarantino, and Jason Ward. Finally, very special thanks to Adam Smith for his diligent research support.

I am extremely grateful to the Mineta Transportation Institute for funding the research for this book, especially the case study chapters (5–9), and to the College of Social Sciences at San Jose State University for providing research grant for this book project.

Errors of fact or interpretation are my responsibility alone.

Chapter 1

The Evolution of Public Transportation Funding in the US

Introduction

The transportation funding stew in the US is a multi-flavored concoction of public and private funding that consists of an array of federal, state and local government programs and mandates, public-private partnerships (PPPs), and private investments. Indeed, as of the year 2008, total government spending in the US on highways and public transportation exceeded $230 billion, of which $55 billion were spent on transit and $182 billion were spent on highways (FHWA, 2010; APTA, 2012). The highway system is almost entirely dependent on government funding, while transit-system-generated revenues accounted for almost a quarter (26.1 percent) of total transit revenues (FHWA, 2010).

The federal role in transportation funding is almost as old as the country itself. However, the beginnings of federal transportation funding were humble. In 1789, 13 years after the US gained independence, the US Congress authorized funds for the construction of lighthouses, beacons and buoys (USDOT, 2009). A couple of decades later, the first federal highway program, the National Road, was commissioned in 1806. Completed in 1839 (Bahadori, 2008), the 824-mile road connected Baltimore, MD and Vandalia, IL, passing through the six states of Illinois, Indiana, Ohio, Pennsylvania, Maryland and West Virginia (FHWA, 2012). The road also served as a model for federal involvement in the development of road transportation projects.

Further impetus to expand the nation's transportation infrastructure was provided in the first half of the nineteenth century by the construction of waterways and railroads. Constructed in 1820, the 363-mile-long Erie Canal for the first time allowed movement of people and goods from the Atlantic Ocean directly to the Great Lakes. In the following decades, similar transportation accessibility was provided by the Chesapeake and Ohio Canal and the Baltimore and Ohio Railroad. Opened in 1831, the 185-mile-long Chesapeake and Ohio Canal boosted trade by linking Cumberland, MD with Washington, DC (NPS, 2011). The Baltimore & Ohio Railroad, the nation's first common carrier railroad, heralded the era of railroads in the country. Construction on a 13-mile stretch commenced in 1828 and ended in 1874. By then, the railroad had linked 13 states through its 811-mile span from Baltimore, MD, to Chicago, IL (America-Rails.com, 2012).

While the National Road and the canals provided accessibility at the regional and inter-state levels, city transportation was dominated by horse- or mule-driven carriages and streetcars until the mid nineteenth century. The horses were given a reprieve with the advent of cable street cars in 1873, when the first cable street car began operating in San Francisco, and electric street cars, called trolley cars, which began operating for the first time in Richmond, VA in 1888 (IEEE Global History Network, 2012). The trolley cars received a big boost in 1890 when Boston decided to replace its fleet of carriages driven by 8000-plus horses with trolley cars (Turner, 2012). Thereafter, the share of trolley cars increased progressively. While in 1880, the 2,050-mile-long streetcar network was entirely horse-driven, a decade later, in 1890, of the 5,800-mile-long streetcar system, approximately 500 miles was cable operated, 1,200 miles was operated with trolley cars, and the remaining 4,100 mile network was horse driven. By 1912, almost the entire 30,000-mile-plus network was trolley-car-driven (Vuchic, 2007). The significant increase in mobility provided by trolley cars allowed people to live further away from the congested and often highly polluted urban core, while still allowing people to the urban core for work. These residential suburban developments are commonly known as streetcar suburbs. Developed all across the country, well known examples of streetcars suburbs include West Hollywood and Highland Park in the Los Angeles area, Chevy Chase in the Washington DC area, and Brighton and Dorchester in the Boston area.

The Decline of Trolley Cars and the Rise of the Automobile

Owned by private companies, several thousand street car systems operated in the country at their zenith in the decade of 1910s, with an annual ridership of approximately 12 billion trips (Schrag, 2002). Thereafter, a multitude of factors, including labor unrest, high operating cost, and competition from buses and personal automobiles, led to the demise of street cars; the age of cars had arrived. Further, it has been argued that vested interests including car, truck, tire, and oil companies, such as General Motors (GM), Mack Truck Company, Firestone Tire and Rubber Company, and Standard Oil, undermined transit companies and hastened the collapse of streetcars in the US. Indeed, in 1947 GM and a few other corporations were indicted on two counts. The first count was conspiring to "monopolize part of the interstate trade and commerce of the United States, to wit, that part consisting of the sale of busses, petroleum products, tires and tubes used by local transportation systems in those cities … in which defendants … owned, controlled or had a substantial financial interest in, or had acquired, or in the future should acquire ownership, control or a substantial financial interest in such transportation systems" (United States *v.* National City Lines, 1951). The second count was conspiring and conducting unlawful activities to gain control of several local transit companies. These companies were only convicted of the first count of conspiring to monopolize interstate bus market, not the second count of conspiring to gain control of local public transit companies. Conviction on the second count was essential for making the case that these companies took control of the transit companies to engineer the downfall of the transit system.

The belief that these companies conspired to affect the downfall of transit did not completely die with the 1949 court verdict. In fact, this belief gained a new lease of life with Bradford Snell's 1974 statement before the US Senate sub-committee on anti-trust and monopoly. Snell was an anti-trust lawyer for the US Senate. His testimony accused GM of conspiring to take control of electric-street-car-based local transit systems and subsequently replace the electric street cars with diesel-based GM buses. Snell argued that the noisy and less convenient buses turned away public transit patrons and ultimately led to the demise of local transit systems across the US (US Senate, 1974). Snell's statement was supported by the testimonies of Mayor Alieota of Los Angeles and Mayor Bradley of San Francisco. Both the mayors noted that automakers, oil companies, and tire companies colluded to eliminate electric streetcars, which were these companies' main competitor in Los Angeles (Slater, 1997). Although the academic literature (see Adler, 1991; Post, 2003; Thompson, 1993; Slater 1997) finds little supporting evidence, this "conspiracy theory" gained the attention of popular media, including a documentary movie titled "Taken for a Ride" (Slater, 1997).

In any case, auto ownership boomed in the ensuing decades, increasing the need for building more and better roads. Road building, which had up until the beginning of the twentieth century remained a largely private enterprise,[1] received national prominence when the Good Roads Movement started in the late nineteenth century by bicycling enthusiasts who very strongly advocated for better quality roads. Soon farmers joined the movement, motivated by the need for drivable roads that would allow the farmers to take advantage of the US Government's Rural Free Delivery (RFD) service, which began in 1896 (Weingroff, 1996b). This service allowed delivery of mail directly to the farms. Finally, the mass production of automobiles that began in the early twentieth century made cars accessible to ordinary people, not just the rich. The Good Roads Movement gathered further steam as ordinary motorists joined the movement.

Road building received a significant boost from the Federal Aid Road Act of 1916. The Act provided $75 million over five years in the form of a 50–50 federal-state match. The federal funds, not to exceed $10,000 per mile, were to be used for the construction of roads that would facilitate mail delivery to rural areas. These roads were designated "rural post roads" (Weingroff, 1996a). Furthermore, the Act required states to create highway agencies that would professionally administer this federal aid program. This Act paved the way for future federal funding for roads.

---

1   More than 5,000 companies operated approximately 30,000–50,000 miles of toll roads (Klein and Majewski, 2008).

Development of the Concept of a National Highway System

The concept of a national highway system matured in the 1920s and 1930s, sharpening into focus in 1941 when President Franklin D. Roosevelt directed the National Interregional Highway Committee to develop a national system of highways to serve the needs of the military during World War II and the anticipated vehicular traffic after the war. The committee provided its recommendations in 1944, the same year the Federal-Aid Highway Act of 1944 was promulgated. The Act provided for designation of up to 40,000 miles of a National System of Interstate Highways. As a result, approximately 38,000 miles of interstate highways were identified over the next three years. However, the Act did not authorize funds for the development of an interstate system, a situation which was not rectified until almost a decade later through the Federal-Aid Highway Acts of 1952 and 1954. The 1952 Act authorized $25 million per year for the construction of interstate highways, with a federal match of 50 percent. The 1954 Act increased federal aid to $175 million per year and the federal match to 60 percent (Williamson, 2012).

Meanwhile, after World War II, government-backed low interest and low down payment home mortgages fueled a housing boom that led to further sub-urbanization (Burchell et al., 1998). Low-density suburbanization, popularly called sprawl, was further aided by local policies, such as zoning laws that necessitated the segregation of land uses and specified minimum lot and home sizes and transportation policies that gave cars supremacy over other modes of transportation. Vehicle ownership had reached 1.43 vehicles per household by 1950 (United States Department of Energy, 2012). This auto-oriented suburbanization was also aided by government-subsidized road development and in turn fueled the need for more and better quality roads. The Federal government responded, both to meet the national defense requirements as well as to connect the major regions and cities of the country.

Federal Funds for the Interstate Highway System

Then a Lt. Colonel in the US Army, President Dwight G. Eisenhower volunteered for a US Army transcontinental motor convoy sent to assess the feasibility of traversing the country on the road. In 1919, the convoy covered the 3,200-mile distance between Washington, DC and San Francisco over a period of 62 days at an average speed of six miles per hour (Weingroff, 1996b). During the trip, the convoy encountered several mechanical failures, broken bridges, muddy or non-existent roads, and personnel injuries. That trip convinced the young Lt. Colonel of the need to connect different parts of the country with better and uniform quality roads for efficient movement of people and goods. That dream was realized when as President he signed the Federal-Aid Highway Act of 1956. The Act authorized an interstate highway system of 41,000 miles and $25 billion in government funding for the period of 1957 to 1969 (United States Department of Interior, 2004) with a 90 percent federal match. The 90 percent match was a significant increase from the then prevalent norm of a 50 to 60 percent federal match.[2] The Act required highways to adhere to uniform design standards and to meet traffic requirement for the year of 1975 (Weingroff, 1996b).[3]

Equally significant from the perspective of transportation finance was the companion Highway Revenue Act of 1956 that created a dedicated revenue source for highway development through the creation of the Highway Trust Fund (HTF). This Act also authorized a one-cent-per-gallon increase to the gas tax. The entire tax increase was dedicated to funding the interstate system (Transportation for America, 2011).[4] The Act also directed revenue from excise taxes on gasoline, tire rubber, and tube rubber and the sales tax on new trucks, buses, and trailers to the HTF (FHWA, 2011a).

The Evolution of Federal Funding for Public Transportation

While roads and highways benefitted from federal aid, federal aid for public transportation was scarce. From the horse-drawn carriages of the eighteenth and nineteenth century to the trolley ways of the late nineteenth and early twentieth century, public transportation had historically relied on private investments. The rapid rise of automobiles in the first half of the twentieth century sent many transit companies out of business, and except for a brief period during the austere World War II period, transit ridership declined from the mid-1920s to the mid-1970s (see Figure 1.1, p.6). At its lowest, only 6.6 billion transit trips were undertaken in 1973. This dip coincided with the heydays of highway building. Since then transit has witnessed a bit of a revival, with 10.2 billion trips undertaken in the year 2010 (APTA, 2012).

Up until the 1960s, public transportation was viewed by most as a local issue, not a national issue. Hence, transit funding was deemed not worthy of federal aid. This line of thought is being refined for three key reasons.

First, public transportation is advocated as key to inner city revitalization. The rapid sub-urbanization after World War II was aided by highway development that opened vast rural hinterland for urban development and that provided an opportunity for households to move out from the congested and polluted urban

---

2   Although scheduled for completion by 1969, the Interstate Highway program is still not complete. However, the federal government share of the cost of Interstate construction ended in FY 1996. By then, $119 billion had been authorized through various Acts to pay the federal share (FHWA, 2011b).

3   The Act was later modified to accommodate traffic forecasts for 20 years.

4   The Gas Tax was first levied in 1932. From 1932 till 1952 it was levied at the rate of one-cent-per-gallon. In 1952 it was raised to two-cents-per-gallon. The entire gas tax revenue went to the US Federal Government General Fund (FHWA, 2011a).

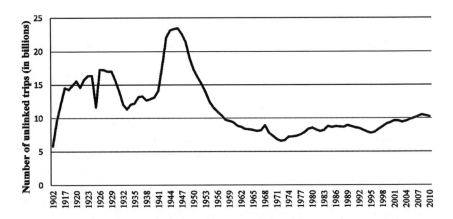

Figure 1.1   Historical trends for transit use in the US
Source: APTA 2012 Public Transportation Factbook, Table 1.

cores of cities. Often, people with the financial means were the first to move out, leaving the poor behind. Furthermore, government policies and private sector activities led to racial and economic segregation (Schill and Wachter, 1995). As a result, the urban cores of major cities found themselves in a downward spiral of decreasing revenues, high crime and poverty, and abandonment. Furthermore, amid declining city population and strong competition from automobiles, private transit companies were either bankrupt or were on the verge of bankruptcy in many large cities, such as Chicago and New York. Such companies were often acquired by the city governments. For example, in 1947, the City of Chicago consolidated two privately-held companies, the Chicago Surface Lines (the trolley car operator) and the Chicago Rapid Transit Company (the elevated rail service operator) into the city's public transit agency, the Chicago Transit Authority (CTA, 2011). Similarly, in the 1940s, New York City acquired several private transit companies including the Brooklyn-Manhattan Transit Corporation, which operated the subway service between Brooklyn and Manhattan, and The Interborough Rapid Transit Company which operated the city's first subway system, a 9.1-mile-long subway line in Manhattan (MTA, 2012). As the owners of transit systems, cash-strapped city governments lobbied for federal aid for transit and highlighted the key role that transit plays in arresting the decline of urban areas and in revitalizing inner city areas (Transportation for America, 2011).

Second, beginning in the late 1960s, citizens concerned about deteriorating environmental quality and the displacement of families due to highway projects became increasingly vocal about the negative impacts of highway development. These concerned citizens often questioned the need for highways. Therefore, in 1969, highway development policies were revised to allow for citizen participation at all stages of highway planning and development, including the early stage of identifying the need for highways (Weiner, 1999).

Third, there was an increasing realization of the need to coordinate land development and transportation policies, and to provide several transportation options to the public.

The above three factors led to the recognition of urban transportation, specifically public transportation, as a national issue worthy of federal attention. In 1962, the stage was set for a direct federal role in urban public transportation to emerge when President Kennedy, on the recommendation of a report on urban mass transportation prepared by the secretary of commerce and the housing and home finance administration, highlighted the key role that mass transportation plays in the viability and livability of American cities (Bianco, 1998). Soon thereafter, the federal government provided direct assistance to public transportation for the first time when Congress authorized up to $150 million per year for public transit under the Urban Mass Transportation Assistance Act (UMTA) of 1964.[5] The federal commitment was expanded under the UMTA 1970, which authorized $3.1 billion for FY 1971 and committed approximately $10 billion over 12 years towards transit capital expenditures on a 50 percent federal match basis. The National Mass Transportation Assistance Act of 1974 expanded the federal role further by authorizing $11.8 billion over six years, allowing the funds at the 50 percent federal match level to be used for transit operating expenses as well and by increasing the federal match for capital expenses from 50 to 80 percent. The Surface Transportation Assistance Act of 1978 increased federal funding for public transportation to $13.6 billion to be spent over four years (Weiner, 1999). Significant strides were made in the development of transit systems during the 1970s and as a result, transit ridership increased by more than 30 percent between 1972 and 1980 (FTA, 2012a).

The federal government under the Reagan Administration significantly cut aid to transit in the decade of the 1980s, including a cut of 20 percent in 1982 alone (Hess and Lombardi, 2005). Consecutively, transit ridership grew only a lethargic three percent during this decade (FTA, 2012a). However, a major new federal-level revenue source was created for transit when the Surface Transportation Assistance Act of 1982 dedicated a one-cent-per-gallon gas tax revenue to transit and required that the revenues be placed in a mass transit account of the HTF (Hess and Lombardi, 2005).

The diminishing contribution of federal funds to public transportation that started in the 1980s continued into the 1990s and well into the twenty-first century. The funding gap was filled by local and state governments. Indeed, during the period from 1994 to 2008, the federal contribution to transit funding ranged between 15 and 18 percent, and the state and local contribution between 36 and 42 percent, and the contribution of system generated revenue ranged from 12 to 17 percent (see Figure 1.2, p. 8). On a positive note, the renewed focus on multimodal transportation provided by the Intermodal Surface Transportation Efficiency Act of 1991 (ISTEA) and the Transportation Equity Act for the 21st Century (TEA-

---

5   However, the actual spending fell well-short of the $150 million per year amount.

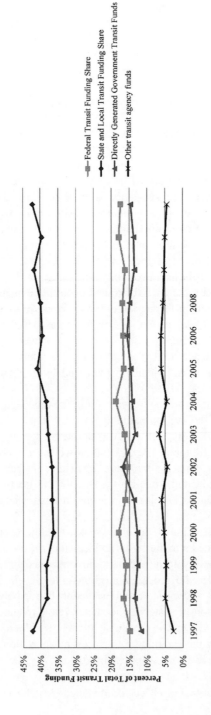

Figure 1.2   Transit funding: 1997–2008

Sources: Transit funds: APTA 2012 Public Transportation Factbook, Table 71; highway funding data from 1957 until 2006: Exhibit 6-7, http://www. fhwa.dot.gov [accessed: 2.11.14]; 2008 highway funding data: Exhibit 6-1, http://www.fhwa.dot.gov/ [accessed: 2.11.14].

21) of 1998 led to higher flexibility in the use of federal funds. For example, the Federal Highway Administration (FHWA) Surface Transportation Program (STP) funds, the Congestion Mitigation and Air Quality Improvement Program (CMAQ), and the Federal Transit Administration (FTA) Urban Formula Funds can be used for both highways and transit (FTA, 2012b).

Public Transportation and Climate Change

Concerns regarding the environmental impact of vehicular emissions were renewed in the 1990s. The nation's population increased by about 150 percent between 1970 and 2012, from 203 to 309 million, while the annual vehicles miles travelled (VMT) increased by more than 250 percent (see Figure 1.3, p. 10), from 11.2 trillion vehicle miles to 29.66 trillion vehicle miles. Furthermore, the transportation sector contributed more than a quarter of the greenhouse gas (GHG) emissions in the country and almost half of the increase in such emissions between 1990 and 2010 (EPA, 2012). Vehicular carbon emissions from cars and light duty vehicles comprised 40 percent of all such transportation sector emissions globally in the year 2003 (Fung, Fung and Feng, 2006, p. 2), with the US contributing almost half of the global carbon emissions emanating from cars and light duty vehicles. Therefore, concerns were raised about the impact of vehicular emissions on local and regional air quality as well as on global warming and climate change.

At the national level, several key pieces of federal legislation sought to reduce the environmental impacts of transportation. While earlier legislation, such as the Clean Air Act of 1970, focused on reducing vehicular emissions though technological improvements and changes to fuel-type and composition, later legislation, such as the Clean Air Act of 1990, the ISTEA and the TEA-21, and more recently the Safe, Accountable, Flexible, Efficient Transportation Equity Act: A Legacy for Users (SAFETEA-LU) of 2005 and the American Recovery and Reinvestment Act of 2009, also focused on travel demand management strategies by encouraging the development of multi-modal transportation systems and by requiring a regional approach to transportation planning and land use-transportation coordination.

At the state level, climate change concerns led California to voluntarily develop initiatives to reduce the state's GHG emissions. Specifically, the California Global Warming Solutions Act of 2006 (AB 32) seeks to reduce GHG emissions by 2020 to the 1990 levels, or a 30 percent reduction from the projected emissions level for 2020 under the "do nothing" scenario (CARB, 2009). The California Air Resource Board (CARB) is the lead agency in charge of achieving these emission targets. Because the transportation sector produces 40 percent of GHG emissions in California, with automobiles and light trucks contributing 75 percent of those emissions, or 30 percent of total GHG emissions (CSAC, 2009), it was evident from the outset that the AB 32 goals can only be met through significant reductions

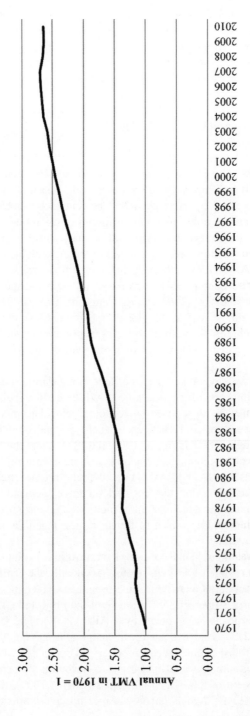

Figure 1.3 Increase in vehicle miles travelled (1970–2010)

Source: US Department of Transportation, Federal Highway Administration, http://www.fhwa.dot.gov [accessed: 2.11.14].

in vehicular GHG emissions. Hence, the state legislature passed the Sustainable Communities and Climate Protection Act of 2008 (SB 375) to reduce GHG emissions from automobiles and light trucks. Specifically, the Act requires the CARB to set regional GHG emission reduction targets for cars and light trucks for each of the state's 18 Metropolitan Planning Organizations (MPOs). Each MPO is required to prepare a Sustainable Communities Strategy (SCS) outlining the steps to achieve reduction in GHG emissions after taking into account the future land use and transportation needs (CALTRANS, 2008).

Elsewhere, many state, regional and local level governments have adopted strategies to mitigate the physical, economic, social and environmental ill effects of sprawl under the broad umbrella of "growth management" or "smart growth."[6] These strategies seek to create more compact walk-, bike- and transit-friendly urban environments that bring various activities together through mixed-use zoning, in-fill development, inner-city revitalization and higher densities. Among other things, these strategies aim to promote the use and provision of public transportation. Indeed, over the last three decades several cities, such as Portland, OR, and Seattle, WA, have either developed new transit systems or are more actively planning for such systems.

Public Transportation: Interest Does Not Match Funding

Concerns about the environmental impacts of vehicular emissions, the ill effects of sprawl and auto dependency have renewed interest in the increased provision of public transportation. However, while well-intended, this interest is not backed with adequate funding for the expansion of public transportation.

Unlike the water, sewer and electricity supplies, transit cannot be funded and operated solely through user fees, specifically, fare box revenues, and therefore needs support to meet its capital and operating expenses. In fact, none of the major transit systems in the US have been able to generate enough farebox revenues to fund their operating expenses, let alone the costs of further developing transit systems. Among the large transit systems, the highest farebox recovery percentages were achieved by the San Francisco Bay Area Rapid Transit District (BART) rail system, which had a farebox recovery percentage of 71.6 percent in 2010 and by the Washington, DC metropolitan rail system, which had a farebox recovery percentage of 62.1 percent (APTA, 2010). However, external support in the form of increased government funding is not forthcoming. In fact, total government funding for public transit as a proportion of total transit expenditures has largely oscillated between 57 and 60 percent during the period from 1994 to 2008 (APTA, 2012). Little wonder that a 2009 American Public Transportation

---

6   See Ye, Mandpe and Meyer (2005) for a review of smart growth strategies. See Downs (2004) for a comparative analysis of the terms "growth management" and "smart growth," and see Gale (1992) for a review of state-level growth management programs.

Association survey found that while transit ridership increased, almost all of the transit systems raised fares or cut services that year as a result of an average of 13 percent year-on-year decreases in local, state and federal funding (APTA, 2009). With all levels of public entities under fiscal stress, any new transit funding source is welcome. Value capture (VC) is one such source.

What is Property Value Capture?

Economic theory suggests people are willing to pay a premium to live, work, eat or play at places that provide amenities, ceteris paribus. These amenities become capitalized into the value of the land and, in turn, into the value of the properties that support such activities. Applied to the field of transportation planning, the theory suggests that the accessibility provided by a transit system should increase the value of station-adjacent property. Property value capture mechanisms seek to identify and capture these value increases. The mechanisms commonly used to fund transit include the following: the joint development of station area public land (including sale or lease of air rights above the transit facilities such as the station or the rail line), the levy of assessments by a special assessment district (SAD), property tax increment capture through a tax increment financing (TIF) district, and transit impact fees.

While the extant literature (see Voith, 1993; Landis, Guhathakutra and Zhang, 1994; Benjamin and Sirmans, 1996; Cervero and Duncan, 2002; Nelson, 1992; Gatzlaff and Smith, 1993; Lewis-Workman and Brod, 1997; Cervero and Landis, 1997; Weinberger, 2000; Mathur, 2008) has extensively demonstrated the property value impacts of transit investments, very little research documents and analyzes the adequacy, stability and growth of VC mechanisms. In fact, Smith and Gihring (2006) note: "it is now time for transit/land-use research to move from hypothesis testing to practical applications of value capture".

A big step in this direction was taken recently when Lari et al. (2009) reviewed the suitability of several VC mechanisms for the State of Minnesota. Earlier, in 2002, the Lincoln Institute of Land Policy offered a course entitled "Tools for Land Management and Development: Land Readjustment" that provided a comprehensive overview of the international use of land pooling to fund urban development. More recently in 2011, the Lincoln Institute of Land Policy organized a conference to examine various aspects of value capture. Furthermore, a US GAO (2010) national-level survey of major transit providers highlights the key obstacles to VC use. These obstacles include a lack of support from public and private entities, poor project formulation and design, and state laws that prohibit or constrain VC use. The study reports the revenues raised by selected VC mechanisms. For example, the study finds that SADs and TIF funded 40 percent ($41 million) of the $103 million Portland Streetcar project; that the SAD alone funded 23 percent ($25 million) of the $110 million New York Avenue

Metro Station in Washington, DC; and that the SADs funded nine percent ($130 million) of the $1.42 billion Los Angeles Metro Red line Segment One. Finally, a simulation study conducted by the Brookings Institution explored the feasibility of funding a street car line between the Minnesota Avenue Metro Station and Union Station in Washington, DC. The study finds that the entire 140 million project cost can be funded through three VC tools, TIF, SAD, and limited PPPs that would allow a public agency to share in the increases in value of streetcar-adjoining private properties (DCST, 2009).

Book Objectives and Organization

This book contributes to the growing VC literature by analyzing 12 transit projects funded across the US using joint development, SADs, TIF, and transit impact fees.[7] In addition, one chapter is devoted exclusively to a review of such mechanisms internationally. The book's focus on project-level analysis should benefit readers in three ways:

a. develop a better understanding of the mediating effects of external factors on the VC mechanisms' ability to fund transit projects across multiple scales and dimensions (regional economy to local community support);
b. identify key steps public entities can take to enhance each mechanism's revenue yield, stability and growth through the review of multiple cases for each VC mechanism; and
c. appreciate the mechanisms' comparative strengths and shortcomings in funding transit, with the aid of the book's findings on selected VC mechanisms.

The rest of the book is organized into nine chapters.

Chapter 2 begins by discussing various factors that impact property values, such as the structural attributes and locational characteristics of the property and the neighborhood and the city, regional and national factors that impact the demand and supply of real estate. Next, the chapter highlights collective action by the local government in the form of the provision of infrastructure and services as the key to the improvement of a property's locational characteristics and the quality of a neighborhood, city and region. Through a review of empirical literature, this chapter discusses increases in property value attributed to such collective action. Next, focusing on the impact of public transportation, the chapter highlights the impact of public transportation on property value, specifically the impact on property value of proximity to a transit station and transit-oriented development (TOD). The chapter then reviews the recent urgency expressed by policy makers

---

7   Joint development, SAD, TIF, and Transit Impact Fee are the four most popular VC mechanisms in use in the US.

at the federal and state levels to capture the value created by public transportation. The chapter concludes by noting that although VC has only recently captured the attention of policy makers and practitioners, it has long been in use in the US and internationally, albeit not extensively. Hence, the next two chapters provide a high-level review of the use of VC internationally and in the US.

Focusing on land pooling and readjustment (LPR), betterment levies, impact fees, sale and lease of land, sale of development rights, joint developments and developer agreements, Chapter 3 reviews the use of VC mechanisms in Europe, Australia, Asia and South America. Specific examples are provided to illustrate the use of VC mechanisms. One such example includes the use of LPR in Gujarat, India.

Chapter 4 begins by highlighting property tax as a widely used VC mechanism. Next, the decline of the property tax and other local taxes in proportion to the total local and state government revenue collected by the governmental taxing bodies is highlighted. The chapter notes two reasons for the need to identify additional sources to fund transit. First, local taxes usually flow into the general fund, where competing demands often result in a low funding priority for transit. Second, farebox revenues do not typically fund the full operating costs of transit, let alone provide capital for the development of new transit systems. The next four sections provide an overview of the four VC mechanisms addressed in this book: SADs, TIF, joint development, and the transit impact fee. Each section begins by briefly describing the mechanism and its use in funding infrastructure in the US. Next, the section reviews the use of the mechanism to fund transit. After discussing the required legal framework, the section concludes by discussing additional factors that should be considered before using the mechanism. These factors differ by the type of VC mechanism under consideration, but, in general, they include equity considerations, political acceptability, the institutional capacity to design, implement and manage the VC mechanism, and the impact of real estate market conditions on the VC mechanism.

Chapters 5 through 8 are organized similarly. Each chapter begins by providing an overview of the case study selection process. The next three sections of each chapter are developed as case studies, one section for each example of a VC mechanism used to fund transit infrastructure.

Chapter 5 reviews the use of SADs to fund the South Lake Union Street Car (Seattle, WA), the New York Avenue Metro Station (Washington, DC) and the Los Angeles Metro Redline Segment 1 (Los Angeles, CA).

Chapter 6 reviews the use of TIF to fund the Contra Costa Center Transit Village (Contra Costa County, CA),[8] the Wilson Yard Station (Chicago, IL) and the Portland Street Car (Portland, OR).

---

8   The Contra Costa Center Transit Village in Contra Costa County, CA employs TIF as well as joint development. Hence, both of these VC mechanisms will be discussed.

Chapter 7 reviews the use of joint development to fund the Dadeland South Joint Development (Miami, FL), the Bethesda Metro Joint Development (Bethesda, MD) and the Resurgens Plaza (Atlanta, GA).

Chapter 8 reviews the use of the following three transit impact fees: the System Development Charge (Portland, OR), the Transit Concurrency Fee (Broward County, FL) and the Transit Impact Development Fee (San Francisco, CA).

Each case study provides an overview of the transit system followed by the VC design, implementation and management process. The case study also highlights the political and policy context, project-specific circumstances and background studies conducted as part of the VC mechanism development process. Finally, each case study concludes with a case analysis sub-section that assesses the impact of the following factors on the success of the VC mechanism: the enabling environment, the institutional capacity of the public agency to design, implement and manage the VC mechanism, stake holder support (including how the support was secured and how opposition was avoided); the impact of the VC mechanism on horizontal and vertical equity, including an analysis on how the inequities were or could have been mitigated and the impact of real estate conditions and other factors on the VC mechanism's revenue yield, stability and growth.

Chapter 9 begins by briefly summarizing the key findings of chapters 5 through 8. Next, this chapter presents a comparative assessment of the suitability of each of the four VC mechanisms with the aim of developing a decision-support matrix that can be used by public transportation policy makers and professionals as they deliberate about the suitability of one VC mechanism or a combination of VC mechanisms to meet project-specific needs. Finally, by developing realistic scenarios that simulate real-world legal, political, policy and project-specific contexts, the chapter operationalizes the decision-support matrix.

The final chapter, Chapter 10, takes stock of the current state of the use of VC mechanisms in the US. By situating VC mechanisms among other public transportation funding sources, the chapter considers the future of VC mechanisms. The chapter concludes by reiterating the book's key findings.

References

Adler, S. 1991. The Transformation of the Pacific Electric Railway: Bradford Snell, Roger Rabbit, and the Politics of Transportation in Los Angeles. *Urban Affairs Review*, 27, 51–86.

American Public Transportation Association (APTA). 2009. *Challenge of State and Local Funding Constraints on Transit Systems: Effects on Service, Fares, Employment and Ridership Survey Results*. Washington, DC: APTA.

American Public Transportation Association (APTA). 2010. *Fare per Passenger and Recovery Ratio* [Online: APTA]. Available at: http://www.apta.com/resources/statistics/Documents/NTD_Data/2010_NTD/T26_2010_Pass_Fare_Recovery_Ratio.xls [accessed: February 22, 2012].

American Public Transportation Association (APTA). 2012. *2012 Public Transportation Fact Book Appendix A: Historical Tables* [Online: APTA]. Available at: http://www.apta.com/resources/statistics/Documents/FactBook/ 2012-Fact-Book-Appendix-A.pdf [accessed: September 1, 2012].

America-Rails.com. 2012. *The Baltimore and Ohio Railroad, Linking Thirteen Great States With The Nation* [Online: American-Rails.com]. Available at: http://www.american-rails.com/baltimore-and-ohio.html [accessed: September 7, 2012].

Bahadori, H. 2008. *A Brief History of Highways and Transportation Funding in America*. Presentation made to the Orange County Transportation Authority (OCTA) Board of Directors on February 25, 2008 [Online: OCTA]. Available at: http://www.octa.net/pdf/022508/trans_fund.pdf [accessed: September 7, 2012].

Benjamin, J. and Sirmans, S. 1996. Mass Transportation, Apartment Rent and Property Values. *Journal of Real Estate Research*, 12(1), 1–8.

Bianco, M.J. 1998. *Kennedy, 60 Minutes, and Roger Rabbit: Understanding Conspiracy-Theory Explanations of The Decline of Urban Mass Transit*. Discussion Paper 98–11. Portland, OR: Center for Urban Studies, College of Urban and Public Affairs, Portland State University. Available at: http:// marthabianco.com/kennedy_rogerrabbit.pdf [accessed: September 1, 2102].

Burchell, R.W. et al. 1998. *The Cost of Sprawl-Revisited*. TCRP Report Number 39. Washington, DC: Federal Transit Administration. Available at: http://onlinepubs.trb.org/onlinepubs/tcrp/tcrp_rpt_39-a.pdf [accessed: August 2, 2012].

California Air Resources Board (CARB). 2009. *Climate Change Scoping Plan: A Framework for Change*. Sacramento, CA: California Air Resources Board [Online: California Environmental Protection Agency: Air Resource Board]. Available at: http://www.arb.ca.gov/cc/scopingplan/document/adopted_scop ing_plan.pdf [accessed: August 29, 2012].

California Department of Transportation (CALTRANS). 2008. *Impacts of SB 375 on Transportation*. Sacramento, CA: California Department of Transportation [Online: California Department of Transportation]. Available at: http://www. dot.ca.gov/hq/tpp/offices/orip/sb375_files/SB_375_Summary-Prepared_by_ Caltrans.pdf [accessed: September 3, 2012].

California State Association of Counties (CSAC). 2009. *SB 375 (Steinberg): Addressing Greenhouse Gas Emissions from the Transportation Sector via Regional Transportation Plans: CSAV Analysis*. Sacramento, CA: California State Association of Counties [Online: California Department of Transportation]. Available at: http://www.dot.ca.gov/hq/tpp/offices/orip/sb37 5_files/csac.pdf [accessed: September 2, 2012].

Cervero, R. and Duncan, M. 2002. Benefits of Proximity to Rail on Housing Markets: Experiences in Santa Clara County. *Journal of Public Transportation*, 5(1), 1–18.

Cervero, R. and Landis, J. 1997. Twenty-Years of the Bay Area Rapid Transit System: Land Use and Development Impacts. *Transportation Research A*, 31(4), 309–333.

Chicago Transit Authority (CTA). 2011. *CTA Facts at a Glance* [Online: CTA]. Available at: http://www.transitchicago.com/about/facts.aspx [accessed: September 1, 2012].

DC Surface Transit, Inc. (DCST). 2009. *Value Capture and Tax-increment Financing Option for Streetcar Construction*. Washington, DC: DCST.

Downs, A. 2004. Introduction, in *Growth Management and Affordable Housing: Do They Conflict?* edited by A. Downs. Washington, DC: Brookings Institution Press.

Federal Highway Administration (FHWA). 2010. Chapter 6, Finance, in the *2010 Status of the Nation's Highways, Bridges, and Transit: Conditions & Performance* [Online: US Department of Transportation Federal Highway Administration]. Available at: http://www.fhwa.dot.gov/policy/2010cpr/chap 6.htm#body [accessed: September 1, 2012].

Federal Highway Administration (FHWA). 2011a. *Highway History* [Online: US Department of Transportation Federal Highway Administration]. Available at: http://www.fhwa.dot.gov/infrastructure/gastax.cfm [accessed: September 1, 2012].

Federal Highway Administration (FHWA). 2011b. *Frequently Asked Questions* [Online: US Department of Transportation Federal Highway Administration]. Available at: http://www.fhwa.dot.gov/interstate/faq.htm#question6 [accessed: August 28, 2012].

Federal Highway Administration (FHWA). 2012. *Historic National Road* [Online: America's Byways]. Available at: http://byways.org/explore/byways/2278/ [accessed: August 28, 2012].

Federal Transit Administration (FTA). 2012a. *Public Transportation in the United States: Federal Funding, National Transit Database, & Livability*. Washington, DC: Federal Transit Administration [Online: APTA]. Available at: http://www.apta.com/members/memberprogramsandservices/international/ Documents/Rita%20Daguillard%20-%20FTA%20Financing.pdf [accessed: August 30, 2012].

Federal Transit Administration (FTA). 2012b. *Flexible Funding for Highway and Transit. Washington, DC: Federal Transit Administration* [Online: FTA]. Available at: http://www.fta.dot.gov/printer_friendly/12867.html [accessed: September 7, 2012].

Fung, J.D., Fung, F. and Feng, A. 2006. *Global Warming on the Road: The Climate Impact of America's Automobiles* [Online: Environmental Defense Fund]. Available at: http://www.edf.org/sites/default/files/5301_ Globalwarmingontheroad_0.pdf [accessed: September 1, 2012].

Gale, D.E. 1992. Eight State-Sponsored Growth Management Programs: A Comparative Analysis. *Journal of the American Planning Association*, 58(4), 425–439.

Gatzlaff, D. and Smith, M. 1993. The Impact of the Miami Metrorail on the Value of Residences Near Station Locations. *Land Economics*, 69(1), 54–66.

Hess, D.B., and Lombardi, P.A. 2005. History, Current Issues, and Recent Evidence. *Public Works and Management & Policy*, 10(2), 138–156.

IEEE Global History Network. 2012. *Milestones: Richmond Union Passenger Railway, 1888* [Online: IEEE Global History Network]. Available at: http://www.ieeeghn.org/wiki/index.php/Milestones:Richmond_Union_Passenger_Railway,_1888 [accessed: September 6, 2011].

Klein, D. and Majewski, J. 2008. *Turnpikes and Toll Roads in Nineteenth-Century America* [Online: EH.net]. Available at: http://eh.net/encyclopedia/article/klein.majewski.turnpikes [accessed: September 1, 2012].

Landis, J., Guhathakurta, S. and Zhang, M. 1994. *Capitalization of Transportation Investments into Single-Family Home Prices*. Working Paper 619. Berkeley, CA: Institute of Urban and Regional Development, University of California.

Lari, A. et al. 2009. *Value Capture for Transportation Finance: Technical Research Report*. Minneapolis, MN: University of Minnesota Center for Transportation Studies.

Lewis-Workman, S. and Brod, D. 1997. Measuring the Neighborhood Benefits of Rail Transit Accessibility. *Transportation Research Record*, 1576, 147–153.

Mathur, S. 2008. Impact of Transportation and Other Jurisdictional-Level Infrastructure and Services on Housing Prices. *Journal of Urban Planning and Development*, 134(1), 32–41.

Metropolitan Transportation Authority (MTA). 2012. *New York City Transit: History and Chronology* [Online: MTA Home]. Available at: http://www.mta.info/nyct/facts/ffhist.htm [accessed: September 2, 2012].

National Park Service (NPS). 2011. *The Building of the Chesapeake and Ohio Canal* [Online: National Park Service]. Available at: http://www.nps.gov/history/nr/twhp/wwwlps/lessons/10cando/10cando.htm [accessed: August 27, 2012].

Nelson, A.C. 1992. Effects of Elevated Heavy Rail Transit Stations on House Prices with Respect to Neighborhood Income. *Transportation Research Record*, 1359, 127–132.

Post, R.C. 2003. Urban Railway Redivisus; Image and Ideology in Los Angeles, California, in *Suburbanizing the Masses: Public Transport and Urban Development in Historical Perspectives*, edited by C. Divall and W. Bond. Aldershot: Ashgate.

Schill, M.H. and Wachter, S.M. 1995. Housing Market Constraints and Spatial Stratification by Income and Race. *Housing Policy Debate*, 6(1), 141–167.

Schrag, Z. 2002. *Urban Mass Transit in the United States* [Online: EH.net]. Available at: http://eh.net/encyclopedia/article/schrag.mass.transit.us [accessed: September 1, 2012].

Slater, M. 1997. General Motors and the Demise of Streetcars. *Transportation Quarterly*, 51(3), 45–66.

Smith, J. and Gihring, T. 2006. Financing Transit Systems through Value Capture. *American Journal of Economics and Sociology*, 65(3), 751–786.

Thompson, G.L. 1993. *The Passenger Train in the Motor Age: California's Rail and Bus Industries, 1910–1941*. Columbus, OH: Ohio State University Press.

Transportation for America. 2011. *Transportation 101: An introduction to Federal Transportation Policy*. Washington, DC: Transportation for America.

Turner, W.R. 2012. *Development of Streetcar System in North Carolina*. [Online: Charlotte-Mecklenburg Historic Landmarks Commission]. Available at: http://www.cmhpf.org/development%20of%20streetcar%20systems.htm [accessed: September 1, 2012].

United States Department of Energy. 2012. Chapter 8, Household Vehicles and Characteristics, in *Transportation Energy Data Book* [Online: Oak Ridge National Laboratory Center for Transportation Analysis]. Available at: http://cta.ornl.gov/data/tedb31/Edition31_Chapter08.pdf [accessed: September 7, 2012].

United States Department of the Interior. 2004. *Federal-Aid Highway Act of 1956: Creating the Interstate System* [Online: nationalatlas.gov]. Available at: http://www.nationalatlas.gov/articles/transportation/a_highway.html [accessed: September 4, 2012].

United States Department of Transportation (USDOT). 2009. *A Chronology of Dates Significant in the Background, History and Development of the Department of Transportation*. [Online: Research and Innovative Technology Administration National Transportation Library]. Available at: http://ntl.bts.gov/historian/chronology.htm#1961 [accessed: September 1, 2012].

United States Environmental Protection Agency (EPA). 2012. *Transportation and Climate: Basic Information*. Washington, DC: United States Environmental Protection Agency [Online: United States Environmental Protection Agency]. Available at: http://www.epa.gov/otaq/climate/basicinfo.htm [accessed: September 1, 2012].

United States Government Accountability Office (GAO). 2010. *Public Transportation: Federal Role in Value Capture Strategies for Transit Is Limited, but Additional Guidance Could Help Clarify Policies*. Washington, DC: United States Government Accountability Office [Online: US Government Accountability Office]. Available at: http://www.gao.gov/new.items/d10781.pdf [accessed: October 6, 2011].

United States Senate Sub-Committee on Anti-Trust and Monopoly. 1974. *Statement of Bradford C. Snell Before the United States Senate Sub-Committee on Anti-Trust and Monopoly*. Available at: http://libraryarchives.metro.net/DPGTL/testimony/1974_statement_bradford_c_snell_s1167.pdf [accessed: August 30, 2013].

United States v. National City Lines. 1951. *United States Court of Appeals for the Seventh Circuit United States v. National City Lines, 1951*. Available at: http://web.archive.org/web/20080608012144/http://www.altlaw.org/v1/cases/770576 [accessed: August 30, 2013].

Voith, R. 1993. Changing Capitalization of CBO-Oriented Transportation Systems: Evidence from Philadelphia, 1970–1988. *Journal of Urban Economics*, 13, 361–376.

Vuchic, V.R. 2007. History and Role of Public Transportation in Urban Development, in *Urban Transit Systems and Technology*. Hoboken, NJ: John Wiley & Sons, Inc.

Weinberger, R. 2000. *Commercial Property Values and Proximity to Light Rail: Calculating Benefits with a Hedonic Price Model*. Paper presented at the 79th Annual Meeting of the Transportation Research Board, Washington, DC.

Weiner, E. 1999. *Urban Transportation Planning in the United States: An Historical Overview*. Westport, CT: Praeger Publishers.

Weingroff, R.F. 1996b. Federal-Aid Highway Act of 1956: Creating the Interstate System. *Public Roads*, 60(1) [Online: US Department of Transportation Federal Highway Administration]. Available at: http://www.fhwa.dot.gov/publications/publicroads/96summer/p96su10.cfm [accessed: September 1, 2012].

Weingroff, R.J. 1996a. Federal Aid Road Act of 1916: Building the Foundation. *Public Roads*, 60(1) [Online: US Department of Transportation Federal Highway Administration]. Available at: http://www.fhwa.dot.gov/publications/publicroads/96summer/p96su2.cfm [accessed: September 1, 2012].

Williamson, J. 2012. *Federal Aid to Roads and Highways since the 18th Century: A Legislative History*. Washington, DC: Congressional Research Service [Online: Federation of American Scientist]. Available at: http://www.fas.org/sgp/crs/misc/R42140.pdf [accessed: August 30, 2012].

Ye, L., Mandpe, S. and Meyer, P.B. 2005. What Is "Smart Growth?" – Really? *Journal of Planning Literature*, 19(3), 301–315.

Chapter 2
Basis of Value Capture:
Value Creation through Public Action

Factors Impacting Property Values

The value of real estate property depends on several sets of factors. These factors for a house, for example, can include structural attributes like the size of the living space, lot size, age of the house, the number of bedrooms and bathrooms, the quality of the structure and other amenities and features, such as a swimming pool or a granite kitchen counter top. The next set of factors includes locational attributes, such as the slope of the land parcel, traffic noise, air pollution, and the views offered by the house (views of a lake, mountain, river, park or open space, for example). The third set of factors includes the neighborhood-level and city-level quality of infrastructure and services, such as the quality of roads, public transportation, police services, fire protection and emergency medical services, schools, parks, recreational facilities, libraries, community centers, and police protection. The fourth set of factors includes the city-level attributes that impact the demand and supply of housing. The demand side attributes comprise employment opportunities, population growth, and property tax rates. The supply side attributes include government regulations, such as those pertaining to urban growth boundaries and large lot zoning. Finally, regional- and national-level economic and demographic drivers impact housing prices and can include unemployment rate, structural changes in the labor force, cost of building construction, population change, and mortgage rates.

The local (city or county) government, a special-purpose government (as in a special district like a school district) or a government or quasi-government agency, such as a redevelopment or transportation agency, usually provides the third set of factors, the neighborhood-level and city-level infrastructure and services that influence property value. Therefore, these infrastructure and services are often labeled "public" infrastructure and services because the public, via government or governmental agencies, pools its collective expertise and funds to plan, implement and maintain these infrastructure and services and because these infrastructure and services are often public goods.[1]

---

1   Non-rivalry and non-excludability are two key characteristics of a public good. For example, a city-level park can be enjoyed by a city resident without reducing some other resident's ability to enjoy the park (non-rivalry). Furthermore, once the park is open to the public, it is very difficult to exclude people from using it.

These public infrastructures and services are typically the result of public actions. For instance, a city's planning department might have developed a master plan identifying the needs and scope of a citywide public transportation system. The transportation department might then have prepared a specific plan further detailing the scope and timing of projects to develop that public transportation system. Finally, the city government might have used its revenues (such as property tax or sales tax revenues) to fund the planning, engineering design, construction and maintenance of the public transportation system.

Logically, if public infrastructure and services benefit individual property owners by imparting a windfall gain in property values, those who benefit from that infrastructure or services should also pay for their benefits, according to the "benefits received" principle. In the context of public transit, if the provision of or enhancements to public transit systems accrue accessibility-related benefits to neighboring properties, these benefits should be positively capitalized into higher property values. The property owners benefit from the public transit systems; therefore, they should help fund the systems.

Conceptual Framework to Understand the Impact of Public Infrastructure and Services on Property Values[2]

Public infrastructure and services impact property prices in several ways. First, infrastructure and services can enhance the locational desirability of properties.

For example, the construction of a new freeway increases transportation accessibility of the surrounding properties. However, it is important to note that property values might not increase if the new infrastructure is provided in an area already well-served (Senior, 2009), such as when light rail service is provided in an area that is already efficiently served by buses or an area where the new infrastructure is under used. The under use could be due to several factors, including the high cost of using the infrastructure and the underlying land use patterns. For example, a very high toll on a bridge and a hard to reach transit station are likely to experience low patronage and may have little impact on surrounding properties. Indeed, Andersson, Shyr and Fu (2010) discover this phenomenon in their study of property value impacts of proximity to high-speed rail (HSR) stations in the Tainan metropolitan area of Taiwan. This study reports little or no property value increase, which is attributed to two key factors. First, the monthly cost to ride the HSR trains is prohibitive at 70 percent of the median monthly wage in Taiwan. Second, the HSR stations are not easily accessible.

---

2   Some portions of the text for this sub-section has been taken verbatim from pp. 283–286 of Chapter 13, entitled "A Note on the Valuation of Jurisdictional-Level Infrastructure and Services," in the John I. Carruthers and B. Mundy edited book entitled *Environmental Valuation: Interregional and Intraregional Perspectives*. Farnham: Ashgate.

Second, some infrastructure and services enhance user's quality of life, hence increasing the demand, and, in turn, the prices of property. For example, the availability of pure water, a sewer connection, good schools, wide roads, and a low crime rate are all known to increase housing prices.

Third, the provision of infrastructure and services adds directly to the cost incurred by the local governments. A part of these costs may be passed on to the developers of new property in the form of development exactions or impact fees. The developers may in turn pass on these costs to the consumers. Furthermore, increases in the prices of new property in turn increase the prices of close substitutes: the existing properties. Indeed, empirical research has shown that impact fees increase the prices of existing housing. For example, Ihlanfeldt and Shaughnessy (2004) find that impact fees increase the price of both new and existing housing by 160 percent of the fee amount, while Mathur, Waddell and Blanco (2004) and Mathur (2007) find the price effect to be 166 percent of the fee amount for new housing and 83 percent for existing housing.

Fourth, broad-based revenue sources like the property tax revenues or the proceeds from general obligation bonds are often used to fund public infrastructure and services. The use of these revenue sources is based on the assumption that the funded infrastructure and services will benefit all residents of a jurisdiction equally. However, to the extent that the benefits are unequally distributed across space—for example, infrastructure may be provided in the suburbs where newer developments will benefit much more than will older, inner-city development—property prices may vary accordingly. Frequently, newer suburban development is also of higher quality than older inner-city development. The provision of infrastructure and services could thus benefit newer, higher-quality property more than it benefits older, lower-quality property. However, while the amenity effect of some public infrastructure and services leads to an increase in property prices, very close physical proximity to these infrastructures may be a disamenity that could dampen property prices. For example, while close proximity to a freeway provides regional access and therefore increases property prices, a building located adjacent to the freeway suffers from the freeway's disamenity effect: the noise and air pollution generated by freeway traffic (Langley, 1976). Similarly, while access to high-quality K-12 education leads to an increase in housing prices, very close physical proximity to schools may decrease housing prices due to schools-associated speed restrictions, noise and traffic (Hendon, 1973). The net property price effect of such infrastructure is the difference in the dollar values of the amenity and disamenity effects.

Finally, proximity to certain public facilities like hazardous waste sites and landfills is very likely to reduce property values. A meta-analysis of approximately 50 studies of waste disposal sites spread across North America finds a consistent negative impact of proximity to such sites on property values (Braden, Feng and Won, 2011). The review also finds that aquatic hazardous sites reduce property values the most. Surprisingly, the price effects of non-hazardous waste disposal sites and of nuclear waste disposal sites are very similar. Furthermore, a meta-analysis of 15 landfills in North America finds that all high-volume landfills (landfills receiving more than 500 tons of waste daily) and approximately three-quarters of low-volume landfills negatively impact the prices of adjacent properties, with an average price reduction of 13.7 and 2.7 percent, respectively (Ready, 2010).

Empirical Evidence of the Effects of Public Infrastructure and Services on Property Values

The property value impacts of public investments are the micro level indirect benefits of public investments as per Banister and Thurstain-Goodwin (2011). The benefits can also be realized at the "macro" and "meso" levels. The macro level benefits include those to the economy, such as an increase in gross domestic product (GDP). At the meso level the economy benefits from agglomeration effects, increased labor participation and productivity, and increased connectivity between various sub-sectors of the economy provided by transportation and telecommunication infrastructure. Focusing on rail investments, this study finds that significant non-transportation benefits are realized at all three levels, especially the meso and micro levels. Indeed, an extensive body of empirical literature finds that various public infrastructures and services positively impact property values. While a small portion of the literature estimates the effect of these factors on non-residential properties such as offices and commercial space, the literature primarily estimates the effects of public infrastructure and services on the price of single-family homes.

We will now review the empirical literature in order to estimate the magnitude of property value impacts attributable to a wide range of public infrastructure and services.

Impact of School Quality on Housing Prices

Several studies find a positive impact of school quality on housing prices. The extant literature has used both input and output measures to estimate the impact of school quality on home prices. The input measures include per pupil school expenditure and student teacher ratio. The output measures typically include some form of standardized test scores. For example, Brasington (2002) finds that a 1 percent increase in proficiency test scores increased the price of a median-priced home in Ohio by $371 in 1991, and Chiodo, Hernandez-Murillo and Owyang (2010) find that a 5 percent increase in elementary school math test scores increased home prices by 10–15 percent in Missouri in 1998.

Studies conducted outside the US find similar impacts. For example, Fack and Grenet (2007) report a 2 percent increase in housing prices due to an increase of one standard deviation in middle school test scores in Paris, France. Davidoff and Leigh (2007) find that a one standard deviation increase in high school test scores increased property values in the Australian Capital Territory by 3.5 percent; Gibbons and Machin (2006) find a 3.8 percent increase in housing prices for a one standard deviation increase in primary school test scores in London, UK.

Similarly, school expenditures positively impact home prices. For example, Mathur (2008) finds that a $1 increase in school expenditure per pupil increased the price of an existing home priced at $200,000 by $0.82 in King County, WA during the period 1991–2000. Mingche and Brown (1980) and Bradbury, Mayer and Case (2001) report similar positive impacts of school expenditures on home prices. Bradbury, Mayer and Case (2001) estimates the impact of school spending on single-family homes for cities and towns in Massachusetts, MA and finds that a jurisdiction that increased its school spending by one standard deviation (8.6 percent) over the average saw an increase in housing prices of about 2 percent more than did a jurisdiction with an average increase in school spending.

Impact of Crime Reduction on Housing Prices

A reduction in crime significantly increases property values. A national-level study by Pope and Pope (2012) estimate the impact of decreases in violent and property crimes over the entire US for the period 1990–2000 and finds that a decrease of 100 violent crimes or of 100 property crimes per 10,000 people increased housing prices by 3.4 and 0.8 percent, respectively. Mathur (2008) finds an even larger housing price effect due to crime reduction. For the same time period (1991–2000) as Pope and Pope (2012), Mathur (2008) reports a decrease of 100 violent crimes per 10,000 people (or a 61 percent decrease in crime for the study dataset) increased housing prices by 15 percent in King County, WA, a magnitude of home price increase comparable to that found by Schwartz et al. (2003) for New York City. This study finds that during the period 1988–1998, a 53 percent reduction in violent crimes increased housing prices by 8 percent. Finally, Lynch and Rasmussen (2001) find that a one standard deviation increase in violent crime decreased home prices by 4 percent in Jacksonville, FL.

Impact of Proximity to Parks and Open Spaces on Housing Prices

Several studies attribute a positive housing price effect to parks and open spaces. For example, a study of green open spaces and parks in a section of central Los Angeles, CA, finds that every 1 percent increase in proximity to parks and every 1 percent increase in the size of green open space increased housing prices by 0.128 and 0.076 percent, respectively (Conway et al., 2010). Similarly, Fullerton and Villalobos (2011) finds that every 1 percent increase in the proximity to parks increased housing prices by 0.045 percent in El Paso, TX. Finally, Nicholls and Crompton (2005), studying the effects of three green open spaces in Austin, TX, find that the greenways raise the price of adjacent homes by as much as 12 percent.

Finally, Molly (2001) finds park size to be an important factor; specifically, smaller parks increase housing prices the most, and the housing price effect of small and medium parks can extend farther than 450 meters from the parks.

Impact of Neighborhood/City-level Infrastructure and
Services on Housing Prices

Estimating the impact of residents' satisfaction with seven city-level services—fire protection, paramedic services, police protection, trash removal, snow removal, street maintenance, and neighborhood parks—on home prices in Dayton, OH, Larsen and Blair (2010) find that a 10 percent increase in satisfaction with fire and paramedic services, with police services and with public works (trash removal, snow removal, street maintenance, and neighborhood parks) increased home prices by 26.81, 13.67 and 24.52 percent, respectively.

Benefield (2009) estimates the impact of several neighborhood-level amenities such as swimming pools, clubhouses, parks, boating facilities, golf courses, and tennis courts for Charleston, SC, for the period of December 2006-June 2007 and finds that tennis courts and boating facilities are the most desirable neighborhood amenities, accounting for 12.4 and 12.2 percent increase in housing prices, respectively.

In the absence of reliable and consistent information about the quality of specific infrastructure and services, researchers often use highly aggregated measures like municipal expenditures per person, as proxies for the quality of infrastructure and services. For example, Mathur (2008) finds that in King County, WA, a $1 increase in municipal expenditure per person increased the price of a newly constructed $200,000 house by $4.20 and increased the price of a similarly priced existing house by $2.40.

Impact of Increase in Auto-oriented Transportation Accessibility
on Housing Prices

The empirical literature that estimates the housing price effects of transportation infrastructure has primarily used two types of measures: the accessibility-based and proximity-based measures. While the proximity-based measures estimate the housing price effect of a specific transportation infrastructure, such as an arterial road, the accessibility-based measures estimate the housing price effects of improvements in overall transportation accessibility. For example, Mathur (2008) uses two accessibility-based measures to assess the impact of auto-oriented transportation infrastructure on housing prices in King County, WA; these measures include the natural log of morning automobile travel time to Seattle's Central Business District (CBD), or downtown, and auto accessibility to retail jobs. The study finds that every 1 percent decrease in travel time to the CBD increased the price of new housing (houses sold within one year of construction) and existing housing by 0.072 and 0.254 percent, respectively. For a $200,000 house, this translates into an increase of $144 and $508, respectively. The price effect is larger for higher-quality new and existing homes—0.125 and 0.377 percent, respectively. The housing price effects of the second measure, auto accessibility to retail jobs are more varied. The study finds that an increase in accessibility to retail jobs increased the price of lower-quality new and existing houses and depressed the price of higher-quality new and existing houses. The study argues that retail jobs are typically low-paying jobs. Therefore, greater accessibility to such jobs is likely to positively impact lower-quality homes (assuming that retail workers are more likely to live in such homes). Moreover, retail jobs are also likely to be close to busy streets and are therefore more likely experience noise pollution, air pollution, and traffic congestion, factors that are likely to significantly impact the price of higher-quality houses. Voith (1993) finds similar positive housing price impacts of increases in transportation accessibility to the CBD of Philadelphia, PA. Increases in CDB access using the region's highway system—specifically, a 1-minute decrease from the mean commute time of 55 minutes, or approximately a 1 percent decrease in travel time—increases housing prices by $880 (approximately 0.7 percent of the housing price).

Several studies have estimated the housing price effect of specific auto-oriented transportation infrastructures like freeways and toll roads. For example, Vadali (2008), estimating the housing price effect of various toll road segments in Dallas County, TX, finds strong evidence of housing price increases for properties located within 0.25–1 mile distance from the freeway, with the maximum housing price increase of as much as 19 percent. The results are mixed for properties located in the 0–0.25 mile distance bands, perhaps reflecting both the amenity effect (transportation accessibility) and the disamenity effect (noise and air pollution and traffic congestion) of proximity to major roads and freeways. A similar housing price premium is found by Boarnet and Chalermpong (2001) in a study of two toll roads in Orange County, CA, the Foothill Transportation Corridor Backbone (FTCBB) and the San Joaquin Hills Transportation Corridor (SJHTC). This study finds that every one mile increase in the distance from the toll roads' on-ramps decreased home prices by $4,600 and $24,000 for the FTBCC and SJHTC, respectively.

The Impact of Accessibility to Public Transportation Infrastructure on Housing Prices

As with studies estimating the housing price effect of auto-oriented infrastructure, the empirical literature on public transportation infrastructure has also used both accessibility-based and proximity-based measures. Proximity-based measures primarily focus on distance to transit access points like train stations and bus stops.

Brandt and Maennig (2012) note that most of studies on the impact of train stations on property prices find a positive price effect (for example, Armstrong and Rodrıguez, 2006; Debrezion, Pels and Rietveld, 2006; Gibbons and Machin, 2005; Henneberry, 1998; Lochl and Axhausen, 2010; McMillen and McDonald, 2004;

Redfearn 2009). The authors primarily attribute the zero or negative price impacts found in some studies (for example, Forrest, Glen and Ward, 1996) to economic recession (Senior, 2009)[3] or to the failure to control for undesirable factors that are correlated with the proximity to train stations. Examples of such correlated variables include crime, railway lines, major streets and busy intersections and undesirable land uses close to the station, such as warehouses and industries. While estimating the impact of a railway station, it is important to control for the effect of proximity to the railway line. Ideally, one would want to live close to the railway station so that access to public transportation is quick, while not being bothered by the noise, vibration and safety issues related with being too close to the railway line. Among US-specific studies, Armstrong and Rodriguez (2006) find a positive impact of railway stations and a negative impact of the railway line on single-family properties in eastern Massachusetts served by the commuter rail service. Specifically, property values are approximately 10 percent higher in cities served by the commuter rail service. Furthermore, property values within 0.5 mile of the train station are approximately 10 percent higher than the values outside this distance band. The study also finds that every additional minute of drive time to the station is associated with a 1.6 percent decrease in property values, providing further evidence of the proximity-related benefits of the train station. Finally, the study finds that proximity to commuter rail lines negatively impacts property values—every 1,000 ft. distance from the line leads to property value increases of $732–$2,897. Similarly, McMillen and McDonald (2004) find that properties located within 1.5 miles of the train stations on the 11-mile long Orange line of the Chicago, IL, city railway system appreciated approximately 7 percent more than the properties farther away from the stations. This translates into a $216 million increase in property value, a benefit to property owners that equals 47 percent of the $410 million Orange Line construction cost. The study also finds that much of the property value increase occurred after the plans for the Orange Line were publicly available but before construction began.

A large number of studies conducted outside the US also find a positive property price impact of the accessibility provided by urban train systems. For example, Pagliara and Papa (2011) report positive property value impacts of proximity to train stations located in the Campania region of Italy. Ibeas et al. (2012) find that each additional rail line increases property value by 1.8 percent in Santander, Spain, and Cervero (1998) reports that the initiation of rail service led to a 57 percent increase in value of commercial properties that were within 50 meters of stations on the Tokaido rail line, Japan. Similarly, Debrezion, Pels and

---

3   Forrest, Glen and Ward (1996) use data for the period 1990–1993 to estimate the property value impacts of Manchester, UK, light rail (Metrolink Phase I). The study finds no effect. The lack of price effect is probably because the study period coincided with an economic downturn and a weak housing market (Senior, 2009), especially because a positive price effect was detected by Ovenell (2007) during a later, healthier economic period of 2004–2005.

Rietveld (2011) report a primarily positive housing price impact of transportation accessibility provided by the public train system in three metropolitan areas in Holland (Amsterdam, Rotterdam, and Enschede). This study devises several measures to estimate the benefits provided by train stations, including the distance to the nearest train station and to the most frequented train station, as well as the overall quality of the closest and the most frequented train stations. The overall station quality is measured using the rail service quality index (RSQI). The RSQI for a station includes factors such as the frequency of train service and the degree of coverage/connectivity provided by the station (measured by the number of direct connections provided by a station, the journey time, and the number of trips originating and ending at a station). While the distance to the railway station provides an estimate of the local accessibility, the RSQI is a measure of a station's regional accessibility. The study argues that in less urbanized metropolitan areas (represented by Enschede in this study), the price effects of the nearest and most frequently used station should be very similar, reflecting the limited station choices available in such areas. In more urbanized areas, such as Amsterdam, the most frequently used station influences property prices more. The study concludes that it is generally more advisable to measure accessibility to the most frequently used station rather than to the nearest train station. The study finds that doubling the distance between a house and the most frequently used station reduces housing prices by 1 and 2.5 percent in Amsterdam and Rotterdam, respectively. For an average priced house this translates to a price decrease of $1,600 and $4,000, respectively.[4] Furthermore, RSQI positively impacts housing prices in two metropolitan areas (Amsterdam and Rotterdam) with a 1 percent increase in RSQI associated with a 0.1 percent increase in housing prices in both the metropolitan areas. The RSQI has an insignificant impact in the Enschede metropolitan area.

Similarly estimating the impact of line four of the Santiago, Chile, metro system on condominium prices, Agostini and Palmucci (2008) find that housing prices increased between 4.2 and 7.9 percent after the construction of the metro line was announced and increased between 3.1 and 5.5 percent after station locations were identified. By converting the property value increases to the increase in property tax revenues, the study concludes that the increase in property tax revenues could have financed 11 to 17 percent of the metro line project.

Another international study of positive impacts of train stations on property values (Karanikolas and Louka, 2012) estimates the housing price effects of the new metro train systems for Thessaloniki, the second largest metropolitan area in Greece after Athens. Focusing on two districts (Ag. Sophia and Flemming District), the study finds an average housing price increase of 5–29 percent and 5–12 percent for residential properties within 100 meters of the metro stations in Ag. Sophia and Flemming District, respectively. Brandt and Maennig (2012) estimate the housing price effect of access to all public railway stations for the city of Hamburg,

---

4   At the January 1, 2002 Euro to US Dollar conversion rate of 1 Euro = 0.886 US Dollars.

Germany, and finds that station access increases prices by approximately 5 percent for condominiums located between 250 meters and 750 meters from the train stations. Finally, Bae, Jun and Hyeon (2003) estimate the impact of Seoul's subway Line 5 on residential property values and finds a housing price increase of 8.9 percent due to a station opening for properties located within 1000 meters of a station.

A growing body of empirical studies reports positive property value impacts of proximity to light rail stations. For example, Hess and Almeida (2007) examining the residential property values surrounding Buffalo, New York's light rail stations, find that for every foot a property is located close to a station, property values increase by $2.31 for straight-line distance and $0.99 for network distance per square foot, or 2–5 percent of the city's median home value. Similarly, Duncan (2011), focusing on the San Diego, CA, metropolitan area's light rail system—the San Diego Trolley—finds that, overall, condominium prices are higher for condominiums located within 1 mile of the trolley station. Furthermore, the study finds that the price increase depends upon neighborhood and station characteristics. For example, the price premium is only 6 percent for a property in an average-quality pedestrian neighborhood, while it more than doubles to 15 percent in neighborhoods with high-quality pedestrian environment.

Although little empirical research examines the property price effect of bus services, a sprinkling of studies find a positive impact. Rodriguez and Mojica (2009) estimate the housing price impact of a line extension of the Bogota, Columbia, Bus Rapid-Transit (BRT) system on surrounding properties' asking prices. The study finds a 13–14 percent increase in asking prices along the BRT line extension. Another Bogota BRT-specific study (Rodriguez and Targa, 2004) finds a similar price premium: a 6.8–9.3 percent price increase for multi-family properties for every 5-minute decrease in walk time to the BRT station. A slightly smaller price premium is found in Quebec City, Canada, where the price premium associated with the BRT system is approximately 7 percent for homes located 50–150 meters from the BRT line and approximately 3 percent for homes located 150–300 meters away (Dube et al., 2011). Furthermore, the study finds that the $8.8 million BRT system accrued $6 million in local government revenues (primarily from increased property tax revenues) and $35 million for property owners in the form of property value increases, and the authors argue that a portion of these value increases should be devoted to funding public transport.

Further, extant literature finds that property value impacts could vary by the specific transit system and the property type. For example, Cervero and Duncan (2002), examining the sales price data for properties surrounding Santa Clara County, CA, light rail and commuter rail stations, report that while stations in both commuter and light rail systems produced measurable property value premiums, some of the largest premiums were found for large apartments within a quarter-mile of light rail stations, which commanded land value premiums of up to 45 percent. Along the same lines, Golub, Guhathamkurta and Sollapuram (2012) find that price impacts of the Phoenix, AZ, light rail system varies by property type. Examining the price impacts on single-family, multi-family, commercial and vacant properties, the study finds that the premium equals 29 percent for a single-family house with mean-level features (for example, a mean house size and a mean lot size) located 200 feet from the light rail station while the premiums for multi-family, commercial and vacant properties at 200 feet from the station equal 37, 73 and 167 percent, respectively. Similarly, Cervero and Kang (2011) find land value premiums of up to 10 percent for houses within 300 meters of Seoul, South Korea, BRT stops, and more than 25 percent for retail and other non-residential uses within 150 meters. The findings of the above three studies are consistent with an older meta-analysis of the price effects of rail stations on commercial and residential property values (Debrezion, Pels and Rietveld, 2007), which finds that commercial properties enjoy a larger proximity benefit from rail stations than do residential properties. Different transit modes also tend to have different effects, with commuter rail apparently enjoying a higher capitalization effect than light and heavy rail.

Key Findings from the Literature

The empirical literature clearly demonstrates that several public infrastructure and services could provide significant economic benefits to property owners. For example, the literature finds that one standard deviation increase in school test scores leads to 1 to 4 percent increases in housing prices, that reducing violent crimes by half could increase home prices by up to 15 percent, and that doubling the proximity to parks and open spaces increases housing prices by 2–10 percent. Similarly, the transportation accessibility provided by roads, freeways and public transportation bestows economic benefits to property owners, with every 1 percent decrease in travel time to the CBD by automobile increasing housing price by 0.07–0.7 percent; proximity to train stations and bus stops could lead to about a 10 percent increase in housing prices and rents.

Because this book focuses on the use of property value capture to fund public transportation, I provide a few key insights from the above-reviewed literature for consideration by jurisdictions planning value capture mechanisms to fund public transportation:

a. While all types of public transportation systems are likely to increase property values, rail-based systems typically accrue greater benefits than bus-based systems.
b. The value increase is dependent upon several factors:
   a. The incremental benefit provided by the transport infrastructure, with smaller marginal increments likely to accrue smaller benefits. For example, opening a new rail station might lead to a smaller property value increase in a part of a city that is already well-served by public transportation compared to a part that has a high demand for rail transportation but very few stations.

b. The quality of transportation mobility provided by the public transportation system. The quality can be measured in terms such as the extent of transportation connectivity and the travel time.
c. The physical quality of the surrounding neighborhood. For example, properties located in pedestrian-friendly neighborhoods around the transit stations are likely to appreciate more than those in poor-quality pedestrian neighborhoods.
d. The property-type. Studies indicate that commercial properties might benefit more compared to residential properties.
c. Frequently, property value increases can accrue long before the public transportation service begins and can continue for a long time after the service is fully functional. Therefore, the full property value increments may be realized over a very long pre- and post-public transportation service period.
d. While access to public transportation may be a benefit, other components of the public transportation system (for example, the rail line) might be disamenities. Therefore, a value capture mechanism should determine the net benefit: economic benefit provided by the access to the transportation system minus the economic loss due to the disamenity effect of the infrastructure.
e. Part of the property value capture would be captured through higher property taxes and real estate transfer taxes. Therefore, a new property value capture mechanism should take into account the property value increment already captured by the existing mechanisms.
f. The property value increase could vary widely. Therefore, detailed study-area-specific studies should be conducted prior to devising a property value capture mechanism.

References

Agostini, C.A. and Palmucci, G.A. 2008. The Anticipated Capitalisation Effect of a New Metro Line on Housing Prices. *Fiscal Studies*, 29(2), 233–256.
Andersson, D.A., Shyr, O.F. and Fu, J. 2010. Does High-speed Rail Accessibility Influence Residential Property Prices? Hedonic Estimates from Southern Taiwan. *Journal of Transport Geography*, 18, 166–174.
Armstrong, R.J. and Rodriguez, D.A. 2006. An Evaluation of the Accessibility Benefits of Commuter Rail in Eastern Massachusetts Using Spatial Hedonic Price Functions. *Transportation*, 33, 21–43.
Bae, C.C., Jun, M.-J. and Hyeon, P. 2003. The Impact of Seoul's Subway Line 5 on Residential Property Values. *Transport Policy*, 10, 85–94.
Banister, D. and Thurstain-Goodwin, M. 2011. Quantification of the Non-transport Benefits Resulting from Rail Investments. *Journal of Transport Geography*, 19, 212–223.

Benefield, J.D. 2009. Neighborhood Amenity Packages, Property Price, and Marketing Time. *Property Management*, 27(5), 348–370.

Boarnet, M. and Chalermpong, S. 2001. New Highways, House Prices, and Urban Development: A Case Study of Toll Roads in Orange County, CA. *Housing Policy Debate*, 12(3), 575–605.

Bradbury, K.L., Mayer, C.J. and Case, K.E. 2001. Property Tax Limits, Local Fiscal Behavior, and Property Values: Evidence from Massachusetts Under Proposition $2^{1/2}$. *Journal of Public Economics*, 80, 287–311.

Braden, J.B., Feng, X. and Won, D. 2011. Waste Sites and Property Values: A Meta-Analysis. *Environmental and Resource Economics*, 50, 175–201.

Brandt, S. and Maennig, W. 2012. The Impact of Rail Access on Condominium Prices in Hamburg. *Transportation*, 39(5), 997–1017.

Brasington, D. 2002. The Demand for Local Public Goods: The Case of Public School Quality. *Public Finance Review*, 30(3), 163–187.

Cervero, R. 1998. *The Transit Metropolis: A Global Inquiry*. Washington, DC: The Island Press.

Cervero, R. and Duncan, M. 2002. Benefits of Proximity to Rail on Housing Markets: Experiences in Santa Clara County. *Journal of Public Transportation*, 5(1), 1–18.

Cervero, R. and Kang, C.D. 2011. Bus Rapid Transit Impacts on Land Uses and Land Values in Seoul, Korea. *Transport Policy*, 18(1), 102–116.

Chiodo, A.J., Hernández-Murillo, R. and Owyang, M.T. 2010. Nonlinear Effects of School Quality on House Prices. *Federal Reserve Bank of St. Louis Review*, 92(3), 185–204.

Conway, D., Li, C.Q., Wolch, J. et al. 2010. A Spatial Autocorrelation Approach for Examining the Effects of Urban Greenspace on Residential Property Values. *Journal of Real Estate Finance and Economics*, 41, 150–169.

Davidoff, I. and Leigh, A. 2007. *How Much Do Public Schools Really Cost? Estimating the Relationship between House Prices and School Quality*. Canberra, Australia: Australian National University Centre for Economic Policy Research Discussion Paper No. 588.

Debrezion, G., Pels, E. and Rietveld, P. 2006. *The Impact of Rail Transport on Real Estate Prices: An Empirical Analysis of the Dutch Housing Market*. Tinbergen Institute discussion paper, TI 2006–031/3.

Debrezion, G., Pels, E. and Rietveld, P. 2007. The Impact of Railway Stations on Residential and Commercial Property Value: A Meta-analysis. *Journal of Real Estate Finance and Economics*, 35, 161–180.

Debrezion, G., Pels, E. and Rietveld, P. 2011. The Impact of Rail Transport on Real Estate Prices: An Empirical Analysis of the Dutch Housing Market. *Urban Studies*, 48(5), 997–1015.

Dubé, J., Des Rosiers, F., Thériault, M. and Dib, P. 2011. Economic Impact of a Supply Change in Mass Transit in Urban Areas: A Canadian Example. *Transportation Research Part A*, 45, 46–62.

Duncan, M. 2011. The Impact of Transit-oriented Development on Housing Prices in San Diego, CA. *Urban Studies*, 48(1), 101–127.

Fack, G. and Grenet, J. 2007. *Do Better Schools Raise Housing Prices? Evidence from Paris School Zoning*. Paris, Ecole Normale Sup´erieure, mimeo.

Forrest, D., Glen, J. and Ward, R. 1996. The Impact of a Light Rail System on the Structure of House Prices: A Hedonic Longitudinal Study. *Journal of Transport, Economics and Policy*, 30, 15–29.

Gibbons, S. and Machin, S. 2005. Valuing Rail Access Using Transport Innovations. *Journal of Urban Economics*, 57, 148–169.

Gibbons, S. and Machin, S. 2006. Paying for Primary Schools: Admissions Constraints, School Popularity or Congestion. *The Economic Journal*, 116, 77–92.

Golub, A., Guhathakurta, S. and Sollapuram, B. 2012. Spatial and Temporal Capitalization Effects of Light Rail in Phoenix: From Conception, Planning, and Construction to Operation. *Journal of Planning Education and Research*, 32(4), 415–429.

Hendon, W. 1973. Property Values, Schools, and Park-school Combinations. *Land Economics*, 49(2), 216–218.

Henneberry, J. 1998. Transport Investment and House Prices. *Journal of Property Valuation and Investment*, 16, 144–158.

Hess, D. and Almeida T. 2007. Impact of Proximity to Light Rail Rapid Transit on Station-area Property Values in Buffalo, New York. *Urban Studies*, 44(5/6), 1041–1068.

Ibeas, A. et al. 2012. Modelling Transport and Real-estate Values Interactions in Urban Systems. *Journal of Transport Geography*, 24, 370–382.

Ihlanfeldt, K.R. and Shaughnessy, T.M. 2004. An Empirical Investigation of the Effect of Impact Fees on Housing and Land Markets. *Regional Science and Urban Economics*, 34, 639–661.

Karanikolas, N. and Louka, E. 2012. The Effects of Metro Station on Commercial Values of Residential Properties: The Case Study of Thessaloniki, Greece Before the Completion of the Metro Project Constriction. *International Journal of Academic Research*, 4(2), 136–143.

Langley, J. 1976. Adverse Impacts of the Washington Beltway on Residential Property Values. *Land Economics*, 52(1), 54–65.

Larsen, J.E. and Blair, J.P. 2010. Public Services Satisfaction and Single-family House Prices in the USA. *International Journal of Housing Markets and Analysis*, 3(4), 278–289.

Lochl, M. and Axhausen, K.W. 2010. Modeling Hedonic Residential Rents for Land Use and Transport Simulation While Considering Spatial Effects. *Journal of Transport and Land Use*, 3, 39–63.

Lynch, A.K. and Rasmussen, D.W. 2001. Measuring the Impact of Crime on House Prices. *Applied Economics*, 33(15), 1981–1989.

Mathur, S. 2007. Do Impact Fees Raise the Price of Existing Housing? *Housing Policy Debate*, 18(4), 635–659.

Mathur, S. 2008. Impact of Transportation and Other Jurisdictional-level Infrastructure and Services on Housing Prices. *Journal of Urban Planning and Development*, 134(1), 32–41.

Mathur, S., Waddell, P. and Blanco, H. 2004. Effect of Impact Fees on Price of New Single Family Housing. *Urban Studies*, 41(7), 1303–1312.

McMillen, D.P. and McDonald, J.F. 2004. Reaction of House Prices to a New Rapid Transit Line: Chicago's Midway Line, 1983–1999. *Real Estate Economics*, 32, 463–486.

Mingche, L. and Brown, J. 1980. Micro-neighborhood Externalities and Hedonic Housing Prices. *Land Economics*, 56(2), 125–136.

Molly, E. 2001. Neighborhood Parks and Residential Property Values in Greenville, South Carolina. *Journal of Agricultural and Applied Economics*, 33(3), 487–492.

Nicholls, S. and Crompton, J.L. 2005. The Impact of Greenways on Property Values: Evidence from Austin, Texas. *Journal of Leisure Research*, 37(3), 321–341.

Ovenell, N. 2007. *A Second Hedonic Longitudinal Study on the Effect on House Prices of Proximity to the Metrolink Light Rail System in Greater Manchester*. Salford, UK: University of Salford, unpublished MSc Transport Engineering and Planning dissertation.

Pagliara, F. and Papa, E. 2011. Urban Rail Systems Investments: An Analysis of the Impacts on Property Values and Residents' Location. *Journal of Transport Geography*, 19, 200–211.

Pope, D.G. and Pope, J.C. 2012. Crime and Property Values: Evidence from the 1990s Crime Drop. *Regional Science and Urban Economics*, 42, 177–188.

Ready, R.C. 2010. Do Landfills Always Depress Nearby Property Values? *Journal of Real Estate Research*, 32(3), 321–339.

Redfearn, C.L. 2009. How Informative are Average Effects? Hedonic Regression and Amenity Capitalization in Complex Urban Housing Markets. *Regional Science and Urban Economics*, 39, 297–306.

Rodriguez, D.A. and Mojica, C.H. 2009. Capitalization of BRT Network Expansions Effects into Prices of Non-expansion Areas. *Transportation Research Part A*, 43, 560–571.

Rodriguez, D.A. and Targa, F. 2004. Value of Accessibility to Bogota's Bus Rapid Transit System. *Transport Reviews*, 24(5), 587–610.

Schwartz, A. et al. 2003. Has Falling Crime Driven New York City's Real Estate Boom? *Journal of Housing Research*, 14(1), 101–136.

Senior, M.L. 2009. Impacts on Travel Behaviour of Greater Manchester's Light Rail Investment (Metrolink Phase 1): Evidence from Household Surveys and Census data. *Journal of Transport Geography*, 17, 187–197.

Vadali, S. 2008. Toll Roads and Economic Development: Exploring Effects on Property Values. *Annals of Regional Science*, 42, 591–620.

Voith, R. 1993. Changing Capitalization of CBD-Oriented Transportation Systems: Evidence from Philadelphia, 1970–1988. *Journal of Urban Economics*, 33, 361–376.

Chapter 3
Use of Value Capture Internationally

Property value capture has a very long history in the US. The simplest value capture mechanism—the sale of land—was used by a cash-strapped New York in 1686 when it sold "water lots" comprised of land between "high" and "low" water marks of the Hudson River, and finally in 1730, sold land 400 feet into the river itself (Appleby, et al. v. City of New York, et al., 1926). The US Federal government subsequently granted land to private companies to facilitate the development of railroads in the nineteenth century, and property owners in New York were allowed to sell air rights (rights to develop over their property) in 1916. Popular value capture mechanisms currently in use in the US include tax increment financing, transfer or sale of development rights, joint development on lands in and around transit stations, exactions and development impact fees, and special assessments.

In Europe, Britain had a long history of betterment levies, charges equivalent to a certain proportion of the estimated increase in property value paid by owners who benefited from a public improvement. For example, in the Middle Ages property owners who benefited from sea defense works paid betterment levies. Similarly, in 1662 the beneficiaries of street widening projects in London and in 1667 the beneficiaries of reconstruction projects undertaken after the Great Fire paid betterment levies. The country tried to revive the use of betterment levies in the twentieth century through the Housing (Town Planning) Act of 1905, the Town and Country Planning Act of 1932, the 1947 Town and Country Planning Act, and the Land Commission Act of 1967 before it was completely repealed in 1971 (Day, 2005). Although betterment levies lost favor in Britain, they have found traction in South America and Asia, especially in Columbia and India.

This chapter provides further insights into the use of value capture internationally through specific examples, which include the use of LPR in Gujarat, India; the sale of development rights in Sao Paolo, Brazil; the use of infrastructure charges in Brisbane, Australia; and the joint development of railway systems and real estate in Hong Kong.

Land Pooling and Readjustment (LPR), Gujarat, India[1]

International Use of LPR

LPR, or its variants, such as Land Readjustment, Land Pooling, and Land Reconstitution, can trace their roots to Holland and Germany in the 1890s. They were quickly adopted for urban development across the globe and played a leading role when urbanization peaked in Seoul and Tokyo from the 1960s until the 1980s (Hayashi, 2002; Lee 2002). LPR was also used in smaller Korean towns and across several other countries, such as Germany, Holland, Nepal, Indonesia, and Australia (Karki, 2004; Larsson, 1997; Archer 1994).

   In LPR, a public agency (often a municipality or a development authority) pools multiple privately held land parcels together. Next, the agency takes a part of the pooled land to provide infrastructure and public facilities and returns the rest of the land to the original landowners in proportion to the sizes of their original land holdings (Archer, 1992). Often, the public agency also reserves a part of the pooled land for future sale.

   LPR offers three key monetary benefits: the public agency does not incur the land acquisition cost; the public agency is able to finance urban development through betterment charges and the sale of land; and landowners gain from the appreciation in the land value due to the provision of infrastructure (Krabben and Needham, 2008). In rapidly growing urban areas, the increase in value of the remaining land parcel often far exceeds the sum of the betterment charges paid by the landowner and the monetary value of the un-serviced land transferred by the landowner to the public agency.

   The practice of LPR varies from country to country and regionally within countries. Some key characteristics of the LPR programs in use internationally are outlined below.

Areas of use

Although LPR is more frequently employed to urbanize peri-urban rural land (Turk 2008), it has also been used to redevelop existing urban areas, such as Rotterdam City Center (Needham 2002), for urban renewal in China (Li and Li, 2007), and for the reconstruction of earthquake-stricken urban centers in Japan (Hein, 2010) and India (Jha, et al., 2010).

Components of LPR

LPR usually includes the provision of infrastructure by a public agency. However, public agencies' roles are limited to land assembly in some countries, such as Germany, Turkey and Indonesia (Turk, 2008, pp. 230–231).

---

1   Parts of this section were originally published in Mathur, S. 2013. Self-financing Urbanization: Insights From the Use of Town Planning Schemes in Ahmadabad, India. *Cities*, 31, 308–316.

Landowner participation

The landowners' participation is usually mandatory. Even where it is voluntary, often the consent of only a simple majority of landowners is required. For example, in Holland, the LPR project requires the approval of either the majority of the landowners, or, if the project is for agricultural purposes, the landowners whose holdings constitute the majority of the land area. Participation is mandatory for other purposes. For example, compulsory readjustment was adopted to rebuild the 158-hectare Rotterdam City Center after World War II (Needham, 2002). Similarly in Japan, the government can initiate LPR projects without landowners' consent where "important planning goals are at stake" (Sorensen, 2002, p. 12). The written consent of the majority of the landowners is required for all other projects.

Techniques used to enhance landowner participation

Techniques are more elaborate where the consent of the majority of the landowners is required. For example, in Japan, the local governments first persuade local community leaders to serve as advocates for LPR schemes and the city planning regulations are LPR-friendly. For example, in the 1980s, to manage uncontrolled urbanization, the federal government divided the area around the cities into two zones—Urbanization Promotion Areas (UPA) and Urbanization Control Areas (UCA). The power to change zoning from UCA to UPA was used to promote LPR, and areas zoned as UCA that agreed to the use of LPR were rezoned as UPA. The written consent of the majority of the landowners was required for LPR projects. Several meetings (on average 72 per project) were held to secure landowner participation. These meetings conveyed the benefits of the project, and provided an overview of the LPR process and the project plan (Sorensen, 2002).

Subsidy for infrastructure funding

Subsidy requirements vary among countries, ranging from entirely self-financing LPR projects in Korea and Gujarat, India, where the betterment charges and revenues from the sale of land fund the project, to Japan where gasoline tax revenues are used to acquire land for the construction of arterial roads (Sorensen 2002). The local governments typically bear a portion of the infrastructure costs in Europe.

Coordination with higher-level planning

LPR projects typically must be consistent with the higher-level (i.e., city and regional) plans. For example, in Holland, a LPR project should be consistent with the regional plan (Needham, 2002). Similarly, in Finland and Japan, it should be consistent with the local or city plan (Sorensen, 2002; Viitanen, 2002).

Land Pooling and Readjustment (LPR) in India

The Bombay Town Planning Act of 1915 was the first legislation to provide the legal framework for the use of LPR in India. The Act enabled the use of Town Planning Schemes (TP Schemes) in the erstwhile Bombay Presidency and later became the basis for the Gujarat's TP Scheme-enabling act, the Gujarat Town Planning and Urban Development Act (GTPUDA) of 1976 (interview with V. Phatak; Ballaney and Patel, 2009). Gujarat's TP Scheme serves 2,000–5,000 residents—similar to a neighborhood in the US. The scheme includes a layout plan that shows the location of various land uses, infrastructure and services. It is accompanied by a detailed estimate of the scheme cost, the betterment charges, and the land received from each landowner.

TP Schemes were widely used in the state of Maharashtra (of which Mumbai, formerly Bombay, is the capital) in the first half of the twentieth century, and large parts of Mahim, Khar and Borivali in Mumbai were developed using TP Schemes. However, TP Scheme use declined when the Maharashtra Regional & Town Planning Act of 1966 shifted the focus from TP Schemes to detailed Development Plans (DPs) for implementing city master plans. In practice, DPs were rarely prepared, while at the same time the use of TP Schemes declined. Furthermore, the long period between a TP Scheme initiation and final government approval (an average of 15 years) and the fact that an ownership dispute over a single land parcel could hold up an entire scheme contributed to the abandonment of TP Schemes (Phatak, 2010).

LPR in Gujarat, India

Gujarat continued using TP Schemes, first through the Bombay Town Planning Act of 1915, which it inherited after seceding from the Bombay Presidency after India's independence, and later through the GTPUDA of 1976.

TP Scheme preparation process in Gujarat
The Notification of Intention (NoI) is the first step in the TP Scheme preparation process. Issued by the appropriate local public agency (typically the municipal corporation or development authority), the NoI identifies the location and scheme boundaries. Next, the public agency collects the land ownership records from the state revenue department and other agencies, such as local village governments. These records also include land parcel details, including the ownership type, encumbrances, the area and value of the land and, wherever applicable, the value of existing structures on the land. The public agency must match and reconcile the land ownership records through a site survey and have the matched records certified by the state revenue department (Ballaney, 2008). The site survey also notes the location of other man-made and natural features; infrastructure and services, such as regional water, power and sewer lines; and the location of major roads already constructed or to be constructed in accordance with the city master plan. A site base map is prepared based on this survey.

Next, a layout plan and an infrastructure plan are prepared. The layout plan shows the street network; the new plots to be returned to the landowners after taking a portion of the land; the location of various services and amenities, such as parks, schools, shops, and electric substations; and the land parcels reserved for future sale by the public agency. The infrastructure plan shows the location of the various infrastructure systems, such as streets and the water, sewer, and electricity supply systems. The plan is accompanied by a detailed cost estimate.

The next major TP Scheme preparation step entails the determination of the following: a) compensation to be paid to the landowners for the land taken from them by the public agency; and b) betterment charges payable by the landowner to the public agency. These charges equal one half of the difference between the pre- and post-TP Scheme land values. The scheme costs that are not recouped from the betterment charges are covered through the sale of the reserved land parcels.

At this stage, the draft TP Scheme (comprised of the layout plan, infrastructure plan, cost estimates, calculation of compensation payable to the landowners, and betterment charge calculations) is presented to the landowners for comments. Next, the scheme is modified to address the comments and forwarded to the state government for approval. Upon receiving the approval of the state government, the scheme is called the "Sanctioned Draft TP Scheme." The TP Scheme preparation process usually takes approximately 14–17 months, or one and one-half years, to reach this stage.

Next, a Town Planning Officer (TPO) is appointed. A state town planning department employee, the TPO undertakes three rounds of public hearings in which the individual landowners can contest the Sanctioned Draft TP Scheme. The first two rounds of hearings focus on the physical issues (such as the location, size and geometry of a land parcel). After the scheme is modified by the TPO based on these hearings, it is submitted to the state government as a "Preliminary TP Scheme." Upon government approval it is called a "Sanctioned Preliminary TP Scheme" (Ballaney and Patel, 2009). The third round of hearings focuses on financial issues such as the betterment charge. The scheme is again modified and submitted for government approval as the "Final TP Scheme." Upon government approval, it is termed the "Sanctioned Final TP Scheme." The TPO has one to two years to prepare the Preliminary and Final TP Schemes. The state government is given two months to approve the Preliminary TP Scheme and three months to approve the Final TP Scheme. However, substantial delays occur in the post-Sanctioned Draft TP Scheme stage due to delays by both the TPOs and the state government (interview with K. Gajjar; Ballaney, 2008). Therefore, a process that should take three to four years may take more than a decade.

Furthermore, the local governments must prepare the schemes in a time-bound manner. However, the state government is not penalized for delaying scheme approval (interview with K. Gajjar). Therefore, the length of time from scheme initiation to completion has not significantly declined.

Finally, the TP Schemes focus primarily on the development of roads and the physical infrastructure that uses road right-of-way, such as water, sewer and electric supply networks. While land parcels are reserved for the other facilities, such as schools, parks, and community centers, the facilities are not constructed. Therefore, the TP Schemes' residents are often uncertain about the timing of provision and the quality of these facilities. Often the land parcels reserved for parks, schools and community centers are either undeveloped or poorly developed.

Lessons from the Gujarat TP Scheme experience
The evolution of any LPR mechanism depends upon several factors, such as the national or state-level legal and policy environment, especially the laws and policies associated with property rights; the demand for land; the history of community cooperation; and the availability and effectiveness of alternative funding mechanisms. These factors may differ significantly among regions and countries. In spite of these variations, Gujarat's experience with the TP Scheme mechanism provides key and widely applicable insights that other regions and countries, especially those experiencing rapid urbanization and sharp increases in the price of serviced urban land, might find useful. The key insights are discussed below.

Revolving funds from the sale of land
Significant up-front capital expenditure on infrastructure and services is highlighted as a major weakness of LPR internationally (Turk and Altes, 2011). The Gujarat TP Scheme mechanism addresses this problem by using the land sale proceeds from previous TP Schemes to fund infrastructure and services in upcoming TP Schemes. The land in the older, well-developed schemes is usually much higher in value compared with the land in the newer schemes; therefore, this revolving fund mechanism allows the local governments to capture significant land value gain and to employ that gain for urban development (interviews with K. Gajjar, B. Patel and D. Mehta).

More accountability is needed for the revenue realized from the sale of reserved land parcels. The revenues are apparently used for the provision of infrastructure benefiting the TP Schemes. However, due to a lack of proper fund accounting, it is not possible to precisely identify the projects funded from these revenues (Interviews with V. Patel and D. Mehta). This lack of fiscal transparency increases the potential for misuse of funds.

Extensive grievance redressal process
The three rounds of hearings conducted by the TPO constitute one effective model of addressing landowner concerns (interview with V. Patel). The TPO is a professional urban planner, and because the TPO is a state government employee, she is unlikely to be unduly influenced by the local governments and the local stakeholders. Finally, the elaborate hearings process has enabled local governments to successfully withstand legal challenges to TP Schemes (interviews with V. Patel, K. Gajjar and N. Munshi).

In spite of the extensive grievance redressal process, landowners express some concerns. They primarily complain that 40 percent land appropriation is excessive. Other concerns revolve around the size and location of the final plots, the fact that the land value and betterment charge calculations are not explained in detail, and inequitable treatment when wider roads and higher floor area ratio (FAR) are often provided in the sections of the scheme where the land is owned by politically influential people. Overall, landowners seem satisfied with this mechanism because they receive an urban level of infrastructure and services and benefit monetarily even after parting with a significant proportion of their land and paying betterment charges (interviews with B. Patel and N. Munshi).

Resolution of land ownership disputes delinked from scheme preparation and approval
LPR can become mired in legal battles over land ownership disputes (Phatak, 2010). This problem is especially acute in developing countries where the land record systems are often not well developed. The Gujarat TP Schemes provide one solution to this problem—delinking such disputes from the LPR process by transferring the ownership disputes to the newly constituted plot (interview with K. Gajjar).

Early development of infrastructure
The early development of infrastructure (roads and water, sewer and electric systems that use road right-of-way) is perhaps the most significant reason behind landowner support for LPR in Gujarat (interview with K. Gajjar). This support also shows that landowners are likely to support planning policies that quickly provide them with clear and significant benefits. The development of backbone infrastructure provides those benefits.

Gujarat amended the GTPUDA in 1999 to allow local governments to appropriate land for road construction and other "priority" infrastructure within the road right-of-way (such as water and sewer pipes, and electricity poles and transmission wires) soon after the state government approves a draft TP Scheme, rather than after final TP Scheme approval. Approval of the draft TP Scheme usually occurs within 15 months of scheme initiation following the publication of a "Declaration of Intent" to prepare a TP Scheme. The approval of the final TP Scheme can take more than a decade.

Self-financing
The betterment charges and revenues from the sale of reserved land finance the entire scheme. Land sale revenues also help local governments hedge against future increases in construction costs, and fund other regional- and city-level infrastructure (interview with K. Gajjar). Due to their self-financing nature and the high level of landowner satisfaction, TP Schemes enjoy a high degree of political acceptability.

Alternative to compulsory land acquisition process
Using TP Schemes means that local governments need not go through the time consuming, confrontational and financially burdensome land acquisition process (Ballaney, 2008). At the same time, they are able to provide infrastructure in a financially sustainable manner.

Suitability of LPR for the US

Several enabling features of LPR are already widely used in the US. These features include the governments' ability to use eminent domain power to acquire property for larger public benefit; the key role of local governments in providing public infrastructure and services; the availability of land and property records; and the active use of government powers to dictate the intensity of use through land use, zoning, and building code regulations.

In the US, peri-urban and rural land is often in the form of large land holdings. Therefore, the need for direct government action to pool a large number of small land parcels to urbanize peri-urban land has not been felt acutely. Nonetheless, there is a long tradition of land owners coming together to form community facilities districts (CFDs) to plan and fund infrastructure that serves multiple land holdings. This infrastructure includes roads, water and sewer systems. The knowledge that their land values would increase once the infrastructure is provided brings these land owners together. Typically, the creation of CFDs requires a super-majority land owner vote (often as high as 75 percent). Due to the large size of land holdings, CFDs might not have to formally pool all of the land parcels together; nonetheless, land owners may have to apportion a part of their land for the provision of infrastructure and services. Furthermore, some states, including California, allow CFDs such as the Mello Roos Districts, to issue bonds to fund infrastructure and development.

LPR can also be used to incentivize redevelopment of urban cores of historical cities, such as New York, where property ownership is often highly fragmented; large-scale compulsory property acquisition can become mired in long, drawn-out legal battles; and developers have to buy-out multiple property owners before development can begin (Sagalyn, 2002). In such a scenario, aligning property owners' interests through LPR could be a better option by making the property owners partners in the development. In such a scheme, selective compulsory land acquisition could still be used to address the "hold out problem" (Turk and Altes, 2010) if the last few property owners refuse to participate for strategic reasons.

Sale of Development Rights, Sao Paolo, Brazil

Land value is determined by a host of factors, such as the characteristics of the land parcel (e.g., parcel geometry, slope and propensity to flood), its locational attributes (e.g., transportation accessibility), and the use allowed on the parcel.

Zoning ordinances prescribe the type of use, such as commercial, industrial, residential and recreational, and the maximum intensity of development allowed on a land parcel. The intensity of development is controlled through parameters such as the maximum permissible floor area to land parcel area ratio (also called the Floor Area Ratio, FAR, or Floor Space Index, FSI), building height restrictions, and minimum setbacks and parking requirements. On the one hand, because zoning ordinances grant land development rights, restrictive zoning reduces land development options and can negatively impact property values. On the other hand, zoning protects property values by not allowing incompatible uses in close proximity to each other; e.g., not allowing a polluting heavy industry in a residential neighborhood.

Traditionally, development rights have been considered to be permanently tied to the land. However, beginning the first half of the twentieth century land ownership was increasingly considered to be ownership of a bundle of development rights. This view was especially popular in the US (Renard, 2007). Treatment of development rights as a bundle opened up the possibility of un-bundling them and selling them independently of the land to which they were originally tied. Tools such as the sale of development rights or the transfer of development rights (TDR) help un-bundle land development rights. Simply put, these programs allow a land owner to sell her land's development rights to the owner of some other parcel of land. The parcel from which development rights are sold or transferred is usually in the "sending area," while the parcel receiving the development rights is in the "receiving area."

The programs employing the sale or transfer of development rights usually limit the intensity of development or prohibit development in the sending area and allow development intensity in the receiving area to be higher than that prescribed by the underlying zoning (Johnston and Madison, 1997). The sending areas often include historic preservation districts, farmlands, environmentally sensitive lands and areas with poor infrastructure and facilities, while the receiving areas usually include areas targeted for high intensity development, e.g. neighborhoods around transit stations, and city centers and downtowns.

Alternatively, the program can be structured such that the sending and receiving areas are one and the same. In such cases, while the overall amount of development remains the same, its location within the area is determined by the sale and purchase of development rights. Finally, in another variant, called the sale of development rights, there is no sending or receiving area. The government agency simply sells development rights (for example, additional floor area) for a fee.

International Use of Sale of Development Rights or TDR

From its first use in the beginning of the twentieth century, when the New York City zoning ordinance of 1916 allowed the sale of air rights to adjacent lots (Giordano, 1988), the use of TDR and the sale of development rights have increased both nationally and globally.

In the US, state-level enabling legislation in 20 states allows cities and counties to use TDR (Landis, McGrath and Smith, 2008). Apart from New York City, where TDR is extensively used to increase density in target areas, other regions, such as King County, WA and Montgomery County, MD have primarily used TDR programs to prevent urbanization of rural lands. Such lands are often environmentally sensitive and resource-rich. Moreover, some jurisdictions, such as Palm Beach County, FL, Seattle, WA, and New York City, NY, use the sale of development rights to promote affordable housing (Landis, McGrath and Smith, 2008; HUD 2009). Palm Beach allows developers to purchase development rights for the construction of affordable housing, while King County and New York City have designated affordable housing developments as an eligible sending area. Such a designation allows land owners to sell unutilized development rights if they construct affordable housing on their land.

The transfer or sale of development rights is growing globally. Sydney, Australia, uses the tool to preserve historic sites (Thompson and Maginn, 2012), while the commune of Lourmarin, France, uses it to protect agricultural areas (Renard, 2007), and Curitiba, Columbia, uses it to preserve both rural areas and heritage sites (Suzuki, et al., 2009). Mumbai, India, allows sale of development rights to incentivize construction of affordable housing by private developers. The developers earn development rights in lieu of constructing affordable housing units and are free to sell these rights in the open market (Business Standard, 2012).

Sale of Development Rights: Case Study of Certificate of Additional Construction Potential Bonds (CEPACs), Sao Paolo, Brazil

National context
Brazil's national-level city planning act, called the Statute of the City (*Estatuto da Cidade*), was passed in 2001 to address the rising social and economic inequities that arose from the country's rapid urbanization. Among other things, the Act empowers local governments to frame policies that balance an individual's property rights with the collective public interest (Instituto Polis, 2002, p. 28). The Act also seeks to minimize real estate speculation by institutionalizing the right of local governments to capture the property value increase that accrues due to public action such as the provision of infrastructure. Further, the Act allows local governments to sell development rights above and beyond the rights allowed by the underlying zoning. Moreover, the Act has created tradable land development rights, called CEPACs, that local governments can auction to fund infrastructure and services in areas targeted for intervention. Such areas, called Urban Operations (UOs), are identified by the city government for targeted public intervention to induce development and attract private investments to improve the UOs economic, social and environmental quality (Sandroni, 2010). The CEPACs grant their bearers the right to construct additional floor area beyond that allowed by the underlying zoning. For example, one CEPAC might grant the buyer the right to develop two square meters of additional floor area. Typical CEPAC-funded projects include road widening, construction of affordable housing, and creation of parks and recreational facilities.

Use of CEPACs by the City of Sao Paolo

With a population of well over 11 million, Sao Paolo is the largest city in Brazil (IBGE, 2010). Currently, almost half a dozen city-council-approved UOs (Sandroni, 2010; Bucalem, 2012) are being actively developed.

CEPACs were first created in 1995 in Sao Paolo to finance development in the Faria Lima UO. However, concerns about the tool's legality stalled its use up until the Statute of the City authorized the use of CEPAC throughout Brazil. CEPACs were approved in 2003 by the CVM (Brazilian equivalent of the U.S. Security and Exchange Commission) as freely tradable securities in the Brazilian Stock Exchange (Ciro, Sandroni and Smolka, 2006). First auctioned for the Faria Lima UO in 2004, the Sao Paolo city government has thus far issued CEPACs for two UOs, Faria Lima and Agua Espraiada (Sandroni, 2010).

The total development rights sold through CEPACs for a UO are calculated based on the estimated development carrying capacity of that UO after the CEPAC-funded infrastructure and services have been provided (Sandroni, 2010). For example, the total additional area to be sold in Agua Espraiada UO corresponds to 3.75 million CEPACs.

The minimum price of a CEPAC is determined by the city government and is based upon the estimated property value increment generated by the exercise of development rights granted by a unit of CEPAC. Further, the development rights granted per CEPAC vary by the location of the land parcel. For example, in the case of Agua Espraiada, in sections of the UO where the land is cheaper, each CEPAC corresponds to three square meters and to one square meter where it is more expensive. In the case of Faria Lima UO, CEPAC values range from 0.8 square meters to 2.8 square meters (Sandroni, 2010).

The sale price of a unit of CEPAC is market-determined through public or private auctions (Ciro, Sandroni and Smolka, 2006). For example, a 2008 auction of 186,740 CEPACs in Agua Espraiada opened with the minimum price of US$230 per CEPAC.[2] Each CEPAC sold for US$555, and the entire revenue of approximately US$104 million was used to fund affordable housing (Albrecht, 2010).

CEPAC generates significant funds

The city of Sao Paolo is using CEPACs to generate significant funds. Sandroni (2010) estimates that CEPAC revenues from just two UOs, Faria Lima and Agua Espraiada, totaled US$812 million over a five-year period, or 58 percent of the property tax revenue of US$1.4 billion from the entire city of Sao Paolo for the year 2007.

Advantages and challenges of CEPACs

CEPACs provide local governments with funds to develop infrastructure and services *prior* to the real estate development. Furthermore, the tool has very limited

---

2   At the rate of one US$ = two Brazilian Real.

downside revenue and construction risk and significant up-side revenue potential. In the worst case scenario where the CEPACs do not sell, local governments do not have to provide infrastructure and facilities and they only incur the cost of organizing the auction. On the upside, local governments get to keep the entire take if the CEPACs sell above the minimum price. To the extent that bidders pay more than the minimum price because their estimates of the CEPAC-generated property value are higher than the local governments' estimates, the local governments receive the maximum possible market-determined estimates of the property value increment. Finally, CEPACs allow local government to access capital markets, thereby significantly expanding the capital-base for urban development.

CEPACs also provide significant benefit to the buyers. First, in many cases, the CEPACs can be used to provide additional floor area as well as for change in land use. Second, they do not have to be used on a specific parcel of land. CEPACs can be used anywhere within the sector of the UO for which they are earmarked. Third, the buyers can employ the CEPACs at the time of their choosing, e.g., during periods of strong real estate demand.

Challenges

While CEPACs bestow significant advantages on the local government and the real estate development industry, they pose several challenges as well.

First, if the use of CEPACs is not part of a comprehensive urban development program, the CEPAC-generated revenues can be misspent on frivolous projects, or local governments may over- or under-estimate the UOs' development potential and offer too many or too few CEPACs for auction. Furthermore, local governments need significant technical and administrative capacity for estimating a CEPAC's fair price. Moreover, CEPAC revenues are dependent upon real estate cycles. CEPACs may not sell well during periods of weak real estate demand. Moreover, similar to any tradable security, CEPACs are prone to speculation. Buyers might purchase CEPACs during periods of weak demand, hold them for speculative purposes, and sell them to the developers at much higher prices during periods of strong real estate demand. In such cases, the financial gain from speculation accrues to the buyers, not to the local governments. Finally, CEPACs are not a recurring revenue source. The revenue flow stops once all the development rights are sold.

CEPACs also pose several challenges to buyers. First, buyers bear the real estate market risk. They might be stuck with CEPACs purchased at very high prices if the real estate market weakens significantly after the purchase. Furthermore, buyers bear significant construction risk if the promised CEPAC-funded infrastructure and service projects (for example, road improvement projects) are delayed, or worse, fail to take off. Moreover, the buyers assume the government risk, which is the risk that new legislation, government policies or corruption may negatively impact the value of the CEPACs (Sandroni, 2010).

Finally, CEPACs, or other similar tools used for the transfer or sale of development rights, are bound to be successful in regions with the following characteristics: strong real estate demand, a legal environment and government culture that allow land development rights to be bought and sold separately from the sale of land, a strong culture of compensating land owners for property value lost due to public action, and sophisticated capital market structures that allow for the auction and subsequent free trade of development rights in the secondary market.

Impact Fee: Brisbane, Queensland, Australia

Infrastructure Charges in Australia

As noted in Chapter 4, an impact fee falls under the broad umbrella of developer contributions. While all states and territories charge developer contributions in Australia,[3] the use of an impact fee, called infrastructure charges in Australia, is less common. Ranging from a few thousand dollars per residence to well above A$50,000, these charges are levied by both state and local governments to fund a variety of infrastructure and services (Commonwealth of Australia, 2011a, pp. 212–213), such as water and sewer systems, roads and public transport, as well as community facilities including community centers, libraries, parks and recreational facilities (Commonwealth of Australia, 2011a, p. 205)

The state-level acts or policies that provide the enabling environment for levying developer contributions also provide the framework for levying infrastructure charges. These acts and policies vary substantially across the country. For example, while New South Wales, Victoria and Queensland allow infrastructure charges to fund local as well as regional infrastructure and facilities, others states restrict their use to local infrastructure and facilities (Commonwealth of Australia, 2011a, p. 206).

The enabling environment also provides varying amounts of flexibility to local governments in charging the fee. For example, the state of Western Australia requires developer contributions in the form of land (or in-lieu fees) for open space, roads and schools; in the form of developer-built infrastructure for off-site water, sewer, drainage and electricity supply and road infrastructure; and monetary contributions for major water, sewer and drainage infrastructure such as water pump stations (Western Australian Government, 2009).

Furthermore, the state allows local governments to seek developer contributions for other infrastructure and facilities, such as community centers, child care, and sporting and recreational facilities (Commonwealth of Australia, 2011b), thereby providing the local governments the authority to levy infrastructure charges. For example, in Perth, the largest city of the state, developers pay infrastructure charges equal to approximately A$20,000 per residential unit of green field development and approximately A$5,000 per residential unit of in-fill development

---

3   The states and territories include Australian Capital Territory, New South Wales, Northern Territories, Queensland, South Australia, Tasmania, Victoria and Western Australia.

(Commonwealth of Australia, 2011a, p. 212). These charges can be levied to fund a wide variety of infrastructure and should be based on either a developer contribution plan or negotiated between the government and the developer. The developer contribution plans, among others, identify the infrastructure needs generated by the new development and the portion of the cost to be charged to the developer.

Infrastructure Charges in Queensland

Queensland is one of the eight states and territories that comprise Australia. The State Planning Act of 2009 provides Queensland's local governments with the enabling environment for levying infrastructure charges. The Act allows these charges to primarily fund trunk water, sewer and transportation infrastructure, and in some cases, local roads (Queensland, 2009, p. 417).

Before the 2009 Act, the legislative framework for levying infrastructure charges was provided by the Local Government (Planning and Environment) Act 1990, and the Integrated Planning Act 1997. However, the high amount levied by some jurisdictions and significant variations in charge calculation methodology and rates led to concerns about the housing affordability impacts and the transparency, reasonableness and consistency of these charges. These concerns were articulated in the Queensland Growth Management Summit of 2010 which was held to generate ideas for managing the state's future (Queensland Government, 2010). In response to stakeholder concerns raised during the Summit, the state government identified infrastructure charge reform as one of the key initiatives, and instituted a task force to recommend reforms. The task force submitted its report in 2011, recommending capping infrastructure charges. The state government acted on the task force recommendations through the State Planning Regulatory Provision (Adopted Charges) 2012, the SPRP, which prescribes a schedule of maximum infrastructure charges that local governments can levy. For example, the charge for a three-bedroom residence is capped at A$28,000 (Queensland Government, 2012). Earlier, some cities charged well above A$50,000.

Infrastructure Charges in Brisbane

The capital city of Brisbane levies infrastructure charges for various uses including residential, commercial, offices, industrial, and recreational uses. Three separate charges are levied for the sewer system; the water supply system; and for transport, community facilities, and storm water (Brisbane City Council, 2011). The infrastructure-charge-funded community facilities include parks and recreational areas, libraries and community centers.

The charges are usually levied at the following three instances:

a. At the time of reconfiguration of a lot, but before Council approves the subdivision plan;

b. During the building application stage before the certification of classification for the building work is issued; or

c. At the time of a material change of use, before the change happens (Brisbane City, 2009a, p. 11).

Apart from assessing charges based on the rate schedule, the city council has the power to enter into a negotiated infrastructure agreement with the developer, usually to "vary the amount, the timing or the form of payment of an infrastructure contribution, for example, to allow the applicant to supply works or land in lieu of part or all of the contribution" (Brisbane City, 2009a, p. 11). The infrastructure charges are estimated based upon the needs identified in the Infrastructure Contributions Planning Scheme Policies (PSPs). The PSPs either focus on selected infrastructure or services (e.g., the city-wide PSP for water supply infrastructure), or a specific geography (e.g., the Fig Tree Pocket PSP for the Fig Tree Pocket suburb of Brisbane, or both (i.e., the city has one PSP for all the community facilities needed in areas with potential for in-fill development) (Brisbane City Council, 2012).

Through the Infrastructure Contribution Unit (ICU) and equivalent tenement (ET), the PSPs link the infrastructure demand generated by a proposed development with the cost of providing the infrastructure. For example, the PSP for city-wide water supply infrastructure estimates that in the Acacia Ridge area of Brisbane, one detached single-family home generates 4,627 ICUs for water infrastructure and that one detached single-family home equals one ET. Furthermore, for the year 2011/12, one ICU equals $1.79. Therefore, the water infrastructure charge for material change of use per detached single-family home equals the number of ICUs times ET times the dollar value of each ICU, which equals A\$8,282 (4,627 x 1 x $1.79) (Brisbane, 2009b).

Comparison of Impact Fee Programs in the US and Australia

Impact fee has firmly established itself as an infrastructure finance mechanism in both the US and Australia. The impact fee programs in both the countries are similar in several ways. For example, they both use the fee to fund a wide variety of infrastructure and services. Furthermore, usually the fee can only be used to fund capital expenses, not the operations and maintenance expenses. Moreover, in both countries the state-level legislative framework provides the basis for charging the fee. Finally, in both countries the fee setting and implementation process takes transparency, equity, and efficiency into consideration.

In spite of the above discussed similarities, there are key differences between these impact fees programs. For example, while in the US impact fees as an infrastructure finance mechanism are only available to the local governments, in Australia the fees can be used to fund infrastructure provided by either local or state governments.

Moreover, while in the US impact fee for each infrastructure project or facility is charged separately, Brisbane's infrastructure charge for transport, community facilities and storm water show that in Australia, one charge may be levied for several infrastructure projects and facilities. For example, the City of Fremont, CA charges the following impact fees for single-family homes: $3,879 traffic impact fee, $17.55 per square foot of affordable rental housing impact fee, $3,336 capital facilities fee, $11,578 park fee, $386 fire fee (City of Fremont, 2012). While charging separate impact fees makes the fee programs more transparent and ensures that the fees meet the nexus and rough proportionality requirements,[4] it makes the tracking of fee revenues onerous.

Finally, local governments in Australia usually have the option to either negotiate the fee with the developers or charge a fixed rate; local governments in the US do not enjoy such flexibility. They have to charge the fee as per a fixed schedule.

Arguably, the flexible nature of the Australian impact fee programs might be better suited for developing countries that usually lack sophisticated financial reporting procedures, and detailed infrastructure plans and cost estimates and, therefore, cannot meet the strong nexus and proportionality requirements of the US impact fee programs.

Hong Kong's Rail Plus Property Development Model

The Mass Transit Railway Corporation Limited (MTRCL) is the agency in-charge of operating and constructing the mass rail transit system in Hong Kong. MTRCL's predecessor agency, the Mass Transit Railway Corporation (MTRC) was founded in 1975 (MTRCL, 2011a). It was fully owned by the Hong Kong Special Administrative Region (HKSAR) Government up until the government sold 23 percent stake to private investors in 2000 (Tang, et al., 2004). MTRC was re-organized as MTRCL in 2007 when it merged with Kowloon–Canton Railway Corporation, KCRC (GovHK, 2012a).

Hong Kong's geography, governance structure, real estate market conditions, and high rail ridership provide unique opportunities to use property development to fund the rail system. Covering an area of 1,104 square kilometers, Hong Kong is situated at the south-eastern tip of China, and is composed of four distinct geographical entities: Hong Kong Island, Lantau Island, the Kowloon Peninsula and the New Territories (GovHK, 2012b). A British colony until 1997, Hong Kong was re-unified with the People's Republic of China (PRC), and given the status of a special administrative region. Under the PRC's "one country two systems" policy, the PRC controls Hong Kong's foreign relations and defense, while Hong Kong has autonomy in matters of commerce and economy (US Department of State, 2012). This autonomy has allowed Hong Kong to pursue an independent

---

4   These requirements are described in Chapter 4.

urban development and public transportation policy tailored to serve its dense urban population.

Hong Kong is 25 percent urbanized, and is one of the most densely populated regions in the world, with a mid-2010 population of 7.07 million and a gross density of 6,504 people per square kilometer, or approximately 17,000 people per square mile (GovHK, 2012d). In comparison, the densest region in the US, the New York-Northern New Jersey-Long Island Metropolitan Statistical Area, only has a density of 2,826 people per square mile (United States Census Bureau, 2010). Furthermore, Hong Kong is a major financial center in the Asia-Pacific region. The combined effect of two major demand side factors (a robust economy and a dense population) has made Hong Kong's residential and office real estate among the priciest in the world. For the year 2010, the ratio of median house price to median household income, a measure of housing affordability, was 11.4 in Hong Kong (median household income of HK$225,400 and a median priced home of HK$2.58 million) (The China Post, 2011), compared to a ratio of 7.8 (US$459,000 median valued home and a median household income of approximately US$59,000) for the New York-Northern New Jersey-Long Island Metropolitan Statistical Area for the year 2006 (ACS, 2006).

The HKSAR Government is quasi-democratic in nature. At present, members of both the executive branch (the Chief Executive and the Election Committee) and a large proportion of the legislative branch (the Legislative Council, or LegCo) are not elected by universal suffrage (GovHK, 2012c).[5] Arguably, this limited form of democracy provides HKSAR a long-term horizon required to implement public transportation projects.

Finally, rail ridership in Hong Kong is impacted by land use in the neighborhoods around the rail stations, station characteristics, and inter-modal coordination. Loo, Chen and Chan (2010) finds commercial and mixed (commercial-residential) land use and residential density are station-area land use characteristics positively associated with rail ridership. Further, stations with ample parking for commuters are more heavily used. Finally, the buses feed passengers into the rail system. Therefore, the number of bus stops around a rail station is positively associated with rail ridership.

Mass Transport System in Hong Kong

Operated by MTRCL, Hong Kong's mass transit system is rail-based, and has grown rapidly since the commissioning of the first rail line in 1979. In 2012 the system served close to five million passengers daily (MTR 2012 Interim Report) through its 82 stations, and consisted of a variety of public transit systems. Nine rail lines totaling 175 km (109 mile) connect Hong Kong Island with Kowloon and the New Territories. A 36.2 km (23 mile) light rail line serves the local

---

5   Universal suffrage is the ultimate goal as per the Basic Law, Hong Kong's constitutional document.

communities of Tuen Mun and Yuen Long in the New Territories, and buses provide feeder service. The MTRCL also operates the Airport Express, a 35.2 km (22 mile) rail line connecting Hong Kong International Airport with the city's exhibition and conference center, AsiaWorld-Expo. Finally, MTRCL's inter-city rail service connects Hong Kong with Guangdong Province, Beijing and Shanghai in the Mainland China (MTRCL, 2011b).

Rail Plus Property Development (R+P) Model

Employing what MTRCL calls a rail plus property development (R+P) business model, the company partners with private property developers to develop commercial, office and residential projects on and around rail stations and depots. The HKSAR Government grants MTRCL the development rights to the station sites and to the government-owned lands along the rail corridors in lieu of a fee, called a "land premium," which is based on the "before rail" land values (UITP, 2011). For example, in 2010, MTRCL paid HK$3.9 billion as land premium for Austin Station Sites C and D along the Kowloon Southern Link (MTRCL, 2011a). The two sites would include six residential towers containing 1,200 apartments with an average apartment size of 99 sq. m. or 1,100 sq. ft. (MTRCL, 2011c).

As of 2011, MTRCL has executed projects around 29 of the 82 stations, providing close to 79,000 housing units and 1.7 million square meters of office and commercial space. Apart from developing property, MTRCL also manages properties throughout Hong Kong, including approximately 82,000 housing units, 12 shopping malls and 5 office buildings totaling three-quarters of a million square meters of office/commercial space. The profit after tax from the property development was between HK$3–4 billion during the period 2008–2011 (GovHK, 2012e). These profits are a significant portion of the company's total profits, accounting for 30 percent of the HK$15 billion after-tax profits for the year 2011 (MTRCL, 2011a).

The property development profits come primarily in two ways: a share in the developers' profits from the sale of real estate and an equity share in the property. Often the residential property is sold while the commercial and office properties are retained as investments (HSBC, 2012).

The R+P Model is not a panacea for all rail development projects. The model works for transit corridors that have or are anticipated to have a high demand for real estate. In fact, among the five rail lines projects undertaken since 2007, only two—the South Island Line (East), or SIL (E), and the Kwun Tong Line Extension, or KTE—are being implemented using the R+P Model. Feasibility studies showed that SIL (E) and KTE would cost HK$12.4 billion and HK$5.3 billion, respectively, and would need funding support from the HKSAR Government to the order of HK$9.9 billion and HK$3.3 billion, respectively. Therefore, in lieu of direct funding support for developing these two rail projects, the HKSAR Government granted MTRCL the property development rights for two government-owned parcels of land for developing the stations, rail depots and other properties.

The other three rail lines do not involve property development. In fact, the entire funding gap for one rail line, the West Island Line (WIL), is being met through a HK\$12.7 billion capital grant from the HKSAR Government (GovHK, 2012f). The other two lines, Shatin to Central Link (SCL) and the Guangzhou-Shenzhen-Hong Kong Express Rail Link (Hong Kong Section) (XRL), are being funded using a concession approach where the MTRCL would manage the construction of the rail lines and the HKSAR Government would bear most or all of the construction cost (LegCo, 2012; Bloomberg, 2010).

Key Contributors to the Success of the R+P Model

Clarity of vision
Provision of public transport and the integration of land use and transportation, are among the five principles guiding the HKSAR Government's Transport Strategy. The Strategy also seeks to enhance the role of rail as the primary public transportation system (HKSAR, 2010). These guiding principles provide a clear policy framework for the HKSAR Government's strong and consistent support for the MTRCL's R+P model, and the policy rationale for the transfer of land development rights from the Government to MTRCL. Assured of government support, MTRCL has been able to rely upon the R+P model as a major long-term business activity, which in turn, has allowed it to develop a high level of expertise in organizationally and financially coordinating its rail development and real estate business.

Close connections with the HKSAR Government
With 77 percent HKSAR Government ownership, MTRCL is effectively government-owned. This close connection with the government has its pros and cons. On the positive side, MTRCL has a monopoly over the transit business in Hong Kong. Furthermore, the company does not have to address the contentious land acquisition process. The HKSAR Government provides land to the company for both rail development and property development. Moreover, these strong connections arguably translate into favorable contract terms for the company. For example, the 2007 merger with the 100 percent government-owned Kowloon-Canton Railway Corporation (KCRC) provided MTRCL access to the New Territories. It is estimated that as part of the merger deal MTRCL only had to pay HK\$7.79 billion in return for KCRC's assets worth HK\$10.57 billion. On the downside, the strong government influence could limit MTRCL's freedom to set fares (HSBC, 2012).

Hong Kong's strong real estate market
As mentioned earlier, Hong Kong real estate is among the priciest in the world. Furthermore, with approximately 80 percent of travel occurring on public transportation (LTA, 2011), Hong Kong is heavily public-transportation-dependent. Therefore, access to public transportation significantly increases land

value in Hong Kong. MTRCL receives land development rights from the HKSAR Government at "before rail" prices, in effect allowing it to capture the full land value increase. This increase is significant for MTRCL-developed properties that are often in prime locations on and around transit stations.

Diversified revenue stream spreads risk
MTRCL has diversified its revenue stream. Up until a few years ago, MTRCL's profits were highly dependent on real estate, with revenue from the sale of real estate accounting for 32 percent of shareholder returns. This dependency has declined to 11 percent of shareholder returns following MTRCL's merger with KCRC. At the same time, the share of revenues from rail operations has increased from 10 to 39 percent. This diversification of the revenue stream has allowed MTRCL to withstand dips in the real estate market and economy (HSBC, 2012).

Applicability of the R+P model to the US

Historically, public transportation and property development in the US were closely linked. For example, much of the private rail road system was built in the nineteenth century through land grants provided by the federal government. Similarly, in the late nineteenth century many land development companies funded and often managed street car infrastructure in order to open rural land for development. However, by the turn of the century the demise of streetcars and the scandals surrounding land grants to railroads brought an end to the close link between public transportation and land development.

The synergistic relationship between land development and public transportation can be revived in the US with adequate regulatory safeguards. Some public transit agencies that own their station lands, such as the BART in the San Francisco Bay Area, have made limited strides in leveraging their station area land to generate revenue through joint development of real estate on these land parcels. The BART partnered with private developers and other local government agencies to develop Contra Costa Center Transit Village, a mixed-use office, commercial and residential development in Contra Costa County, CA. This development is further reviewed in Chapter 7.

The primary obstacles limiting the large-scale adoption of the R+P model, or its variants, in the US are two-fold: first, the lack of zoning powers, let alone land ownership, by transit agencies, and second, the opposition to high density development from the neighboring community. Often when transit stations fall within or at the periphery of low density residential neighborhoods, the residents fear that high density development on or around the transit station will depress the value of their homes and bring noise, air pollution and traffic congestion into their neighborhood. However, nascent US-specific empirical research provides some evidence that residents' fears about negative property value impacts of TODs might be ill-founded. For example, Mathur and Ferrell (2013) find that a sub-urban TOD in San Jose, CA, increased the value of surrounding single-family homes.

Similarly, in 1994, rents were $34 per month higher for apartment within one-quarter mile of the Pleasant Hill, CA, BART station compared to the apartments outside this distance band (Bernick and Cervero, 1996; Cervero, 1998). Finally, some transit agencies such as the MDT, Miami-Dade Transit,[6] have powers that allow them some influence over transit-proximate real estate development. Even before the Metrorail in Miami-Dade County, FL became operational in 1984, the Miami-Dade Board of County Commissioners recognized coordination of land use and transportation as vital to a viable rail system. Therefore, seeking to develop a cohesive transit-conducive zone along the heavy-rail corridors, the County adopted an ordinance in 1978 that requires the County and municipality to jointly adopt development standards that are acceptable to both the County and the municipality. Such influence over zoning could potentially be used by the transit agency to grant rights in return for a fee to develop such land or to share the profits derived from the development of such land, similar to the way MTRCL derives income from the R+P model.

References

Appleby et al. v. City of New York et al. No. 15, 271 U.S. 364, 46 S.Ct. 569, 70 L.Ed. 992 (1926, N.Y.). Available at: https://bulk.resource.org/courts.gov/c/US/271/271.US.364.15.html [accessed: 29 November 2012].

Day, P. 2005. *Incentives and Disincentives: The Potential of Property Taxes to Support Public Policy Objectives* [Online: Griffith University]. Available at: www.griffith.edu.au/__data/assets/pdf_file/.../urp-ip04-day-2005.pdf [accessed: 29 November, 2012].

Land Pooling and Readjustment (LPR), Gujarat, India

Archer, R.W. 1992. Introducing the Urban Land Pooling/Readjustment Technique into Thailand to Improve Urban Development and Land Supply. *Public Administration and Development*, 12, 155–174.

Archer, R.W. 1994. Urban Land Consolidation for Metropolitan Jakarta Expansion, 1990–2010. *Habitat International*, 18(4), 37–52.

Ballaney, S. 2008. *The Town Planning Mechanism in Gujarat, India*. Washington, DC: The World Bank.

Ballaney, S. and Patel, B. 2009. Using the Development Plan-Town Planning Scheme Mechanism to Appropriate Land and Building Urban Infrastructure, in *India Infrastructure Report*, edited by N. Mohanty, P. Sarkar and A. Pandey. New Delhi, India: Oxford University Press.

Hayashi, K. 2002. *Land Readjustment as a Crucial Tool for Urban Development*. Cambridge, MA: Lincoln Institute of Land Policy.

---

6   MDT is a department under the Miami Dade County.

Hein, C. 2010. Shaping Tokyo: Land Development and Planning Practice in the Early Modern Japanese Metropolis. *Journal of Urban History*, 36(4), 447–484.

Jha, A.K., Barenstein, J.D., Phelps, P.M., et al. 2010. *Safer Homes, Stronger Communities: A Handbook for Reconstructing after Natural Disasters.* Washington, DC: The World Bank [Online: World Bank]. Available at: http://www.housingreconstruction.org/housing/sites/housingreconstruction.org/files/SaferHomesStrongerCommunitites.pdf [accessed: 29 November 2012].

Karki, T.K. 2004. Implementation experiences of land pooling projects in Kathmandu Valley. *Habitat International*, 28, 67–88.

Krabben, E. and Needham, B. 2008. Land Readjustment for Value Capturing: A New Planning Tool for Urban Redevelopment. *Town Planning Review*, 79(6), 651–672.

Larsson, G. 1997. Land Readjustment: A Tool for Urban Development. *Habitat International*, 21(2), 141–152.

Lee, T. 2002. *Land Readjustment in Korea.* Cambridge, MA: Lincoln Institute of Land Policy.

Li, L. and Li, X. 2007. Land Readjustment: An Innovative Urban Experiment in China. *Urban Studies*, 44(1), 81–98.

Needham, B. 2002. *Land Readjustment in The Netherlands.* Cambridge, MA: Lincoln Institute of Land Policy.

Sorensen, A. 2002. *Consensus, Persuasion, and Opposition: Land Readjustment Organizing in Japan.* Cambridge, MA: Lincoln Institute of Land Policy.

Sagalyn, L.B. 2002. *Land Assembly, Land Readjustment and Public/Private Redevelopment.* Cambridge, MA: Lincoln Institute of Land Policy.

Turk, S. 2008. An Examination for Efficient Applicability of the Land Readjustment Method at the International Context. *Journal of Planning Literature*, 22(3), 229–242.

Turk, S. and Altes, W. 2011. Potential Application of Land Readjustment Method in Urban Renewal: Analysis for Turkey. *Journal of Urban Planning and Development*, 137(1), 7–19.

Turk, S. and Altes, W. 2010. How Suitable is LR for Renewal of Inner City Areas? An Analysis for Turkey. *Cities*, 27, 326–336.

Viitanen, K. 2002. *The Finnish Urban Land Readjustment Procedure in an International Context: What Can Be Learned Commonly.* Cambridge, MA: Lincoln Institute of Land Policy.

Interviews

Interview with Bimal Patel, an Ahmadabad-based urban planning consultant, March 7, 2010.

Interview with Vidyadhar Phatak, ex-Principal Chief, Town and Country Planning Division, Mumbai Metropolitan Region Development Authority, February 1, 2010.

Interview with Kaushik Gajjar, staff, Ahmadabad Urban Development Authority, February 22, 2010.
Interview with Vatsal Patel, staff, Ahmadabad Municipal Corporation, February 24, 2010.
Interview with Neela Munshi, staff, Ahmadabad Urban Development Authority, December 22, 2009.
Interview with Dinesh Mehta, Professor Emeritus, Center for Environmental Planning and Technology, Ahmadabad, December 21, 2009.

Sale of Development Rights, Sao Paolo, Brazil

Albrecht, D. 2010. *How to Finance Public Infrastructure from the Private Investors' Pockets in Urban Development Projects: The Examples of Brazilian CEPAC*, Marketplace on Innovative financial solutions for development, Paris, France, March 4–5, 2010.
Bucalem, M. 2012. *Sustainable Urban Development of São Paulo: Challenges and Opportunities*, fourth meeting of the World Cities World Class University network, University of Sao Paulo, Sao Paolo, Brazil, March 28–30, 2012. Available at: http://www.city.ac.uk/__data/assets/pdf_file/0007/129949/Secretary -General-Sao-Paulo_Day1.pdf [accessed: October 4, 2012].
Business Standard. 2012. *Maharashtra CM for Amending TDR Rules in Mumbai.* Available at: http://www.business-standard.com/india/news/maharashtra-cm-for-amending-tdr-rules-in-mumbai/464246/ [accessed: October 4, 2012].
Ciro, B., Sandroni, P., and Smolka, M. 2006. Large-scale Urban Interventions: The Case of Faria Lima in Sao Paulo. *Land Lines* 18(2): 8–13. Available at: https://www.lincolninst.edu/pubs/dl/1111_April%2006%20Land%20Lines%20final.pdf [accessed: October 4, 2012].
Giordano, M. 1988. Over-stuffing the Envelope: The Problem with Creative Transfer of Development Rights. *Fordham Law Journal*, 16, 43–66.
Instituto Brasileiro de Geografia e Estatística (IBGE). 2010. *2010 Census Results: 2010 Census: Brazilian Population Amounts to 190,732,694 Persons* [Online: IBGE]. Available at: http://www.ibge.gov.br/english/presidencia/noticias/noticia_visualiza.php?id_noticia=1766&id_pagina=1 [accessed: October 4, 2012].
Instituto Polis. 2002. *The Statute of the City: New Tools for Assuring the Right to the City in Brasil* [Online: Universal Periodic Review]. Available at: http://www.upr-info.org/IMG/pdf/UNH_BRA_UPR_S1_2008_UnitedNat ionsHABITAT_uprsubmission.pdf [accessed: October 4, 2012].
Johnston, R. and Madison, M. 1997. From Landmark to Landscapes: A Review of Current Practices in the Transfer of Development Rights. *Journal of the American Planning Association*, 63(3), 365–378.
Landis, M., McGrath, K. and Smith, L. 2008. Transferring Development Rights in New York City. *New York Law Journal*. Available at: http://www.phillipsnizer.

com/pdf/Article-NYLJ-RE-TransDevRights-ML-KMc-LS-9–29–08.pdf [accessed: October 4, 2012]

Renard, V. 2007. Property Rights and the Transfer of Development Rights: Questions of Efficiency and Equity. *Town Planning Review*, 78(1), 41–60.

Sandroni, P. 2009. A New Financial Instrument of Value Capture in São Paulo: Certificates of Additional Construction Potential, in *Municipal Revenues and Land Policies*, edited by G.K. Ingram and Y. Hong. Cambridge, MA: Lincoln Institute of Land Policy.

Suzuki, M., Dastur, A., Moffatt, S. and Yabuki, N. 2009. *Eco2 Cities: Ecological Cities as Economic Cities*. Washington, DC: The World Bank. Available at: http://www.preventionweb.net/files/11282_Eco2CitiesFullReportConfEdition6260.pdf [accessed: October 4, 2012].

Thompson, S. and Maginn, P. 2012. *Planning Australia: An Overview of Urban and Regional Planning*. Cambridge, UK: Cambridge University Press.

United States Department of Housing and Urban Development (HUD). 2009. Transfer of Development Rights and Affordable Housing. *Breakthroughs*, 18(5). Available at: http://www.huduser.org/portal/rbc/newsletter/vol8iss5_2.html [accessed: October 4, 2012].

Impact Fee: Brisbane, Queensland, Australia

Brisbane City Council. 2012. *Infrastructure Contributions Planning Scheme Policies*. Available at: http://www.brisbane.qld.gov.au/planning-building/development-assessment/infrastructure-charges/infrastructure-contributions-planning-scheme-policies/index.htm [accessed: October 1, 2012].

Brisbane City Council. 2011. *Brisbane Adopted Infrastructure Charges Resolution (No. 2) 2011*. Available at: http://www.google.com/url?sa=t&rct=j&q=brisbane%20city%20council%20brisbane%20adopted%20infrastructure%20charges%20resolution%20%28no.%202%29%202011&source=web&cd=1&cad=rja&ved=0CB8QFjAA&url=http%3A%2F%2Fwww.brisbane.qld.gov.au%2Fdownloads%2Fplanning_building%2Fdevelopment_assessment%2FAdopted_infrastruture_charges_resolution_2.DOC&ei=iT9uUPrPI-_oiwKTt4HYDg&usg=AFQjCNEZyiNbIVSGKhe5mBPI9QKk4ye2eQ [accessed: October 1, 2012].

Brisbane City. 2009a. *Infill Community Purpose Infrastructure Contributions Planning Scheme Policy*. Available at: http://www.brisbane.qld.gov.au/2010%20Library/2009%20PDF%20and%20Docs/2.%20Planning%20and%20Building/2.7%20After%20development%20approval/after_development_approval_infill_community_purposes_infrastructure_contributions_psp.pdf [accessed: October 1, 2012].

Brisbane City. 2009b. *Water Supply Infrastructure Contributions Planning Scheme Policy*. Available at: http://www.brisbane.qld.gov.au/2010%20Library/2009%20PDF%20and%20Docs/2.%20Planning%20and%20Building/2.7%20After%20

development%20approval/after_development_approval_water_supply_
infrastructure_contributions_psp.pdf [accessed: October 1, 2012].

Commomwealth of Australia. 2011a. *Performance Benchmarking of Australian Business Regulation: Planning, Zoning and Development Assessments.* Productivity Commission Research Report, Volume 1. Available at: http://www.pc.gov.au/__data/assets/pdf_file/0003/108840/planning-volume1.pdf [accessed: October 1, 2012].

Commomwealth of Australia. 2011b. *Appendix F: Jurisdictional Infrastructure Contribution Arrangements* in Performance Benchmarking of Australian Business Regulation, Planning, Zoning and Development Assessments, Productivity Commission Research Report, Volume 2. Available at: http://www.pc.gov.au/__data/assets/pdf_file/0009/108864/07-planning-appendixf.pdf [accessed: October 1, 2012].

City of Fremont. 2012. *Fee Schedule (With Developer Deposit Schedule).* Available at: http://www.fremont.gov/DocumentCenter/Home/View/3939 [accessed: October 4, 2012].

Queensland. 2009. *Sustainable Planning Act 2009.* Available at: http://www.legislation.qld.gov.au/legisltn/acts/2009/09ac036.pdf [accessed: September 27, 2012].

Queensland Government. 2012. *State Planning Regulatory Provision (Adopted Charges).* Available at: http://www.dsdip.qld.gov.au/resources/laws/state-planning-regulatory-provision/sprp-ict.pdf [accessed: October 1, 2012].

Queensland Government. 2010. *Shaping Tomorrow's Queensland: A response to the Queensland Growth Management Summit.* Available at: http://www.dsdip.qld.gov.au/resources/plan/growth-summit-response.pdf [accessed: October 1, 2012].

Western Australian Government. 2009. *State Planning Policy 3.6: Development Contributions for Infrastructure.* Available at: http://www.planning.wa.gov.au/dop_pub_pdf/sps3.6_dev_contributons.pdf [accessed: October 1, 2012].

Hong Kong's Rail Plus Property Development Model

American Community Survey (ACS). 2006. *American Community Survey Data Products for: New York-Northern New Jersey-Long Island, NY-NJ-PA* [Online: State of New Jersey Department of Labor and Workforce Development]. Available at: http://lwd.dol.state.nj.us/labor/lpa/census/acs/metro/New%20York-Northern%20New%20Jersey-Long%20Island,%20NY-NJ-PA.xls [accessed: November 1, 2012].

Bernick, M. and Cervero, R. 1996. *Transit Villages in the 21st Century.* New York: McGraw Hill.

Bloomberg. 2010. *MTR Corporation MTR Re Contract* [Online: Bloomberg]. Available at: http://www.bloomberg.com/apps/news?pid=newsarchive&sid=aXotoGvFTI.E [accessed: November 1, 2012].

Cervero, R. 1998. *The Transit Metropolis: A Global Inquiry.* Washington, DC: The Island Press.

GovHK. 2012a. *Review of the Fare Adjustment Mechanism of the MTR Corporation Limited* [Online: GovHK]. Available at: http://www.gov.hk/en/residents/government/publication/consultation/docs/2012/MTR.pdf [accessed: March 7, 2013].

GovHK. 2012b. *Hong Kong—the Facts* [Online: GovHK]. Available at: http://www.gov.hk/en/about/abouthk/facts.htm [accessed: November 1, 2012].

GovHK. 2012c. *Hong Kong: The Facts: Government Structure* [Online: GovHK]. Available at: http://www.gov.hk/en/about/abouthk/factsheets/docs/government_structure.pdf [accessed: November 1, 2012].

GovHK. 2012d. *Hong Kong: The Facts: Population* [Online: GovHK]. Available at: http://www.gov.hk/en/about/abouthk/factsheets/docs/population.pdf [accessed: November 1, 2012].

GovHK. 2012e. *Press Releases: LCQ6: MTR property development, Annex 3* [Online: GovHK]. Available at: http://gia.info.gov.hk/general/201204/25/P2 01204250310_0310_92955.pdf [accessed: November 1, 2012].

GovHK. 2012f. *Press Releases: LCQ6: MTR property development* [Online: GovHK]. Available at: http://www.info.gov.hk/gia/general/201204/25/P2012 04250310.htm [accessed: November 1, 2012].

Government of the Hong Kong Special Administrative Region, The (HKSAR). 2010. *Speech by Commissioner for Transport at Seminar on Environmentally Friendly Transport System*. Available at: http://www.td.gov.hk/en/publicatio ns_and_press_releases/speeches/20100605/index.html [accessed: November 1, 2012].

International Association of Public Transportation (UITP). 2011. *Project/initiative South Island Line (East): Implementing the "Rail + Property" financing model* [Online: International Association of Public Transportation]. Available at: http://www.ptx2uitp.org/sites/default/files/showcase_pdf/37_china.pdf [accessed: November 2, 2012].

LegCo. 2012. *LC Paper No. CB(1)1327/11–12: Updated background brief on Shatin to Central Link* [Online: Legislative Council of the Hong Kong Special Administrative Region of the People's Republic of China]. Available at: http://www.legco.gov.hk/yr11–12/english/panels/tp/tp_rdp/papers/tp_rdp0 323cb1–1327-e.pdf [accessed: November 1, 2012].

Loo, B.P.Y., Chen, C. and Chan, E.T.H. 2010. Rail-based transit-oriented development: Lessons from New York City and Hong Kong. *Landscape and Urban Planning*, 97, 202–212.

LTA. 2011. *Passenger Transport Mode Shares in World Cities* [Online: Land Transport Authority Singapore Government]. Available at: http://ltaaca demy.gov.sg/doc/J11Nov-p60PassengerTransportModeSHares.pdf [accessed: November 1, 2012].

Mathur, S. and Ferrell, C. 2013. Impact of Sub-urban Transit-oriented Developments on Residential Property Values. *Transportation Research Part A*, 47, 42–55.

Mass Transit Railway Corporation Limited (MTRCL). 2011a. *Growth in Motion: Annual Report 2011* [Online: MTR Corporation Limited]. Available at: http://www.mtr.com.hk/eng/investrelation/2011frpt_e/EMTRAR2011F.pdf [accessed: November 2, 2012].

MTRCL. 2011b. *Business Overview* [Online: MTR Corporation Limited]. Available at: http://www.mtr.com.hk/eng/publications/images/business_over view_e.pdf [accessed: November 2, 2012].

MTRCL. 2011c. *Austin Station: Austin Station (Site C & Site D)* [Online: MTR Corporation Limited]. Available at: http://www.mtr.com.hk/eng/properties/ ksl_site_cd.html [accessed: November 2, 2012].

Mass Transit Railway Corporation Limited (MTRCL). 2012. *Growth in Motion: Interim Report 2012* [Online: MTR Corporation Limited]. Available at: http:// www.mtr.com.hk/eng/investrelation/interim2012/EMTRIR12.pdf [accessed: November 2, 2012].

Tang, B.S. Chiang, Y.H., Baldwin A.N. and Yeung, C.W. 2004. *Study of the Integrated Rail-Property Development Model in Hong Kong* [Online: Reconnecting America]. Available at: http://reconnectingamerica.org/assets/ Uploads/mtrstudyrpmodel2004.pdf [accessed: November 1, 2012].

The China Post. 2011. Hong Kong has world's least affordable housing: survey. *The China Post* [Online 26 January]. Available at: http://www.chinapost.com. tw/business/asia/hong-kong/2011/01/26/289059/Hong-Kong.htm [accessed: November 1, 2012].

The Hong Kong and Shanghai Banking Corporation (HSBC). 2012. *Industrials Conglomerates Equity—Hong Kong: MTR (66)* [Online: HSBC Global Research]. Available at: https://www.research.hsbc.com/midas/Res/RDV?p=p df&key=S5y5G1AKbR&n=330961.PDF [accessed: November 1, 2012].

United States Census Bureau. 2010. *Patterns of Metropolitan and Micropolitan Population Change: 2000 to 2010*. Available at: http://www.census.gov/prod/ cen2010/reports/c2010sr-01.pdf [accessed: November 1, 2012].

US Department of State. 2012. *U.S. Relations With Hong Kong*. Available at: http:// www.state.gov/r/pa/ei/bgn/2747.htm [accessed: November 1, 2012].

Chapter 4
Use of Property Value Capture in the US

The local governments in the US have traditionally funded municipal infrastructure and services through broad-based tax revenues such as the property tax and sales tax revenues, and through federal and state aid. However, in recent decades, citizens have opposed tax increases. The most vocal of such opposition was California's Proposition 13. Passed in 1978, the proposition limited the property tax rate to 1 percent of the assessed value of the property, put restrictions on local governments' ability to increase property taxes over time, and raised the bar to impose new taxes. Constrained by their lack of ability to raise revenues through taxes, local governments have come to rely more on non-tax revenue sources such as user fees. However, local taxes and user fees do not meet transit funding needs adequately. Local taxes usually flow into the general fund, where competing demands often result in a low funding priority for transit. Farebox revenues do not typically fund the full operating costs of transit; let alone provide capital for the development of new transit systems. Therefore, the use of VC mechanisms to fund transit projects is gaining increasing attention. This chapter will provide an overview of the four VC mechanisms addressed in this book—SADs, TIF, joint development, and the transit impact fee. As mentioned earlier, these four are among the most commonly used VC mechanisms in the US.

Property Tax: The Traditional Property Value Capture Mechanism

Although not often viewed as such, the property tax is the most widely used property value capture tool in the US. Typically levied on land and any improvements on the land, the tax has many desirable qualities. It is progressive, meaning that those with a greater ability to pay, as evidenced by their ownership of more valuable property, are charged more tax. It is broad-based, that is, paid by a large group of people, the property owners. If designed well, the property tax is efficient because it does not distort consumer behavior; if the property tax rate in one jurisdiction is similar to the tax rate in another equivalent-quality jurisdiction, the tax does not create an incentive for the property owners to sell their property and move to the other jurisdiction.

The tax does a commendable job of capturing property value. In Chapter 2, we discussed the normative basis for employing property value capture tools—public action significantly increases the property value, and therefore, the entity undertaking these public actions, typically the city or the county government, has the right to capture at least some of the value increase. Because property tax is an ad valorem tax, charged as a percentage of the property value, it, in its purest form, simply but effectively captures any increase in property value.

While property taxes constitute the primary source of local government revenue, the property tax share of local tax revenue has declined from 80.5 percent in 1977 to 73.9 percent in 2009 (Tax Policy Centre, 2010). Even starker is the decline of property taxes as a proportion of the total local and state government revenue, plummeting from approximately one-quarter of such revenues (35.6 percent) in 1972 to one-sixth (16.6 percent) in 2005 (Reuben and Rosenberg, 2008). In fact, this decline is in line with the American's opposition to taxes in general and their ability to cap local and state tax rates. These revenues also fell from slightly under two-thirds (65.4 percent) of all local and state government revenue in 1972 to approximately half (54.3 percent) in 2005.

The revenues from property taxes and other local broad-based taxes, such as sales and local income and business taxes, usually flow into a jurisdiction's general fund and can be spent on almost any local government function. In practice, the lion's share of the general fund revenue is spent on education, police and fire protection, with the rest largely spent on wages and salaries. Little is often left for other infrastructure and services, including transit. Furthermore, as mentioned in Chapter 1, unlike water, sewer and electricity supply, transit cannot be funded and operated solely through user fees, specifically, fare box revenues. Moreover, transit agencies in US are under tremendous fiscal stress. Therefore, while funding for transit is limited, an increasing number of state and local governments are building public transit systems to revitalize their urban cores and grow in a sustainable manner. Portland, OR, and Seattle, WA, developed streetcar systems in the last decade and Charlotte, NC, and Atlanta, GA, are following suit. The federal emphasis on land use-transportation integration through the Intermodal Surface Transportation Efficiency Act (ISTEA), the Transportation Equity Act for the 21st Century (TEA-21), the Safe, Accountable, Flexible, Efficient Transportation Equity Act: A Legacy for Users (SAFETEA-LU), and more recently, the American Recovery and Reinvestment Act has further reinforced the need for transit. Indeed, transit use is growing. Almost 11 billion transit trips were undertaken in 2008—the highest number since the Interstate Highways System was approved in 1956 (Nelson Nygaard, 2009).

With all levels of public entities under fiscal stress, any new transit funding source is welcome. Non-property tax-based value capture tools are one such source. These tools include the imposition of public transportation impact fees, the sale or joint development of public land or property in proximity to the transit system, the lease or sale of air rights above the transit stations, the levy of special assessments, the capture of property tax increments through a TIF district, and land value taxation (LVT). With the exception of LVT, which is used only by a small number of Pennsylvania cities, these tools are rapidly gaining national interest, and hence will be further examined in this book.

While any one of the above identified value capture tools can be used to fund transit, the actual use of any of these mechanisms would depend upon several factors, such as the following:

- Legal provisions—does a state allow the use of TIF for public transportation?;
- Political acceptability—is a land value tax politically acceptable to the state and local governments?;
- Revenue yield—is an impact fee likely to yield adequate revenues, or would joint development be a better option? Can you use both the tools?;
- Administrative capacity—does the local government have the financial, administrative and technical capacity to undertake joint development?; and
- Equity—would use of impact fees adversely impact housing affordability?

Before we begin to examine the use of these tools, we will further define them. The remainder of this chapter provides an overview of the four value capture tools—transit impact fees, assessment districts, tax increment financing, and joint development. Further, through examples of specific transit infrastructure funded by these tools, this book will explore the various factors to be considered by local governments as they plan and implement these tools.

Non-property Tax-based Value Capture Tools

Impact Fee

An impact fee is a type of development exaction. A development exaction requires real estate developers to contribute public facilities, infrastructure and/or services either financially or in-kind (for example, through land donation). The term impact fee is used strictly to describe financial exactions (Altshuler and Gomez-Ibanez, 1993).

Standardized rather than negotiated (Nelson, Nicholas and Juergensmeyer, 2009), an impact fee is charged to recoup the capital costs of providing services and infrastructure (Smith, 2008). The fee has various names depending upon its purpose, including "capacity fee," "facility fee," "impact development fee," or "utility connection fee." However, the basic principle behind all types of impact fees is the same—the developer pays money to the local government for the development of infrastructure and services that will serve the new development.

How is an impact fee used?

Impact fees are used to fund a wide variety of public infrastructure and services. The most common uses are potable water and sanitary sewer facilities, followed by transportation projects, such as roads and highways. Impact fees are also used to fund libraries, parks, schools, police and fire facilities, and emergency medical facilities (Smith, 2008; Nelson, et al., 2008).

How widespread is impact fee use nationally?
Several nation-wide changes over the past decades have contributed to the rise of impact fees. These changes include: (1) the rapid rise in inflation beginning in the 1970s and early 1980s, which diminished the effectiveness of fixed-base taxes, such as the motor fuel tax, in funding transport infrastructure; (2) the reduction in federal funds for infrastructure that began in the early 1980s; and (3) property owners' opposition to property taxes (Nelson, Nicholas and Juergensmeyer, 2009). In addition to these changes, Americans have come to expect a level of service that is higher than ever before, raising the service provision cost.

The above changes increased the cost and shifted the fiscal burden of providing infrastructure away from the federal and state governments to the local governments (Nelson, Nicholas and Juergensmeyer, 2009). As a result, alternative funding mechanisms, such as impact fees, have become popular.

Impact fees are used in all 50 states. State-level enabling legislation is not a prerequisite for charging an impact fee. In fact, only half of the states have passed such legislation. Further, the use of the fee is not evenly distributed; it is used most heavily in the South and the West and is less common in the Northeast and Midwest (Nelson, Nicholas and Juergensmeyer, 2009).

How widespread is transit impact fee use?
While impact fee use is common for automobile-related transportation projects, such as roads, highways, and bridges, the fee is not commonly used for public transportation (Nelson, et al., 2008). At least 14 states prohibit transit impact fees, while 20 states have adopted legislation explicitly allowing the use of impact fees for transit (Smith, 2008).

Although allowed in several states, there are a few instances of the actual use of transit impact fees. A 2008 study finds few such cases and notes two main reasons for the infrequency of the use of impact fees. First, state laws often require impact fees to fund only capital expenditures and prohibit their use for operations. Transit capital expenditures are often already paid through federal subsidies. Therefore, the transit agencies see little use for the impact fee. Second, the entity responsible for charging the fee is often separate from the entity providing the transit service. While impact fees are collected by the municipal government or county as part of the permitting or zoning approval process, transit investments often fall under the purview of a separate authority that might be run by a state or local agency. This organizational separation of powers can complicate the appropriation of impact fee funds for transit. Further, the close coordination required between the municipal government and the transit agency to charge impact fees rarely occurs (Smith, 2008).

Legal framework for charging impact fees
From a legal standpoint, an impact fee is not a tax, but a fee (Altshuler and Gomez-Ibanez, 1993). While local jurisdictions usually have broad power to protect public health, safety, and welfare under the "police power," very often they may

not have the power to tax without voter consent (Nelson, et al., 2008). Hence, local jurisdictions have relied on their police power to legally justify the use of impact fees (Smith, 2008).

Characterizing an impact fee as a fee, rather than a tax requires that the service for which the developer pays the impact fee have a direct relationship to the development. In legal terms, the fee must have a "rational nexus" and "rough proportionality" to the use for which it is assessed (Altshuler and Gomez-Ibanez, 1993).

Two decisions by the US Supreme Court, popularly known as *Nolan* and *Dolan*, held that exactions (of which impact fees are a special case) must be related to the land development (the "nexus" requirement), and that there must be "rough proportionality" between the exaction and the land development impacts (Smith, 2008).

Major considerations for impact fee use:

Political acceptability

Impact fees may not always be politically feasible. For example, jurisdictions with low or negative population growth may view impact fees as obstacles to growth. In their view, impact fees may discourage growth by increasing land development costs. However, to provide new growth-serving infrastructure and services without increasing the existing residents' tax burden, rapidly growing jurisdictions may increase existing fee rates or charge new fees (Peters, 1994).

Critics have also questioned the constitutionality of impact fees, especially where state enabling statutes do not exist. They claim charging an impact fee is an abuse of local governments' police power (Peters, 1994). They further argue that impact fees are discriminatory, violate equal protection principles, and infringe on property rights (Nelson, et al., 2008).

Real estate market conditions and growth rate

Impact fees are suitable for rapidly growing jurisdictions with strong real estate demand (Tischler, 1999). Rapid growth often results in the demands for public services and infrastructure outstripping the local government's fiscal capacity. In such cases, impact fees can facilitate growth by providing an additional revenue source for the local governments (Altshuler and Gomez-Ibanez, 1993).

Institutional capacity

Impact fee-enabling legislation varies considerably among states. Many states lack clear guidelines regarding the uses eligible for impact fee funding. Courts have struck down many local impact fee ordinances, holding jurisdictions responsible for refunding the fees. Therefore, impact fees can be risky for local governments in the absence of clear state legislation. The fees may also require significant administrative and technical expertise to institute and manage (Lillydahl, et al., 1988).

Equity considerations

Several studies have found that impact fees increase housing prices. In King County, WA, the fee raised the price of new housing by 166 percent of the fee amount (Mathur, 2007). Furthermore, an impact fee was found to raise the price of existing housing by 60 percent in Miami-Dade County, FL. The fee is the highest in California, where a 2008 study finds that the average non-utility impact fees paid per single-family house equals $19,536, significantly higher than the nation-wide average of $11,276 (Nelson, Nicholas and Juergensmeyer, 2009).

Pointing out impact fees' negative impact on horizontal equity,[1] critics note that the fee can disproportionately affect certain land uses and types of development. For example, in one jurisdiction, apartment dwellers might pay the same amount of school impact fees as residents of single-family homes despite housing far fewer school-going children (Nelson, et al., 2008).

In some cases, the criteria for determining the impact fee amount may be vertically inequitable.[2] For example, many jurisdictions charge a park impact fee per dwelling unit even though smaller homes may have lower values and house fewer people than larger homes. Therefore, a per-unit park impact fee tends to place a greater burden on the smaller homes. To the extent that lower-income households own smaller homes, impact fee causes vertical inequity (Nelson, et al., 2008).

Finally, the fee is often charged without adequate consideration of the ripple effects of the impact fee-paying development. For example, a new office development may be charged an impact fee. However, the new office development may cause an influx of construction workers and, eventually, of people who will work in the office buildings. In the absence of an adequate housing supply, impact fee-enabled rapid office growth can create job-housing mismatch, requiring workers to live far from their jobs (Altshuler and Gomez-Ibanez, 1993). Courts have allowed the use of impact fees to pay for attendant housing needs and other "soft" services under the "rational nexus" principle (Nelson, et al., 2008).

Special Assessment Districts

A special district is a government entity that provides one or more services, but is often not administered by a general governing body, such as a city or a county. A special district employs a cost recovery system that is based on the benefits-received principle (Snyder and Stegman, 1986). The district can charge a user fee

---

1 Beneficiary-to-pay (BTP) principle operationalizes the horizontal equity rule in the field of public finance. Underlying principle behind the popularity of user fees, impact fees, tax increment financing and special assessments, BTP calls for those benefitting from a public infrastructure/service to pay for it in proportion to the benefit derived.

2 Operationalized through the ability-to-pay principle, vertical equity has its roots in welfare economics. In the field of public finance, vertical equity rule calls for the rich to pay more than the poor for government-provided goods and services.

(for example, a water district), receive a portion of property taxes (for example, a library district), or levy assessments (for example, a transportation benefit district).

Uses of special districts
Special districts have long been used to provide a wide variety of services and infrastructure. Most special districts provide service and infrastructure in one of these six areas: electric power, transportation, hospitals, housing and community development, water, and sewers (Porter, Lin and Peiser, 1992).

Growth of special districts
States have used special districts since the mid-nineteenth century, and all 50 states currently do so. Beginning in the early twentieth century, special districts became popular due to rapid urbanization and the attendant need to build new infrastructure. During the Great Depression, many special districts became insolvent due to falling property values. However, their use increased again as the depression ended and has grown ever since. The districts have been particularly popular in fast-urbanizing un-serviced rural or peri-urban areas (Lari, et al., 2009; Porter, Lin and Peiser, 1992).

Special assessment districts: A sub-set of special districts
Special assessment districts (SADs) are a sub-set of special districts that charge property owners mandatory fees, called assessments, in lieu of the benefits provided by the SAD to the property owner (Lari, et al., 2009). Like private financing, these districts are structured so that those who benefit from the improvements pay for them (Snyder and Stegman, 1986).

Use of SADs to fund public transportation
The use of SADs to fund public transportation has grown in recent decades. In the 1980s, several metropolitan areas, including Los Angeles, CA, and Washington, DC, began using SADs to finance rail projects. In the last decade, several cities, such as Seattle, WA and Portland, OR, have used them to finance transit infrastructure, such as street cars and light rails, while Charlotte, NC and Atlanta, GA, plan to use them to finance local transit projects (Lari, et al., 2009).

Properties within SADs are assessed fees based on attributes, such as property value, parcel size, street frontage, and use (Nelson, et al., 2008). Street front footage, or the length of the property along the transit infrastructure, is the traditional method of determining the benefit in a SAD. However, new methods are becoming more popular, as the frontage method has proven inequitable (Snyder and Stegman, 1986). These new methods include the following:

- The "benefits assessed" or "increased value" method: This method estimates the increase in value for each property to determine the fee amount.
- The "zone" method: This method uses the proximity to the amenity to determine the fee amount. For example, properties may be divided into

zones depending on their proximity to the transit infrastructure, with the fee rate increasing with the proximity.
• The "area" method: In this method, assessments are proportional to the size of the land parcel on which the property is located (Lari, et al., 2009).

The infrastructure and services within a SAD can be financed using the "pay as you go" method, that is, by spending funds as they are collected, or the "pay as you use" method, where SAD revenue-backed bonds (commonly called special assessment bonds) fund the infrastructure project. Special assessment bonds cover the up-front costs of building infrastructure. These bonds have the added advantage of being more politically feasible than general obligation bonds in some states, such as California, where a simple majority is needed to approve them, rather than the two-third super-majority required for the general obligation bonds (Mathur, 2009).

The enabling legal framework
The states' legal requirements impact SAD formation. In most cases, the majority property owners must support SAD formation. After the property owners vote for the SAD, a preliminary study outlining the project details is conducted, and the city or county council votes to approve or deny SAD formation. Next, each property within the SAD is assessed a fee. Property owners are given the option to appeal the fee. If an appeal is upheld, the fee is reassessed (Lari, et al., 2009).

Other considerations for use:

Political acceptability
Unlike exactions and impact fees that only apply to new developments, SADs can also affect existing developments. Therefore, some states require SADs to be contiguous and to include already developed properties. This requirement makes SADs politically unpopular with the current residents. To reduce voter opposition, the exclusion of existing developments is becoming the norm in states that do not require contiguous application of a SAD (Snyder and Stegman, 1986).

Government fragmentation
The proliferation of special districts could lead to multiple government agencies serving the same population. These agencies often perform similar or related services. This functional overlap makes coordinated service provision complex. The overlap might also reduce the efficiency of service provision. For example, special districts have enabled the creation of "phantom cities" (highly urbanized pockets in the county area) in California. The residents of these phantom cities use SADs to provide essential services that are typically provided by a city, thereby obviating the need to become part of a city. Critics argue that special districts' proliferation puts a burden on nearby cities as well. The residents of phantom cities are often unwilling to contribute to regional initiatives. In addition, phantom

cities often provide a low level of service (such as poor police protection or few parks) leading to negative spillover effects (Snyder and Stegman, 1986). These effects include spillover of criminal activity to the surrounding cities and higher demand for the parks located in the surrounding cities.

Quasi-governmental entities with less public oversight

Highlighting the undemocratic nature of special districts, critics note that voting privileges are sometimes determined based on property qualifications rather than residency (McCabe, 2000). Additionally, special districts can often fly under the public radar, as residents may assume that the districts are a part of the local city or county government. The resulting lack of public oversight may decrease transparency in the functioning of the special districts (Porter, Lin and Peiser, 1992).

A way to by-pass bond issuance limits

Special districts are more likely to be created when states restrict local governments' taxing or borrowing powers. In such situations, fiscally constrained local governments can face difficulty meeting their constituents' service demands (McCabe, 2000). As the debt raised by the special districts does not qualify as traditional municipal debt, special districts can be formed to fund infrastructure and services otherwise provided by the local government.

Impact of real estate market conditions

SADs need a strong real-estate market to thrive. The impact of the real estate market can be particularly significant on SADs formed to fund newly urbanizing areas. These SADs typically rely on the future urban growth. Existing property owners can bear heavy assessment burdens if the anticipated growth does not materialize (Meisner and Firtell, 1990).

Equity considerations

If not structured carefully, SADs can negatively impact vertical equity by putting a high burden on those with a low ability to pay. Assessments are regressive when they do not take into consideration the property owner's income level, thereby putting a financial burden on lower income property owners (Downing and Bierhanzl, 1995).

Assessments can reduce horizontal equity if certain groups of properties, often the residential properties in already built-up areas, are exempt from paying assessments or pay lower assessments, even though they benefit from the assessment-funded infrastructure or service.

Tax Increment Financing

Tax increment financing (TIF) is a funding mechanism primarily intended to remove physical blight, and enable economic development.

TIF is implemented by creating a geographic district administered by a TIF authority, usually a redevelopment agency. After the district is created, the assessed property value is frozen for a period of time, usually ranging from 10 to 25 years (Paetsch and Dahlstrom, 1990). As new funds are invested, the property values in the district increase, and so do the property tax revenues. The property tax increment (the new property tax minus the property tax on the frozen property values) is diverted to the TIF authority rather than the agencies that would usually receive it. Such agencies include the city, county and school districts. The tax increment is reinvested in the TIF district.

Under the TIF mechanism, there are two ways to raise funds for initial infrastructure development: a pay as you go approach or a pay as you use (sometimes called "rebate" or "up front") approach (Smith, 2008). The pay as you go approach can be a slow process, as the development is financed as and when the tax increment revenue is realized. The other approach requires the TIF authority (or the local government) to issue bonds backed by the future tax increment revenue. Bond proceeds can be used immediately or "up front" to finance the development. The "up front" approach, while inherently riskier than the pay as you go approach, is the most common for the simple reason that the TIF agencies often need money up front to kick-start capital projects (Paetsch and Dahlstrom, 1990).

For what purpose is TIF used?
In most states, TIF districts can only be created to fight blight. Although the exact definition of blight varies among states, the blighted areas are usually characterized by physical deterioration, unsanitary conditions, and a high rate of tax delinquency. Ideally, TIF removes severe blight, directs public funds to a community plan or policy, addresses environmental remediation, and finances infrastructure (CDFA, 2007; Paetsch and Dahlstrom, 1990).

Although there is much debate as to whether TIF should be used to develop areas that are not truly blighted, several states do so. For example, TIF can be used to promote economic development as well as to promote redevelopment in Ohio, Vermont, Connecticut, Kentucky, Delaware and North Carolina. Vermont has the most lenient legislation, allowing TIF to be used for development, job creation, or even simply to increase tax revenue (Marks, 2005).

How widespread is TIF use nationally?
TIF was first used in California in 1952. By 1970, only a few western states and Ohio had TIF-enabling state legislation. However, TIF use spread quickly across the country as local governments sought ways to fill the financing void left by the federal funding cuts of the 1970s. By the late 1980s, few states lacked TIF-enabling legislation. Eventually, with the exception of Arizona, all of the states and Washington, DC enacted such legislation (CDFA, 2007; Paetsch and Dahlstrom, 1990).

However, some states, such as Illinois, use TIF more than others, such as New Jersey, Arkansas, North Carolina, and Louisiana. TIF can be used to fund several types of public infrastructure projects, including sewer and storm drainage systems, streets, park improvements, streetscape improvements, landscaping, libraries, environmental remediation, emergency service facilities, schools, and public transportation (CDFA, 2007).

Is TIF used to fund public transportation?
Though growing, the use of TIF to fund transit projects is not common. In fact, a 1985 study notes that the Embarcadero station in San Francisco was the only known use of TIF to fund transit (Johnson and Hoel, 1986). Since then, several new instances of TIF use for transit have been documented.

A 2008 report identifies four states where TIF had been used to fund transit and transit-related projects—Illinois, Pennsylvania, Georgia and Oregon. The TIF areas in these states are referred to as special taxing districts, development authority districts, community facilities districts, or community management districts (Smith, 2008). Several instances of TIF-funded TODs have also been noted (CDFA, 2007).

TIF can be used to fund transit or TODs in several ways. In the first or traditional way, a transit station or other transit infrastructure may fall completely within a TIF district. The funds collected from the TIF district are then used to fund several projects within the TIF district, *including* the transit infrastructure. This is the case in Chicago, where TIF funds are being used to redevelop three transit stations (Smith, 2008). Another, more recent, way is by creating a special transit taxing district, where funds are used to pay for the transit or the TOD. In this method, funding transit-related projects is the sole purpose of the TIF district. One such example is in Pennsylvania, where Transit Revitalization Investment Districts (TRIDs) are created to fund TODs. These districts differ from SADs. TRIDs use *tax increments* as the revenue source, whereas SADs assess *fees*.

The legal framework
States almost always require that two criteria be met before a TIF district can be formed: a finding of blight and the "but for" requirement. The "but for" requirement necessitates proving that the area within the proposed TIF district would not develop "but for" the creation of the district. There must be adequate proof that the area would not improve without public intervention. Most states also require preliminary project plans, a redevelopment plan, public hearings, and plan approval by elected officials (Paetsch and Dahlstrom, 1990).

Other considerations for TIF use:

Stakeholder support
Public buy-in is extremely important for TIF success. The neighborhood residents are often most affected by the TIF-led changes. In many cases, TIF funds might be used for high impact projects, such as building demolition and construction. While some stakeholders may find this demolition and rebuilding aesthetically desirable

and economically beneficial, others may be concerned about the displacement of existing residents, destruction of historic buildings, and other changes to the neighborhood character (CDFA, 2007).

Buy-in from other government agencies and the business community is also necessary. The Council of Development Finance Agencies (CDFA) lists four groups that are critical for TIF success. They are the following:

- Development authorities: Cities use development authorities to make key development decisions and administer TIF.
- Finance agencies: These agencies often lend money for TIF projects, and set lending terms and conditions.
- Chamber of commerce: Chamber of commerce boards often comprise powerful business leaders who could provide essential support and broker TIF project deals.
- Private and non-profit entities: Private for-profit entities, such as energy providers, can be key supporters because they may have business interests in the TIF-funded development. Non-profit agencies are also important stakeholders. They often work closely with the TIF development (for example, a TIF-aided affordable housing development) and could provide political and financial support.

Real estate market conditions

The success of a TIF district hinges on the TIF-funded development project's ability to raise property values within the district. If the property values do not rise, or worse, fall, the district might face difficulty repaying the TIF-backed bonds. Therefore, the consistency of TIF revenues is important. Due to the financial risk involved in the TIF-funded projects, it is contingent upon the local government to conduct an extensive financial viability analysis of the TIF district. Such an analysis must show a steady and continuous growth in property values within the TIF district. In addition, it is essential that the redevelopment plan accurately anticipate the market conditions, and that it be carried out on schedule (CDFA, 2007).

Institutional capacity

The process of creating and maintaining a TIF district requires significant institutional capacity. TIF is complex, often requiring input from multiple experts, such as municipal bond financing experts, economic development experts, real estate appraisers, civil engineers, financial analysts and consulting planners (Paetsch and Dahlstrom, 1990).

Equity considerations

Housing prices in the TIF district may rise due to the TIF-funded improvements, pricing out many existing residents. To the extent that these residents are likely to be low-income households,[3] TIF can negatively impact vertical equity. Some states, such as California, have tried to address this problem by allotting a portion of TIF funds to affordable housing. However, demographic shifts could still occur (CDFA, 2007).

TIF can also negatively impact horizontal equity. To the extent that the property taxes would have increased without the use of TIF, the capture of the entire property tax increment by the TIF district results in the loss of tax revenues for other taxing agencies, such as the school district, county or city. In such a scenario, TIF can negatively impact other essential services, such as schools or health care. It is often politically difficult to create TIF districts amidst opposition from the school or hospital districts (Johnson and Hoel, 1986). Some states, such as California, have tried to address this situation by allowing other taxing districts to share the tax increment with the TIF authority.[4]

Joint Development

Joint development involves cooperation between private and public entities—often a transit agency/local government and a real estate developer—to develop a real estate project. From the local government perspective, joint development partnerships aim to raise revenue for the transit agency and/or increase ridership. Three features are unique to joint development:

- Joint developments are legally binding agreements between the two parties;
- The private party must compensate the public entity through payments or cost-sharing arrangements; and
- Agreements are voluntary for all the parties involved (Cervero, et al., 2004).

Joint development benefits for the transit agency
Joint developments can benefit transit agencies in a number of ways. First, private developers could compensate transit agencies for the right to develop on the agency land (ground lease payments) or over the land (air rights lease) or for the physical connection between their property and the transit station (station connections fee). Furthermore, private developers can share the costs of construction and/or maintenance of the station and other facilities, such as the heating and ventilation systems (Cervero, et al., 2004).

Apart from the more straight forward revenue and cost sharing, joint developments could bring other benefits to the transit agencies, including

---

3 Low-income households are likely to be concentrated in the blighted neighborhoods targeted for TIF-funded redevelopment.

4 Effective February 1, 2012, redevelopment agencies (RDAs), the public agencies in-charge of TIF, have been dissolved in California. TIF was charged with siphoning-off property tax revenues from other taxing governments such as the school districts and counties.

increased transit ridership by increasing station-area density or adding destinations on transit lines. The increased ridership can, in turn, raise the transit agency's farebox revenue. Transit agencies may also enter into joint agreements to promote economic development and job growth or create affordable or transit-accessible housing (Cervero, et al., 2004).

Typical joint development arrangements
Three major types of joint development arrangements are in use, primarily based on the ways in which the transit agencies and developers can derive benefit. These include: i) revenue sharing arrangements; ii) cost sharing arrangements; and iii) use of incentives, or a combination of the above three (Cervero, et al., 2004; Lefavre, 1997).

The sale or lease of property is the most common revenue sharing arrangement. The transit agency grants developers the right to develop or occupy a piece of agency-owned land. Leases could include air rights leases, ground leases, or subterranean leases, based on whether the transit agency leases land or space above, on, or below the land (for example, space below the transit station) to the developer.

Operations and construction cost sharing is the second most common arrangement, in which transit agencies and private developers jointly pay for the construction and/or ongoing operations and maintenance. The station connection fee is next, where tenants or landowners pay a fee to the transit agency to access the station (Lefavre, 1997). Incentive agreements are the fourth most common arrangement. Developers are granted density bonuses or other benefits in exchange for contributing to the transit agency's objectives. This type of agreement is most common in New York City, where density bonuses are extremely valuable to developers. The other arrangements (such as negotiated private contributions) are less common and make up only a small percentage of joint development agreements nationwide (Cervero, et al., 2004; Landis, Cervero and Hall, 1991).

The major cost sharing arrangements include the following: incentive-based agreements (including negotiated private contributions)—the transit agency grants developer special privileges, such as a density bonus, in exchange for a fee that is typically used to fund transit infrastructure; voluntary agreements (including construction cost sharing and operations cost sharing)—agreements to coordinate and fund planning, construction, or operations or other agreements that can reduce the costs to both the transit agency and the developer; and equity participation—both the transit agency and the developer contribute construction funds (Cervero, et al., 2004).

Barriers to joint development
The most significant barrier to joint development is the prohibition by several states and counties—such as Pennsylvania and New Jersey, and Miami-Dade County, Florida—of transit agencies engaging in land use activities and real estate development. With little control over the type and intensity of uses allowed on

and near the transit stations, the agencies are unable to create joint development proposals that are attractive to private developers. Even if allowed to undertake land use activities, the transit agencies may face internal opposition. Many transit agency board members simply do not believe that their agency should be involved in real estate development (Cervero, et al., 2004).

Transit agencies may also have other policies that inhibit joint development. For example, the BART has a one-for-one parking replacement policy that often requires construction of prohibitively expensive multi-storied parking garages to compensate for displaced surface parking.

Transit agencies may also lack understanding of the complicated private real estate development process. Agencies have been known to mismanage and overestimate the value of their property (Lefavre, 1997).

Finally, other public agencies, such as city governments or redevelopment agencies may oppose joint development or may not view real estate development as within the purview of transit agencies. These public agencies may not co-operate with the transit agencies (Cervero, et al., 2004).

Private developers can also lack joint development experience. Additionally, public agencies may impose requirements that developers perceive as risky, such as requiring a mix of housing types or socio-economic groups that, in the private developers' view, may negatively impact real estate market demand. Other risks include the following: the planning process and regulations can be highly complicated and place unknown and undue burdens on the developers; the request for proposal (RFP) process, often employed to choose the developer, is inherently risky for the developers; the unknowns of partnering with a transit agency may limit the expectations of a developer in terms of what they can build; and other requirements imposed by the transit agency may reduce profits, such as the requirement to sell a certain number of units at below-market rate (Lefavre, 1997).

Political opposition to joint development projects may also be a barrier. The surrounding communities may oppose these developments on a number of grounds, including traffic congestion, air and noise pollution, or the fear of lower-income residents moving into their neighborhoods.

History of joint development projects
Joint development in the US became popular in the early 1980s, when 10 new rail systems were completed (Cervero, 1994). A 1990 study reports 117 joint development projects in 24 cities throughout the USA. A more recent, 2010 GAO study reports 166 such projects, of which just three agencies (Los Angeles Metro, Washington Metro, and Metropolitan Atlanta Rapid Transit, or MARTA) were responsible for 58 (USGAO, 2010). Dallas, San Diego, and the San Francisco Bay Area have also used joint development extensively (Cervero, et al., 2004).

Supportive federal policies also contributed to the popularity of joint development projects. The Young Amendment to the National Mass Transportation Act of 1974 and the Surface Transportation Act of 1978 allowed the use of federal funds for joint development projects. Under the Reagan Administration during the 1980s, the federal government began requiring that transit agencies receive more funds from local sources and operate more efficiently, which led agencies to seek funding through non-traditional sources, such as joint development. Additionally, after a long period of decline, the real estate market began to revive in central cities in the 1980s and 1990s, attracting new investors and making joint development feasible in inner-city areas (Landis, Cervero and Hall, 1991).

Overview of joint development projects nationally
As noted above, although over 166 in number nationally, joint development projects are concentrated in a small number of urban areas. The projects located in some of the major urban areas are discussed below.

The Washington Metropolitan Area Transit Agency (WMATA) has been particularly active in joint development, with over 33 completed projects since the 1970s (The Schumin Web Transit Center, 2011; Cervero, et al., 2004; Landis, Cervero and Hall, 1991). WMATA has used a diverse set of tools, including air rights, service connection fees, and cost sharing agreements. The agency has been successful in undertaking joint development projects in part because it created a real-estate development department that actively seeks out joint development opportunities.

Rather than trying to standardize the process, WMATA considers each opportunity on its own merits. The WMATA has devised a rating system to assess the potential of new sites and developed guidelines to ensure project success. Seeking to attract new riders, increased revenue, and expand the tax base, these guidelines include maximizing the use of transit, linking land use to transit, mixing housing types and uses, and bringing vibrancy to urban spaces (Cervero, et al., 2004). While WMATA is proactive in seeking out joint development opportunities, devoid of any land use powers, it must rely on the local jurisdictions for the actual joint development approvals.

New York City actively pursues joint development to renovate and redevelop existing stations, primarily using cost sharing agreements to pay for such improvements. The regional transportation agency, the Metropolitan Transportation Authority (MTA), has worked with the planning department to provide incentives, such as the floor-area ratio bonuses, while requiring property owners to improve subway facilities adjacent to their buildings. The city planning department has also incentivized joint development by relaxing station-area zoning limitations (Cervero, et al., 2004, Landis, Cervero and Hall, 1991).

Miami-Dade County, FL, has used a different cost sharing tool, known as the Rapid-Transit Zone (RTZ), to encourage joint development. Created along the rapid transit lines, RTZ lessens private developers' risk by standardizing the zoning ordinances among all municipalities within the zone. Miami has encouraged joint development along rail transit corridors outside of the RTZ with incentive-based agreements, such as density bonuses, and by supporting rail stations with new infrastructure (Cervero, et al. 2004).

Completing five joint developments by 2011 (Tarantino and Ward, 2011), Atlanta, GA, has encouraged joint development, especially along its Peachtree corridor, by modifying zoning ordinances to allow for greater density and taller buildings. These modifications resulted in the construction of several new office buildings on or adjacent to MARTA stations (Landis, Cervero and Hall, 1991).

In the San Francisco Bay Area, BART has used joint development to promote TODs near stations. Recent projects include mixed-use Contra Costa Centre Transit Village and Fruitvale Station Transit Village. BART has also encouraged cooperation between other agencies and private developers to facilitate new growth around transit stations.

In the southern part of the San Francisco Bay Area, the Santa Clara Valley Transportation Authority (VTA), unhampered by restrictive policies, such as BART's one-for-one parking replacement policy, has been able to develop TOD projects in former surface parking lots.

San Diego, CA, has used incentive-based agreements to encourage TODs. By streamlining the development process along transit corridors, the city has been able to prevent developers from building auto-oriented developments or to require them to include affordable or senior housing in exchange for a streamlined development permit approval process (Landis, Cervero and Hall, 1991).

Other considerations for joint development use:

Stakeholder acceptance

Joint developments must be internally acceptable to the transit agencies' board members and the other transit agency decision makers, and externally acceptable to the local communities, other public agencies and the city or county governments.

A clear joint development policy or even an unofficial internal consensus could garner significant acceptance of joint developments. For example, an agency should identify its key goals in pursuing a joint development. Should joint developments primarily benefit the community (for example, through the development of affordable housing) or be devoted to the highest and best use? Agencies that lack clear policy objectives can become plagued by disagreements or lack of direction.

External stakeholder acceptance is important. Joint development must win community support and obtain government approval. This is especially important for transit agencies operating in multiple jurisdictions. Such agencies might have to collaborate with several local governments and public agencies and win the support of multiple community groups.

Real estate market conditions

Joint developments are impacted by market conditions. Weak market conditions can reduce revenue yield. Many leases protect transit agencies from market risk by requiring minimum guaranteed lease payments.

Institutional capacity
The institutional capacity needed for joint developments varies based on the project type and size. Nonetheless, most joint developments require considerable institutional capacity to conceptualize the developments, determine their scope, invite developers to partner in project development, review the developers' proposals, negotiate agreements with developers, and manage the project during and after the construction stage.

Equity considerations
Equity considerations in joint development revolve around horizontal equity. Private developers and/or transit agencies typically finance joint developments. The project risk is therefore borne by the developer and/or the transit agency. Equity should be considered in the lease structure or other financial arrangements that allocate joint development benefits, costs and risks. Horizontal equity can be achieved if the benefits are in proportion to the costs incurred and risks taken.

What Can We Learn from the Current State of Property Value Capture Use in the US?

The above overview of the value capture tools used in the US show that local governments are interested in using these tools. However, significant barriers to their use exist, ranging from state law limitations on the use of impact fees for operating expenses to the lack of land use power inhibiting transit agencies' ability to undertake joint developments in and around transit stations. The successful use of value capture tools also hinges upon the public agencies' institutional capacity and willingness to mitigate inequities that may arise due to poor design or implementation of these tools. Stakeholder acceptance and real estate market conditions also have impacts.

Finally, these value capture tools are often dependent upon timely completion of large construction projects. For example, Oregon and many other states in the US allow collection of assessment fees only after completion of the infrastructure project for which the fees are to be collected. Significant delays or cost overruns in constructing the infrastructure project could delay levying assessment fees. Such delays are likely to result in smaller than planned assessment fees revenue contributions to the overall project cost. In cases where assessment fees are charged before the infrastructure is developed, the assessment-fee-paying property owners may be frustrated with construction delays and oppose fee payment. Similarly, TIF or impact fee revenues that are dependent upon the construction of one or two large projects (such as a large TOD) might not accrue as planned if the projects are delayed, scaled back, or even fail to break ground.

Extant literature, especially studies focusing on mega projects and projects developed through public-private-partnership (PPP), note that transportation projects world-wide routinely suffered delays and cost overruns (Flyvbjerg,

Bruzelius and Rothengatter, 2003; Little, 2011; Marrewijk, et al., 2008; Primeus, Flyvbjerg and Wee, 2008; Singh, 2010). For example, an extensive study of 258 transportation projects in 20 countries and 5 continents notes that 90 percent of projects experienced cost overruns. The situation is especially worrisome for rail projects. Final rail projects costs exceed the estimated costs by an average 45 percent, and actual ridership averages 51 percent below the forecast (Flyvbjerg, Holm and Buhl, 2002). Furthermore, many projects are prone to significant financial risk because environmental impacts are underestimated, often deliberately, to enhance the chances of project approval. This situation could lead to underestimation of the environmental mitigation costs resulting in cost overruns due to higher than anticipated final environmental impact mitigation costs. Project delays could occur due to the additional time required to mitigate the unanticipated environmental impacts. Other factors that could derail a large project include foreign exchange risk, which is especially important if a significant portion of the project cost, such as the cost to purchase train cars, is incurred in foreign currency, as well as sector-policy risk, which is the risk that project's regulatory environment might change during the project development period (Flyvbjerg, Bruzelius and Rothengatter, 2003). Finally, enthusiasm to develop a "signature" project often makes funding agencies and public overlook the project cost overruns and construction delays. This phenomenon, termed "optimism bias" (Althsuler and Luberoff, 2003), is shown to be an important factor that drove much of the decision-making process for the San Francisco-Oakland Bay Bridge in northern California (Frick, 2008).

In summary, the key factors that impact the successful use of property value capture mechanisms include the following: the legal and policy environment; public agencies' institutional capacity to plan, design and implement value capture mechanisms; the stakeholders' acceptance of these mechanisms and the public agencies' ability to secure that acceptance; the mechanisms' revenue yield, stability and ability to effectively increase the yield and stability; the ability of the public agencies to minimize horizontal and vertical inequities generated by these mechanisms; and the timely and within-budget completion of the construction projects that are likely to create value.

The subsequent chapters discuss several instances of the use of impact fees, SADs, TIF and joint development to develop transit. These chapters identify key lessons that will help governments, transit agencies and other stakeholders plan, design and implement more effective value capture mechanisms.

References

Altshuler, A. and Luberoff, D. 2003. *Mega-projects: The Changing Politics of Urban Investments*. Washington, DC: Brookings Institution Press.

Altshuler, A. and Jose Gomez-Ibanez, J. 1993. *Regulation for Revenue: The Political Economy of Land Use Exactions.* Washington, DC: The Brookings Institute, and Cambridge, MA: The Lincoln Institute of Land Policy.

American Public Transportation Association (APTA). 2010. *Fare per Passenger and Recovery Ratio* [Online: APTA]. Available at: http://www.apta.com/ resources/statistics/Documents/NTD_Data/2010_NTD/T26_2010_Pass_ Fare_Recovery_Ratio.xls [accessed: February 22, 2012].

American Public Transportation Association (APTA). 2009. *Challenge of State and Local Funding Constraints on Transit Systems: Effects on Service, Fares, Employment and Ridership Survey Results.* Washington, DC: APTA.

Cervero, R. 1994. Rail Transit and Joint Development. *Journal of the American Planning Association,* 60(1), 83–94.

Cervero, R., et al. 2004. *Transit-Oriented Development in the United States: Experiences, Challenges, and Prospects.* TCRP Report 102. Washington, DC: Transportation Research Board [Online: Transportation Research Board]. Available at: http://onlinepubs.trb.org/onlinepubs/tcrp/tcrp_rpt_102. pdf [accessed: February 1, 2012].

Council of Development Finance Agencies (CDFA). 2007. *Tax Increment Finance Best Practices Reference Guide.* Cleveland, OH: CDFA, and New York, NY: International Council of Shopping Centers [Online: International Council of Shopping Centers]. Available at: www.icsc.org/government/CDFA.pdf [accessed: November 12, 2011].

Downing, P. and Bierhanzl, E. 1995. User Charges and Special Districts, in *Management Policies in Local Government Finance,* edited by J.R. Aronson and E. Schwartz. Washington, DC: International City/County Management Association.

Flyvbjerg, B., Bruzelius, N. and Rothengatter, W. 2003. *Megaprojects and Risk: An Anatomy of Ambition.* Cambridge, UK: Cambridge University Press.

Flyvbjerg, B., Holm, M.K. and Buhl, S.L. 2002. Underestimating Costs in Public Works Projects: Error or Lie? *Journal of the American Planning Association,* 68(3), 279–295.

Frick, K.F. 2008. The Cost of the Technological Sublime: Daring Ingenuity and the New San Francisco-Oaklabd Bay Bridge, in *Decision-Making on Mega-Projects: Cost-Benefit Analysis, Planning and Innovation,* edited by H. Priemus, B. Flyvbjerg and B.V. Wee. Cheltenham, UK and Northampton, MA, USA: Edward Elgar.

Gary, J. and Hoel, L.A. 1986. *An Inventory of Value Capture Techniques for Transportation.* A University of Virginia Technical report. Washington, DC: US Department of Transportation.

Landis, J., Cervero, R. and Hall, P. 1991. Transit Joint Development in the USA: An Inventory and Policy Assessment. *Environment and Planning C: Government & Policy,* 9(4), 431–452.

Lari, A. et al. 2009. *Value Capture for Transportation Finance: Technical Research Report*. Minneapolis, MN: University of Minnesota Center for Transportation Studies.

Lefaver, S. 1997. *Public Land with Private Partnerships for Transit Based Development*. Mineta Transportation Institute Report 97-1. San Jose, CA: Mineta Transportation Institute.

Lillydahl, J.H., Nelson, A.C., Ramis, T.V., et al. 1998. The Need for a Standard State Impact Fee Enabling Act. *Journal of the American Planning Association*, 54(1), 7–17.

Little, R. 2011. The Emerging Role of Public-Private Partnerships in Megaproject Delivery. *Public Works Management Policy*, 16(3), 240–249.

Marks, L. 2005. The Evolving Use of TIF. *Review*, 8(1), 1–2 [Online: CDFA]. Available at: http://www.cdfa.net/cdfa/cdfaweb.nsf/ordredirect.html?open&id =evolvingtif.html [accessed: 12 November, 2011].

Marrewijk, A.V. et al. 2008. Managing Public–private Megaprojects: Paradoxes, Complexity, and Project Design. *International Journal of Project Management*, 26(6), 591–600.

Mathur, S. 2009. Financing Community Facilities: A Case Study of the Parks and Recreational General Obligation Bond Measure of San Jose, California. *Theoretical and Empirical Researches in Urban Management*, 2(11), 34–49.

Mathur, S. 2007. Do Impact Fees Raise the Price of Existing Housing? *Housing Policy Debate*, 18(4), 635–659.

McCabe, B. 2000. Special-District Formation Among the States. *State and Local Government Review*, 32, 121–131.

Meisner, L.J. and Firtell, L. 1990. *Private Funding for Roads*. Planning Advisory Service Report No. 426. Chicago, IL: American Planning Association.

Nelson, A.C., Nicholas, J.C. and Juergensmeyer, J.C. 2009. *Impact Fees: Principles and Practice of Proportionate-Share Development Fees*. Chicago, IL American Planning Association.

Nelson, A.C., Bowles, L.K., Juergensmeyer, J.C. and Nicholas, J.C. 2008. *A Guide to Impact Fees and Housing Affordability*. Washington, DC: Island Press.

Nelson Nygaard. 2009. *Stranded at the Station: The Impact of the Financial Crisis in Public Transportation*. Washington, DC: Transportation for America.

Paetsch, J. and Dahlstrom, R. 1990. Tax Increment Financing: What It Is and How It Works, in *Financing Economic Development: An Institutional Response*, edited by R. Bingham, E. Hill and S.B. White. Newbury Park, CA: Sage, 82–98.

Peters, R. 1994. The Politics of Enacting State Legislation to Enable Local Impact Fees: The Pennsylvania Story. *Journal of the American Planning Association*, 60(1), 61–69.

Porter, D., Lin, B. and Peiser, R. 1992. *Special Districts: A Useful Technique for Financing Infrastructure*. Washington, DC: Urban Land Institute.

Priemus, H., Flyvbjerg, B. and Wee, B. 2008. *Decision-making on Mega-Projects: Cost-Benefit Analysis, Planning and Innovation*. Edward Elgar: Cheltenham, UK and Northampton, MA, USA.

Rueben, K. and Rosenberg, C. 2008. *State and Local Government Revenues* [Online: Tax Policy Center]. Available at: http://www.taxpolicycenter.org/UploadedPDF/1001173_state_local.pdf [accessed: February 21, 2012].

Smith, G.C. 2008. *Use of Fees or Alternatives to Fund Transit*. Transit Cooperative Research Program: Legal Research Digest 28. Washington, DC: Transportation Research Board [Online: Transportation Research Board]. Available at: http://onlinepubs.trb.org/onlinepubs/tcrp/tcrp_lrd_28.pdf [accessed: October 30, 2011].

Snyder, T. and Stegman, M. 1986. *Paying for Growth: Using Development Fees to Finance Infrastructure*. Washington, DC: Urban Land Institute.

Singh, R. 2010. Delays and Cost Overruns in Infrastructure Projects: Extent, Causes and Remedies. *Economic & Political Weekly*, 160(21), 43–54.

Tarantino, T. and Ward, J. 2011. *Staff, Joint Development Group, Metropolitan Atlanta Rapid Transit Authority*. Interview by Mathur, S., on December 6.

Tax Policy Centre. 2010. *Local Property Taxes as a Percentage of Local Tax Revenue, Selected Year 1997–2008* [Online: Tax Policy Center]. Available at: http://www.taxpolicycenter.org/taxfacts/Content/PDF/dqs_table_84.pdf [accessed: 21 February 21, 2012].

The Schumin Web Transit Center. 2011. *Bethesda* [Online: The Schumin Web Transit Center]. Available at: http://transit.schuminweb.com/transit/wmata/redline.php?station=A09 [accessed: October 16, 2011].

Tischler, P. 1999. *Introduction to Infrastructure Financing*. International City/County Management Association (ICMA) IQ Service Report 31(3). Washington, DC: ICMA.

United States Government Accountability Office (USGAO). 2010. *Public Transportation: Federal Role in Value Capture Strategies for Transit is Limited, but Additional Guidance Could Help Clarify Policies*. Washington, DC: United States Government Accountability Office [Online: GAO]. Available at: http://www.gao.gov/new.items/d10781.pdf [accessed: 6 October, 2011].

Chapter 5

Special Assessment District

Special assessment districts (SADs) have been extensively used to fund urban development throughout the US, especially the road, water and sewer systems. In the last couple of decades their use to fund public transportation has also grown. In this chapter we will review four such projects. These projects include Seattle South Lake Union Streetcar, Seattle, WA; New York Avenue Metro Station, Washington, DC; and Los Angeles Metro Red Line Benefit Assessment District, Los Angeles, CA. The fourth case, Portland Streetcar, Portland, OR, uses both SAD and TIF. It is discussed in Chapter 7 among the TIF cases. These projects meet the following selection criteria: First, SAD revenue must be used to fund the construction, operation, or maintenance of public transportation infrastructure, such as stations, rail lines, and rolling stock. Second, assessments must be a major revenue source. Third, a variety of transportation modes must be involved. Finally, data must be available.

South Lake Union Streetcar, Seattle, WA

Overview

With a population of about 608,000, Seattle is the largest city in the Seattle–Tacoma–Bellevue metropolitan statistical area (US Census Bureau, 2010a). The city has a relatively well-developed and diverse public transportation system, including an extensive bus system, light rail, streetcars, and monorail (City of Seattle, n.d.). Like many cities in the United States, Seattle had a streetcar system in place in the late nineteenth and early twentieth centuries, but the system was abandoned with the advent of the automobile. In recent decades, streetcars have made a resurgence across the country, and Seattle joined this trend with the completion of the Seattle South Lake Union Streetcar (referred to in this discussion simply as the streetcar) in 2007 (City of Seattle, n.d.).

The streetcar operates between Seattle's downtown and South Lake Union neighborhood. It serves the Denny Triangle and Belltown neighborhoods as well. With 11 stops along a 2.6-mile route (see Figure 5.1, p. 88), it connects with Seattle's other local and regional public transit systems, including the Metrobus, Sound Transit buses, trains and light rail, and the monorail at the Westlake Hub/ Pacific Place Station (Shedd Allen Brackett, 2006; City of Seattle, n.d.). The streetcar line was approved by the City Council as part of a larger investment intended to revitalize the South Lake Union neighborhood (Mulady, 2005).

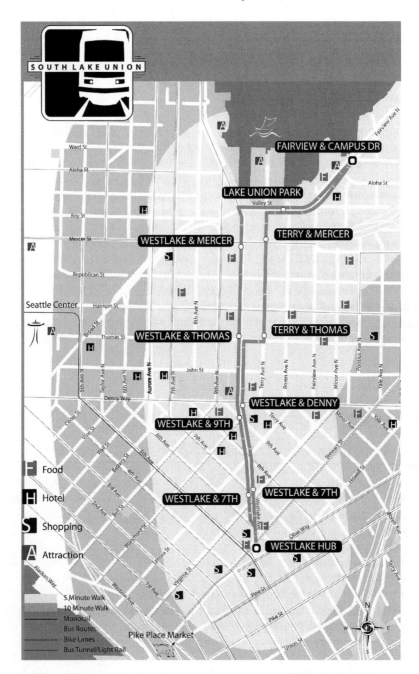

Figure 5.1   Route map of the Seattle Union Streetcar
Source: Seattle Streetcar.

Discussions about bringing a streetcar to the neighborhood had been under way since the early 2000s. The city of Seattle conducted several preliminary studies, including one of local improvement district (LID) assessment methodology (SADs are officially called LIDs in the state of Washington). After property owners approved the LID in 2005, the City Council approved funding for the project and formation of the LID (Shedd Allen Brackett, 2006). The streetcar began operating in 2007 (City of Seattle, n.d.).

Assessment Methodology and Revenue Generated

The LID funded more than half of the streetcar project. The city issued bonds to pay up front for the capital costs. The bonds are being paid back through the LID assessments (Shedd Allen Brackett, 2006).

For the purposes of calculating assessments, each parcel was considered on an individual basis as if owned "fee simple," i.e., these were assessed as if the property was owned outright. The assessments are based on the estimated increase in the property value resulting from the introduction of the streetcar system. They assume that traffic congestion would have prohibited certain properties from developing to their highest and best use if the streetcar had not been built. That is, by building the streetcar, the city was essentially allowing property owners to use their property to the fullest extent, thereby increasing its value (Shedd Allen Brackett, 2006).

The property appraisal was conducted in 2004 and published in 2006. The 760 parcels considered were classified into the following major groups: land or vacant/interim uses, apartments, condominiums, hotels, retail, industrial, office, and other (Shedd Allen Brackett, 2006).

Vacant properties and interim-use properties (not developed to their highest and best use) were estimated to benefit most from the streetcar (see Table 5.1, p. 90). Apartments, condominiums, hotels, and retail uses were expected to be the next-highest beneficiaries, and properties already developed to their highest and best use (industries, offices, and other) were expected to benefit the least (Shedd Allen Brackett, 2006).

The amount of the assessment fee for each property was based on proximity to the streetcar line. The analysis areas were grouped as follows:

- Area A: frontage on the streetcar, north of the central business district (CBD) core
- Area B: one block from the streetcar or with frontage near the south terminus
- Area C: two to three blocks from the streetcar, north of Denny Way
- Area D: two to three blocks from the streetcar, south of Denny Way
- Area E: four or five blocks from the streetcar (Shedd Allen Brackett, 2006).

The special assessment fee provided $25.7 million (52 percent of the total project cost). The rest of the project funding came from federal and state grants

Table 5.1   Projected percentage increase in valuation resulting from introduction of the Seattle Streetcar

Analysis area	Apartment	Condo	Hotel	Retail	Land	Industrial	Office
A	3.00%	3.00%	3.00%	3.00%	8.00%	1.50%	1.50%
B	2.25%	2.25%	2.25%	2.25%	6.00%	1.00%	1.00%
C	1.50%	1.50%	1.50%	1.50%	4.00%	0.75%	0.75%
D	1.00%	1.00%	1.00%	1.00%	3.00%	0.50%	0.50%
E	0.50%	0.50%	0.50%	0.50%	1.00%	0.00%	0.00%

Source: Deborah A. Foreman and Matthew C. Sloan, "Seattle CBD to South Lake Union Streetcar Final Special Benefits Study" (May 2006).

Table 5.2   Seattle Streetcar project funding sources

Funding source	Amount total	Percent of total project cost
LID Assessments (Net)	$25,700,000	51.71%
Federal/ State Grants	$18,500,000	37.22%
Maintenance Base	$2,200,000	4.43%
Property Sale	$3,300,000	6.64%
Total	$49,700,000	100.00%

Source: Allen Brackett Shedd, "Final Special Benefits Study for South Lake Union Streetcar," p. 4.

(see Table 5.2, above). As of 2007, nearly $17 million in assessment fees had been paid (City of Seattle Department of Finance, 2007).

Property owners were provided the opportunity to seek amendments to the fee, and some assessments were successfully amended because mistakes were found in the assessment process. Among the largest reductions, the Pacific Place assessment was reduced by $209,235 (54 percent), the Seattle Times assessment was reduced by $156,853 (68 percent), and the Comprise Venture assessment was reduced by $141,897 (52 percent) (Young, 2005; Shedd Allen Brackett, 2006).

Property owners were given the option of paying the fee up front or over 18 years at an interest rate of 4.4 percent. If a property is sold before the full fee is paid, the entire balance is payable at the time of closing. The 18-year payment option and the associated interest rate reflect the tenure and interest rate associated with the city-issued general obligation bonds that funded the up-front costs of the streetcar project (Ethan Malone, Streetcar Program Manager, City of Seattle, interview by Shishir Mathur, April 15, 2011).

Case Analysis

Enabling environment

Washington has clear LID-enabling legislation that allows the use of LIDs for transportation. Without such legislation, the 12 property owners who were opposed to the LID and had threatened a lawsuit might have had a better chance of winning a lawsuit and might have decided to go ahead with the legal challenges. The enabling legislation put the city on solid legal ground.

Stakeholder support

LIDs require property-owner buy-in. LIDs are "personal," in that while most construction projects can disrupt traffic and inconvenience people, LIDs ask that the owners put up with the disruptions and directly fund the disruption-causing projects. Therefore, LIDs have the potential to be very unpopular (Municipal Research and Services Center and American Public Works Association, 2009).

However, the Seattle Streetcar project was very popular among property owners, 98 percent of whom agreed to finance more than half of the total project cost through a LID. The streetcar was backed by few major players, including Microsoft co-founder Paul Allen's company, Vulcan; the Mayor; and the City Council.

The city was able to resolve disputes and complaints from unhappy property owners. The 12 property owners who objected to the assessment represented ownership of only 1.5 percent of the assessed value of the properties within the LID (Young, 2005). Property owners were given a chance to review their assessments with the appraisers, and most of the issues were resolved at this stage. The few still unsatisfied property owners were referred to a hearing examiner. The property owners agreed with the examiner's rulings (Ethan Malone). Moreover, those who threatened to sue the city did not carry out their threat because of prohibitive legal costs (Young, 2005).

Real estate market

The fee was assessed in 2004 and approved in 2005. The streetcar began operating in 2007, just months before the housing crisis and the economic recession deepened. Had the LID formation process begun during the recession, say in 2009, the outcome of the entire project might have been much different. The property owners would probably have lost some of their equity during the recession and might have been less enthusiastic about paying assessments.

Institutional capacity

Significant institutional capacity may be needed to form, implement, and manage LIDs. Specifically, capacity is required to conduct the benefit study, secure property owner buy in, obtain City Council approval, and levy the fee (Municipal Research and Services Center and American Public Works Association, 2009).

Horizontal and vertical equity
The large variety of property types within the Seattle LID required the city to devise a transparent and equitable benefit assessment calculation methodology, one that is bit more complex than one simply based on street frontage or parcel size. The city successfully developed a calculation methodology, basing assessments on the increase in property value if the property is developed to its highest and best use and the property's proximity to the streetcar. As each property had to be individually assessed, this methodology required much more work than simpler methodologies. However, it was viewed by property owners as bringing a sense of fairness and probably minimized opposition to the LID.

Even with a fair methodology, LIDs have the potential to adversely impact lower-income or fixed-income property owners, such as low-income senior citizens. Therefore, Chapter 84.38 of the Revised Code of Washington (RCW) and RCW 35.43.250 and 35.54.100 allow indefinite deferment of LID payments for certain qualifying senior citizens. In addition, economically disadvantaged individuals may defer payments for up to five years.

The LID assessment calculation methodology is also horizontally equitable—the amount each property pays is in proportion to the estimated financial benefit received.

Revenue yield, stability, and growth
Because assessments are determined at the time a LID is established, the assessment revenues can be very reliably estimated for an already developed area. The balance assessments are due when the property is sold, so revenues can be reliably estimated even when the property owners pay over a long period.

In summary, the Seattle Streetcar case shows that even after accounting for the risk of public opposition or legal action, SADs are a low-risk financing option when used in an established urban area with a strong real estate market and a robust enabling environment.

New York Avenue Metro Station, Washington, DC

Overview of Washington Metropolitan Area Transit Authority

The Washington Metropolitan Area Transit Authority (WMATA) was created in 1967 to build a regional transit system in the Washington, DC, area (WMATA, n.d.a). WMATA operates the regional bus and Metrorail system. It acquired four bus systems in 1973, and the first Metrorail line became operational in 1976. The bus system has more than 300 routes, and the Metrorail has five lines, 84 stations and 103 miles of track (WMATA, n.d.b). The Metrorail routes and opening dates are listed in Table 5.3 (p. 93).

Table 5.3   WMATA metrorail routes and opening dates

Name	Began operating	Route
Red line	1976	Shady Grove—Glenmont
Orange line	1978	Vienna/Fairfax—New Carrollton
Blue line	1977	Franconia-Springfield—Largo Town Center
Yellow line	1983	Huntington-Fort Totten/Mount Vernon Square/7th Street—Convention Center
Green line	1991	Branch Avenue—Greenbelt
Silver Line (planned)	2016 (planned)	Route 772—Sadium Armory

Source: WMATA, "Metro Facts," http://www.wmata.com [accessed: 7.27.11].

New York Avenue Metro Station

The New York Avenue Metro Station was developed as a result of a partnership between the local landowners; the Washington, DC, government; the federal government; and WMATA (PB Consult, n.d.). The station is located in the north-of-Massachusetts, or NoMa, area on the Red Line between the Union Station and Rhode Island Ave–Brentwood stations. The Red Line was in use for almost three decades before the New York Avenue Station opened in 2004.

During the 1990s, NoMa was an underdeveloped neighborhood with freight rail yards, abandoned buildings, warehouses, and vacant lots. The station site was identified by the Washington, DC, planners as a prime redevelopment opportunity due to its location near the downtown area. However, as the NoMa area was already congested, the station was considered a prerequisite for the further redevelopment of the neighborhood (PB Consult, n.d.).

Construction of the New York Avenue Station began in 2002, and the station opened in 2004 (National Council for Public Private Partnerships, n.d.). See Table 5.4 (p. 94) for the time line. The construction funds came from a variety of sources—the landowners; the Washington, DC, government; and the federal government. The property owners supported the station construction and agreed to pay assessments for 30 years to raise funds for it because they understood the benefits the station would bring to the local community, including significant investment from the federal government (PB Consult, n.d.).

Reasons for Landowners' Willingness to Fund the Station Costs

Prior to the station's development, several owners of the NoMa neighborhood's brownfield industrial land parcels had sought the city government's permission to develop offices on their land. Traffic on the local roads was at capacity, so the government determined that land development was possible only if a Metro station was built. Heeding the government's advice, the landowners petitioned

Table 5.4   Time line of development and construction of the New York Avenue Metro Station

1997–1998	District completes a strategic plan that identifies NoMa as a strategic investment area and identifies the need for an infill Metro Station
1997–1998	Negotiations with private landowners
March 1998	DC government funds a feasibility study to explore whether an infill station could be built in the NoMa area.
November 1998	The new metro station becomes an important part of DC's strategic economic development plan.
December 1998	Private landowners agree to contribute $25 million
1999	WMATA conducts a feasibility study for the station
June 1999	DC agrees to contribute $34 million to the new station
October 2000	Congress commits $25 million to the project
Fall of 2000	Preliminary engineering completed
Fall of 2000	Design was approved by the Nation Capitol Planning Commission and the Commission of Fine Arts
December 2000	Ground breaking on the project site
November 2002	Ground breaking on the station
November 2004	Station opens

Source: PB Consult, "New York Avenue-Florida Avenue-Galludet University Metro Station: A Case Study," p. 6.

for Metro station construction (Rick Rybeck, Former Deputy Associate Director for Policy & Planning, District Department of Transportation, interview by Shishir Mathur, June 24, 2011). However, as public funds were scarce, the director of the DC Department of Transportation suggested that the NoMa property owners share the cost. The city government administration thought that this suggestion would not be well received by the property owners, but much to its surprise, the property owners expressed their willingness to contribute $25 million toward the construction costs. The Mayor's office was so pleased with the proposal that it simply accepted the deal without negotiating with the property owners (Rick Rybeck). Building the station was logistically difficult. It had to be constructed without disrupting the already busy Red Line, which added to the project's complexity and expense. The WMATA approached key US Congress representatives with a request for additional funds. The representatives expressed interest in the proposal, primarily because the federal government needed a site for relocating the Bureau of Alcohol, Tobacco, Firearms and Explosives (ATF) headquarters from its existing location by 2003–2004, and the representatives liked the idea of locating it in the vicinity of the New York Avenue Station. Therefore, Congress struck a deal with WMATA. Both parties agreed on the 2003–2004 construction completion deadline (Rick Rybeck).

Given the deadline, the Washington, DC, Council needed to minimize property-owner opposition in order to quickly set up a SAD. As the owners of residential properties were very likely to oppose paying assessments, these properties were exempted. This exemption allowed the process to move forward quickly and enabled the construction to be completed before the 2003–2004 deadline (Rick Rybeck).

Stakeholder Participation Process

The supporters of the Metropolitan Branch Trail initially opposed the station construction, since it interfered with their plans to build a trail through the neighborhood that would be part of the larger eight-mile Metropolitan Branch Trail. WMATA addressed the concerns of the trail supporters by building a bridge over the railroad track to accommodate the trail (PB Consult, n.d.).

The DC Department of Housing and Community Development New York Avenue Task Force, later called Action 29, was also instrumental in garnering support for the station construction (PB Consult, n.d.). Overall, the project received wide community support.

Securing the landowners' financial support was a bit more difficult (PB Consult, n.d.). The landowners were initially willing to pay the assessment fee in exchange for credit on future property taxes. They felt they would be "double-billed" if they were required to pay assessments as well as taxes on their properties' increased value. However, the Washington, DC, government argued that a tax credit would defeat the purpose of the assessment fee. Therefore, the government hired a professional economist to investigate the landowners' double-billing claim. The economist found that the land-value gain would be more than 100 times the station cost. This finding led the landowners to abandon the double-billing charge (Rick Rybeck) and agree to fund $25 million of the project through a SAD without receiving property tax credits (PB Consult, n.d.).

Total Station Cost

The station cost a total of $109.9 million (WMATA, n.d.c). Table 5.5 (p. 96) provides a breakdown of the project funding sources.

A SAD was created to pay for a portion of the station cost, and the city issued general obligation bonds to cover the up-front capital costs. The SAD was set up with the following criteria: the assessment amount would be based on the current value of the property and would not change over time (PB Consult, n.d.); properties assessed must be within one-half mile of the station but not within 1,250 feet (one-quarter mile) of the Union Station. Properties served by the Union Station would be deemed to receive no benefit from the New York Avenue Station (WMATA, n.d.b); properties must be zoned as commercial; property owners must own more than 10,000 contiguous square feet of land; assessments would be retroactive to December 2000; residential properties would not pay assessments; and properties

Table 5.5   Funding sources for the New York Avenue Metro Station

Funds	Source
$53.4 million (48%)	DC Government (for station)
$6.5 million (6%)	DC Government (for Metropolitan Branch Bicycle Trail)
$25 million (23%)	Special Assessment District–Private Landowners
$25 million (23%)	Federal Government

Source: WMATA, "Metro's New York Ave-Florida Ave-Gallaudet U Metrorail station opens today on the Red Line," http://www.wmata.com [accessed: 12.10.11]; WMATA, "Project Overview Relative to a Proposed New Station at Potomac Yards," http://www. scribd.com [accessed: 12.10.11].

exempt from paying property taxes (for example, churches and hospitals) would also be excluded from paying assessments (District of Columbia Official Code, 2001).

The assessments are collected over a 30-year period, with the annual amount being 1/30th of the total amount. The assessments are calculated by multiplying a special assessment factor (SAF) with the total assessed value for each land parcel in 2000. The SAF is determined by dividing the annual special-assessment amount by the aggregate assessed value of the properties. In other words, each property pays in proportion to its year 2000 value. The SAF can be adjusted to meet the annual special-assessment collection target (District of Columbia Official Code, 2001).

Some of the owners of station-adjacent land parcels donated their land temporarily for construction staging and storage, and some donated part of their land permanently for station access. These landowners greatly benefited from these strategic donations, since their land would be close to, or in some cases, right at the station entrances (Rick Rybeck). The DC government issued general obligation bonds and paid $25 million from the bond proceeds to WMATA. In exchange, WMATA pledged 30 years of assessment revenues to the government (District of Columbia Official Code, 2001).

Lessons Learned

The New York Avenue Metro Station case shows that property owners' commitment to pay part of a project cost can help leverage federal funds. In this case, the federal investment also brought the local landowners on board. The federal government agreed to match their contribution and to build a new ATF headquarters, which would employ 1,100 workers.

This federal commitment made the landowners confident of the station's success (PB Consult, n.d.). The station has been successful in attracting investment in the NoMa neighborhood. More than $1.5 billion in private investment has been

Table 5.6   New York Avenue Metro Station ridership

Dates	Monthly ridership
Nov. 2004 to Oct. 2005	55,863
Nov. 2005 to Oct. 2006	71,970
Nov. 2006 to Oct. 2007	85,701
Nov. 2007 to Oct. 2008	104,404
Nov. 2008 to Oct. 2009	121,298

Source: WMATA, "Metro's New York Ave-Florida Ave-Gallaudet U Metrorail station celebrates five years of service," http://www.wmata.com.

planned within walking distance of the station and ridership more than doubled between 2004 and 2009 (see Table 5.6, above). The total property value in the 35-block area around the station increased more than four times in six years, from $535 million in 2001 to $2.3 billion in 2007 (WMATA, n.d.b).

Case Analysis

Enabling legal environment
The New York Avenue Metro Station construction was made possible by the New York Avenue Metro Special Assessment Authorization Emergency Act of 2001 (District of Columbia Official Code, 2001). While the Washington, DC, government had the authority to create SADs, the Act operationalized the use of this authority (Rick Rybeck).

Institutional capacity
The Action 29 campaign to gain local support was an expensive endeavor. The group held numerous meetings with neighborhood and community members and went through an elaborate negotiation process with the landowners. Action 29 was able to secure a $100,000 grant from the city government and raised $140,000 in private funds (PB Consult, n.d.). Apart from Action 29's capacity to gain local support, the institutional capacity of the other major stakeholders—the DC government and WMATA—also must be considered. WMATA has a long-standing reputation of delivering joint development projects and has an entire department dedicated to them. However, the DC government's capacity to undertake such projects seems limited. This lack of capacity is evident in its hasty acceptance of the landowners' offer to contribute $25 million. A government-sponsored economic study later found that the land-value gain would be more than 100 times the station cost, reinforcing the notion that the landowners should have contributed a larger proportion of the costs.

Stakeholder support
Landowner contribution paid for nearly a quarter of the total project cost, demonstrating their support for the project. Furthermore, the government acknowledged the standing of a broad spectrum of stakeholders and worked closely with those initially opposed to the station. In particular, the $6.5 million dedicated to building the trail bridge demonstrated WMATA's commitment to working with the community.

Horizontal and vertical equity
The assessment calculation methodology is very simple: the property owners pay assessments in proportion to their properties' year 2000 assessed value. Only large commercial properties (more than 10,000 square feet in area) within walking distance of the station pay assessments.

The assessment methodology is vertically equitable, as smaller commercial properties do not pay assessments. The methodology is also horizontally equitable, as only properties likely to benefit from the station pay assessments. The sphere of benefits is defined as a radius of a quarter-mile from the station.

Horizontal equity could be further strengthened by requiring all the properties that benefit from the station to pay assessments. However, residential properties were deliberately excluded to expedite the project.

Finally, the assessments are based on the assessed property values in 2000, not on the estimated future benefits. The assessment calculation methodology reduces horizontal equity to the extent the 2000 property values are not a good indicator of future station-related benefits.

Revenue yield, stability, and growth
The proceeds of a general obligation bond provided $25 million for the station construction. The assessment-fee revenues will repay the bonds. The revenue yield is predetermined, does not need to grow over time as it is amortized over 30 years (much like a home mortgage), and there is no reason to believe that the landowners would oppose paying the annual assessments in the future.

Los Angeles Metro Red Line Benefit Assessment District, Los Angeles, CA

Overview

The Los Angeles Metrorail system is a combination of heavy- and light-rail systems operating in Los Angeles County, CA. With nearly 10 million residents, Los Angeles County is one of the largest counties in the United States (US Census Bureau, 2010b). The Metrorail system is operated by Los Angeles County Metropolitan Transit Authority (LACMTA). The LACMTA was created from a 1993 merger of the Southern California Rapid Transit District (SCRTD) and the Los Angeles County Transportation Commission (LACTC) (LACMTA, 1994).

Metrorail Time Line

The Metrorail's five currently operational lines opened during the 1990s and early 2000s (see Table 5.7, p. 100, for the chronology, description, and routes). Red Line Segment 1, which is the focus of this case study, was the second segment to open, after the Blue Line, and was the only segment financed partially through a SAD.

Red Line Segment 1 is a heavy-rail transit system that operates in downtown Los Angeles. The Red Line and the Purple Line are the only Metrorail lines that operate completely within the city limits of Los Angeles—the Red Line runs from downtown Los Angeles to North Hollywood. The Red and Purple are also the only heavy-rail lines in the county; the other three lines are light-rail lines. Red Line Segment 1 cost $1.42 billion, of which $130 million, or nine percent, was paid for by two benefit assessment districts (BADs) (SADs are called benefit assessment districts in Los Angeles), Districts A1 and A2 (GAO, 2010). District A1 includes four Red Line stations: Union, Tom Bradley/Civic Center, Pershing Square, and 7th Street Metro. District A2 includes one Red Line station, Westlake/MacArthur Park (Sikes, 2008). See Figure 5.2 (p. 101) for the station location.

Assessment Calculation Methodology

Districts A1 and A2 supported two bonds, also called A1 and A2, which were passed in 1992. In 2001, two new bonds were issued to partially pay off the 1992 bonds. A1 generated $123.7 million, and A2 generated $6.5 million, to fund capital improvements (Sikes, 2008). A number of other BADs were planned for subsequent segments of the Red Line, but they never materialized because of the passage of CA Proposition 218 in 1996, which requires two-thirds-majority approval from property owners to form a BAD (California Legislative Analyst's Office, n.d.). This law has made BAD formation next to impossible in California, especially since there is significant property-owner opposition in the already developed areas that have fragmented property ownership.

Commercial properties, including vacant land, offices, parking facilities, retail stores, hotels, and motels, have paid assessments. In District A1, properties within one-half mile of the rail stations (1,300 properties with a total area of 64 million square feet) paid the fee. District A2 is much smaller, having only 200 properties (with a total area of 3.5 million square feet) within one-third mile of the Westlake/Macarthur Station (Sikes, 2008).

Residential properties, religious institutions, and nonprofits were exempted from paying the fee, which was charged at a variable rate (up to $0.33) per square foot of the building or parcel, whichever is greater. Specifically, the rate was $0.17 for first five years (1992–1997), $0.27 for the next five years (1997–2002), and $0.33 for the next seven years (2002–2009), for an average of $0.25 per square foot for the entire 17-year assessment period.

Table 5.7   Metro rail lines in Los Angeles County

Line name	Opened	Rail type	Route
Blue Line	1990	Light rail	D'town LA—Long Beach
Red line Segment 1	1993	Heavy rail (subway)	D'town LA Union Station—MacArthur Park
Red line Segment 2a	1996	Heavy rail (subway)	MacArthur Park—Vermont
Red line Segment 2b	1999	Heavy rail (subway)	Vermont—H'wood/Vine
Red line Segment 3	2000	Heavy rail (subway)	H'wood/Vine—North H'wood
Purple Line	1993	Heavy rail (subway)	D'town LA—Mid-Wilshire District
Green Line	1995	Light rail	Redondo Beach—Norwalk and LAX
Gold Line	2003	Light rail	E. LA—Pasadena via D'town

Source: LACMTA, "Past Visions of L.A.'s Transportation Future," http://www.metro.net [accessed: 10.6.11]; Robert P. Sechler, "The Seven Eras of Rapid Transit Planning in Los Angeles" Southern California Scenic Railway Association (January 1999), http://www.scsra.org [accessed: 10.6.11].

Property owners were allowed to pay the fee over a 17-year period, over a five-year period, as a one-time payment in advance (with a discount), or as a one-time payment when the line opened. The fee is used to pay back the bonds that were sold to fund the up-front construction costs (Sikes, 2008).

The State Law Authorizing BADs for the Red Line

California State Code 3300 authorized the use of BADs for the Red Line. Unlike the Oregon and Washington codes, which apply statewide, Code 3300 was specifically written for the SCRTD (now LACMTA). The Code essentially gave the SCRTD the authority to create BADs with a two-thirds vote of the Board of Supervisors. The Code limits the use of assessment funds to rail transit stations and related facilities. It also limits the bond issuance to 40 years and the interest rates on the bonds to 12 percent annually. The Code has a special provision for also allowing creation of BADs through an election if 25 percent of the property owners petition for them. The property owners within a BAD can then vote for the BAD—only a simple majority is needed. Cast only by the property owners, one vote is allotted per $1,000 of property value. While the LACMTA assessed the fee, Los Angeles County was responsible for levying and collecting it (California Tax Data, n.d.). Districts A1 and A2 were created using the two-thirds board majority option.

Go Metro

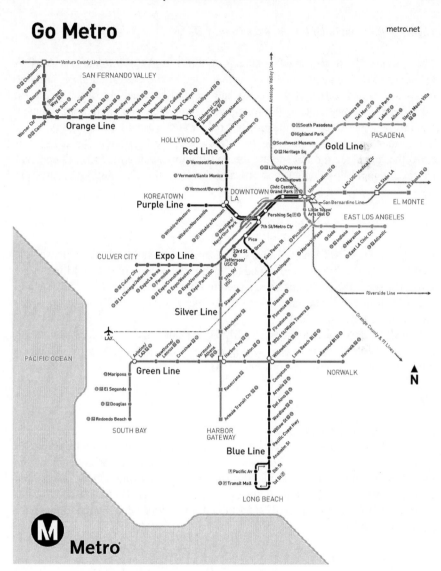

Figure 5.2   Los Angeles Metro system map

Source: Map image courtesy of Metro (Los Angeles County Metropolitan Transportation Authority).

Legal Challenges to the Los Angeles County BADs

There was at least one legal challenge to the Los Angeles County BADs. A challenge to their constitutionality was overruled by the California State Supreme Court in 1992. A state appellate court had previously struck down the BADs on the grounds that they violated the "one-person, one-vote" constitutional guarantee. Under CA State Code 3300, the property owner vote was based on property value, not on the "one-person, one-vote" rule. However, the California Supreme Court ruled that the Code did not violate the constitution, stating that a BAD does not exercise general government powers, and therefore the constitutional protection does not apply (Stein and Hager, 1992).

Revenue Generated from the BADs

In 1992, the LACMTA issued two sets of bonds to fund the construction of the Red Line. The A1 bonds were issued to finance the section of the Red Line in the A1 BAD, while the A2 bonds were issued to finance the section in the A2 BAD. A second pair of bonds was issued in 2001 to refinance the debt. Both sets of bonds were paid in full by FY 2010.

The BAD revenues increased steadily. By FY 2005, the BADs were generating more than $20 million per year (see Figure 5.3, p. 103). Revenue from the BADs more than doubled between 2001 and 2010.

Case Analysis

Enabling legal environment
A special state-level act was passed to enable BAD funding for the Los Angeles Metro. However, passage of Proposition 218 in California in 1996 has made the use of BADs for transit difficult. Property owners can now simply vote them down. In fact, the LACMTA did not even try to set up BADs for the Metro after the passage of Proposition 218, even though the initial plans included them for Segments 2 and 3 of the Red Line.

Institutional capacity
Significant institutional capacity is required to set up BADs, issue bonds, levy and collect assessments, and, if required, defend them in court. Like SADs in Seattle and Portland, implementation of BADs takes staff time and resources, especially in the beginning stages, when public outreach is needed to address property-owner concerns. In the Los Angeles case, further capacity was needed to defend the BADs in a lengthy court battle.

Stakeholder support
While Portland and Seattle used assessments to fund a large portion of their streetcar systems, funding the line was not the main impetus for creating the Red Line

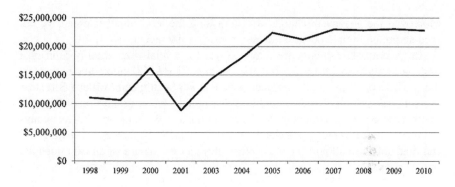

Figure 5.3   Los Angeles Metro Redline Segment 1: Annual revenues from Benefit Assessment Districts

BAD. The BAD revenues funded a small but significant portion of the construction costs, but demonstrating local support for the project to receive federal funding was perhaps the primary reason for the BAD formation (LACMTA, 1994).

While the Red Line BADs were successful in attracting federal funding, they met with some property-owner opposition. The Metro staff highlighted the importance of majority resident support and unified private sector, local, state, and federal support for any assessment district's success (Sikes, 2008).

Horizontal and vertical equity

The Los Angeles BADs assessed a fee on a per square foot of the built-up area or the lot area basis. This calculation method may result in a fee that is not proportional to the benefit received. For example, a large hotel that operated at full capacity before the Red Line was constructed would have received little benefit but would have had to pay a very large assessment because of its sizable floor area. In contrast, a restaurant running below potential might have doubled its business, having paid only a very small assessment fee. In summary, the fee calculation methodology does not take actual benefits into account. It does not even try to account for the variations in the benefit received by different land uses but instead uses a one-size-fits-all approach. Furthermore, only commercial properties paid the fee. Residential properties benefited as well but were exempted from paying.

The fee was vertically equitable to the extent that the owners of smaller properties have lower ability to pay than the owners of larger properties. The option to pay the assessments over time further enhanced vertical equity.

Revenue yield, stability, and growth

An assessment district in already developed urban areas, such as Los Angeles, typically has a predictable and stable revenue yield, because the number of assessment-paying properties is known at the time of the district formation.

Moreover, the agency in charge of establishing the assessment rate can, within predetermined limits, increase the rate in case of any revenue shortfall.

In general, assessments are likely to pay for a relatively small portion of a large rail project such as Metrorail. The Segment 1 BADs funded nine percent of the project cost. For smaller projects, such as the Seattle and Portland Streetcar projects, assessment districts might be able to fund a larger proportion of the cost. In any case, as demonstrated in Portland, Seattle, and Washington, DC, local buy-in is critical for leveraging state and federal funding. Therefore, even when BADs can fund only a small portion of a project, they can still have a significant financial impact overall.

Concluding Remarks

The four case studies discussed in this book demonstrate that SADs can be used to fund a variety of public transportation projects, from streetcars to heavy rail to train stations. However, SADs are only able to capture the micro-level property value benefits of the transportation infrastructure, not the meso and macro level benefits, such as the city level economic development impacts of transportation infrastructure.[1] Therefore, SADs are able to generate revenue limited to the amount of assessments paid by neighboring properties that are usually within ¼ to ½ mile from the transport infrastructure. These revenues are often enough to fund a substantial portion of smaller projects, such as the Seattle South Lake Union Streetcar line, but only a fraction of capital-intensive projects, such as the heavy-rail-based Los Angeles Red Line. Nonetheless, SAD use demonstrates local support for public transportation projects. This support could be used to leverage state and federal funds.

SADs are very likely to encounter property owner opposition. The case studies reveal several proactive and a few reactive strategies to address this problem. The proactive strategies include residential property owner exemption from paying assessments, payment over a long period of time, and strong local businesses support for SADs. The reactive strategies include instituting a process to redress grievances and defense against property owner initiated lawsuits.

Ideally, assessment fees should be based upon the property's value from a purely value capture perspective. However, such fee calculation methodology leaves the fee revenue susceptible to real estate market downturn. Therefore, public agencies base the fee on a metric unlikely to decline over time to minimize revenue instability. For example, assessment fees for the various phases of the Portland Central Streetcar Project were based on the area of the land parcel (see Table 7.8, p. 145) or the length of the street frontage of the land parcel. The land/building area method was also used to calculate assessment fees for the BADs

---

1   In the defense of SADs it is worth noting that the city-wide and regional benefits might be muted anyway (Flyvbjerg, Bruzelius and Rothengatter, 2003).

created for Segment 1 of the Los Angeles Metro Red Line. The assessment fee calculation methodology for Phase 3a of the Portland Central Streetcar Project indicates that even when an assessment fee is calculated using the property value method, real estate market risk can be minimized by calculating the fee using both the property value method and the land/building area method and then charging the higher of the two fees. Other ways to minimize real estate market risks include charging the fee as a proportion of the property's previously assessed value, which was adopted in the case of New York Avenue Metro Station, or a portion of a fixed property value increment, which was adopted in the case of Seattle South Lake Union Streetcar Project.

References

South Lake Union Streetcar, Seattle, WA

City of Seattle. n.d. *About the Streetcar* [Online: Seattle Streetcar]. Available at: http://www.seattlestreetcar.org/about/ [accessed: July 13, 2011].

City of Seattle Department of Finance. 2007. *2007–2012 Adopted Capital Improvement Program* [Online: City of Seattle]. Available at: http://www.seattle.gov/financedepartment/0813adoptedcip/transportation_fund.pdf [accessed: July 13, 2011].

Mulady, K. 2005. South Lake Union Streetcar Cost Shocks Neighbors. *Seattle Post-Intelligencer*, October 4, 2005 [Online: Seattle Post-Intelligencer]. Available at: http://www.seattlepi.com/default/article/South-Lake-Union-streetcar-cost-shocks-neighbors-1184408.php [accessed: July 13, 2011].

Municipal Research and Services Center and American Public Works Association, Washington State Chapter. 2009. *Local and Road Improvement Districts Manual for Washington State* [Online: Municipal Research and Services Center]. Available at: http://www.mrsc.org/publications/lid-rid09.pdf [accessed: December 2, 2011].

Shedd Allen Brackett. 2006. *Final Special Benefits Study for South Lake Union Streetcar*. Seattle, WA: City of Seattle.

US Census Bureau. 2010a. *Profile of General Population and Housing Characteristics: 2010* [Online: Amercian Factfinder]. Available at: http://factfinder2.census.gov/faces/tableservices/jsf/pages/productview.xhtml?pid=DEC_10_DP_DPDP1&prodType=table [accessed: December 2, 2011].

Young, B. 2005. Land Owners Hop Aboard Lake Union Streetcar Line. *Seattle Times*, November 12, 2005 [Online: Seattle Times]. Available at: http://community.seattletimes.nwsource.com/archive/?date=20051112&slug=slustreetcar12m [accessed: July 13, 2011].

New York Avenue Metro Station, Washington, DC

District of Columbia Official Code 2001. § 47-881–885.
National Council for Public Private Partnerships. n.d. *New York Avenue Metro Station, Washington DC* [Online: National Council for Public Private Partnerships]. Available at: http://www.ncppp.org/cases/nystation.shtml [accessed: December 19, 2011].
PB Consult. n.d. *New York Avenue-Florida Avenue-Galluadet University Metro Station: A Case Study* [Online: AASHTO Center for Excellence in Project Finance]. Available at: http://www.transportation-finance.org/.../New_York_Avenue_Case_Study.pdf [accessed: July 27, 2011].
Washington Metropolitan Transit Authority (WMATA). n.d.a. *Railfanning, Railroad Profiles* [Online: Railfanning.org]. Available at: http://railfanning.org/profiles/metro.htm [accessed: July 27, 2011].
WMATA. n.d.b. *Metro's New York Ave-Florida Ave-Gallaudet U Metrorail Station Opens Today on the Red Line* [Online: Washington Metropolitan Area Transit Authority]. Available at: http://www.wmata.com/about_metro/news/PressReleaseDetail.cfm?ReleaseID=3182 [accessed: July 27, 2011].
WMATA. n.d.c. *Metro's New York Ave-Florida Ave-Gallaudet U Metrorail Station Opens Today on the Red Line* [Online: Washington Metropolitan Area Transit Authority]. Available at: http://www.wmata.com/about_metro/news/PressReleaseDetail.cfm?ReleaseID=3182 [accessed: July 27, 2011].
WMATA. n.d.d. *Project Overview Relative to a Proposed New Station at Potomac Yards* [Online: Washington Metropolitan Area Transit Authority]. Available at: http://www.scribd.com/doc/3424590/Potomac-Yard-Metro-presentations-08 0527 [accessed: July 27, 2011].

Los Angeles Metro Red Line Benefit Assessment District, Los Angeles, CA

California Legislative Analyst's Office. n.d. *Understanding Proposition 218* [Online: Legislative Analyst's Office]. Available at: http://www.lao.ca.gov/1996/120196_prop_218/understanding_prop218_1296.html [accessed: October 6, 2011].
California Tax Data. n.d. *California Codes: Public Utilities Code Section 33000–33020* [Online: California Tax Data]. Available at: http://www.californiataxdata.com/A_Free_Resources/legislation/SoCalRapidTransit.asp [accessed: October 6, 2011].
LACMTA. 1994. *The Benefit Assessment District Program-1994* [Online: Youtube]. Available at: http://www.youtube.com/watch?v=4s4gOqxwwps [accessed: October 6, 2011].
Sikes, D. 2008. *Benefit Assessment Districts Program*, It's Time to Move LA Conference, Los Angeles, CA, January 10, 2008, Available at: www.movela.org/pptdocs/LACTFC_BenefitAssessment.ppt [accessed: October 18, 2011].

Stein, M. and Hager, P. 1992. Red Line Tax Approved by High Court. *Los Angeles Times*, January 31, 1992 [Online: Los Angeles Times]. Available at: http://articles.latimes.com/1992–01–31/news/mn-909_1_metro-red-line [accessed: October 18, 2011].

US Government Accountability Office (GAO). 2010. *Public Transportation: Federal Role in Value Capture Strategies for Transit Is Limited, but Additional Guidance Could Help Clarify Policies* [Online: U.S. Government Accountability Office]. Available at: http://www.gao.gov/new.items/d10781.pdf [accessed: October 6, 2011].

US Census Bureau. 2010b. *2010 Census Data Redistricting Data* [Online: United States Census 2010]. Available at: http://2010.census.gov/2010census/data/ [accessed: October 6, 2011].

Concluding Remarks

Flyvbjerg, B., Bruzelius, N. and Rothengatter, W. 2003. *Megaprojects and Risk: An Anatomy of Ambition*. Cambridge, UK: Cambridge University Press.

Chapter 6
Joint Development Projects

Four joint development projects are examined in this book. They are: Bethesda Metro Joint Development Project in Bethesda, MD (this is a WMATA project); Dadeland South Joint Development Project in Miami-Dade County, FL (this is a Miami-Dade Transit [MDT] project); Resurgens Plaza, Atlanta, GA (a MARTA project); and CCC Transit Village in Contra Costa County, CA (this project is on BART property). Except for the CCC Transit Village, which has been discussed among the TIF cases in Chapter 7, the projects also use air rights as a revenue source. These projects were chosen on the basis of the following criteria: First, the project must endow direct financial benefit to the transit agency through revenue- and/or cost-sharing arrangements. Second, the value of transit service must be captured—in other words, the project was developed with the intention of using transit benefits, including increased real estate demand and transportation accessibility. Third, the project is in, on, or contiguous to a transit station. Fourth, is in an urban area that is actively pursuing joint development. Fifth, the project uses multiple joint development tools, including air rights. Finally, data availability was a major consideration while choosing the project. The first three criteria excluded projects in which a public agency gained no direct financial benefit (for example, when TODs are subsidized in the hope that the development would increase transit ridership).

Bethesda Metro Joint Development, Bethesda, MD

Overview of WMATA's Public Transportation System

Located approximately nine miles northwest of downtown Washington, DC, the 3.5-acre Bethesda Metro Joint Development (BMJD) is built above the Bethesda Metrorail subway station, on the Metro Red Line. The station opened in 1984, and the joint development was constructed a year later (Schumin Web Transit Center, n.d.).

Overview of WMATA's Joint Development Policy

WMATA has a long history of using joint development to spur economic growth, facilitate TOD development, and create a long-term revenue source for itself. Its projects are intended to create dense and pedestrian-friendly mixed-use communities that integrate transit with land use and reduce dependence on automobiles (Schumin Web Transit Center, n.d.).

As of 2010, 33 joint development projects had been developed at 27 Metrorail stations. The total lease revenues from these projects since the opening of Metrorail in 1976 exceed $250 million (Schumin Web Transit Center, n.d.). Indeed, revenues from these projects have been a significant source of income for WMATA in recent years (see Table 6.1, p. 111).

Despite the fact that joint development projects bring in revenues of several million dollars annually, this represents less than one percent of WMATA's billion-dollar-plus annual operating budget (see Table 6.2, p. 111).

Overview of the Bethesda Metro Joint Development

Bethesda, MD, is an affluent suburb of Washington, DC. The BMJD, which sits on top of the Bethesda Metrorail station (Cervero, et al., 2004), contains one 17-story office tower with 368,000 square feet of office space, 41,600 square feet of retail space (including a 19,000-square-foot food court), a 390-room hotel, and a five-story garage with 1,305 parking spaces (Malasky, 2010; Meridian Group, n.d.). Bethesda Metro Center Limited Partnership (BMCLP), a Maryland-based organization, owned, operated, and maintained BMJD until 1999, after which the majority partner in BMPCL—CRI—sold its stake to the Meridian Group, Inc. At present, the Meridian Group owns and operates the BMJD (Meridian Group, n.d.).

On December 1, 1981, the BMCLP entered into a lease agreement with WMATA, pursuant to which the BMCLP leased the land on which BMJD is built for 50 years. The lease can be renewed at the BMCLP's option for an additional 49 years (SEC Info, 1999).

Generating minimum annual lease revenue of $1.6 million, BMJD is WMATA's most successful joint development project. Apart from air-rights lease revenues, WMATA also gains from sharing the construction and operations costs (Cervero, et al., 2004). The lease agreement requires the BMJD's owner (earlier BMCLP, now Meridian Group) to pay WMATA a minimum annual rent of $1.6 million. Finally, since 1986, the owner has been obligated to pay WMATA additional rent in an amount equal to 7.5 percent of annual gross revenue in excess of $31 million (SEC Info, 1999).

Case Analysis

Enabling environment
Joint developments for WMATA are intended to work in tandem with the Metrorail system. This coordination is achieved by integrating land use with transportation through the development of TODs. The TODs are sought out not simply to increase revenue but to provide transit riders as well. Furthermore, WMATA has developed joint development policies and guidelines (last updated in 2008) that lay out the following: roles and responsibilities of various stakeholders involved

Table 6.1   Revenue from WMATA joint development projects

	Year							
	2011	**2010**	**2009**	**2008**	**2007**	**2006**	**2005**	**2004**
Revenue ($ millions)	6.450[a]	9.848[b]	8.161[b]	8.8.	10.5	7.8	4.7	3.5

Note: [a] WMATA, Approved in FY 2011 budget, p. III-1, http://www.wmata.com [accessed: 7.6.11]; [b] WMATA, "Approved in FY 2011 budget," p. III-1, http://www.wmata.com [accessed: 7.6.11].
Source: WMATA, Comprehensive Annual Financial Reports 2009 and 2010, http://www. wmata.com [accessed: 5.4.11]; WMATA, "Monthly Financial Report, January 2005," http://www.wmata.com [accessed: 5.4.11].

Table 6.2   Percentage of WMATA operating budget provided by joint developments

Fiscal year	2010	2009	2008	2007	2006	2005	2004
WMATA operating budget ($ millions)	1,358	1,360	1,200	1,130	1,040	940	909
Percent of operating budget revenue from joint development	0.73[a]	0.60[a]	0.73	0.93	0.75	0.50	0.38

Note: [a] WMATA, "Approved in FY 2011 budget," p. III-1, http://www.wmata.com [accessed: 7.6.11].
Source: WMATA, "Comprehensive Annual Financial Reports, FY 2004–2010," http:// www.wmata.com [accessed: 11.23.11].

in the joint development process; the procedure for selecting developers for the joint development projects; community involvement in scoping and developing projects, following guidelines to facilitate the success of TODs (WMATA, 2008).

While these guidelines are in place to ensure project success, joint development projects are limited by zoning and community acceptance. WMATA operates in several jurisdictions, but it is unable to control the local zoning ordinances and is therefore able to engage in joint development only in locations with supportive local zoning (MWCOG, n.d.).

Institutional capacity
WMATA's Planning and Joint Development Department manages the joint development program. The department staff proactively identifies joint development opportunities. WMATA also actively solicits potential developers through its request for qualifications (RFQ)/RFP process. The RFQ/RFP process

is outlined in documents describing WMATA's joint development policies and guidelines. These documents are available on WMATA web site.

In summary, by devoting significant staff and financial resources, WMATA has created substantial institutional capacity to identify, develop, and manage joint development projects.

Horizontal and vertical equity

As mentioned earlier, the equity concern for joint development projects primarily revolves around whether the development agreements benefit the involved parties in proportion to their stake and risk in the development (horizontal equity). Of particular concern is whether the interests of the public sector agency, in this case WMATA, have been protected.

Analysis of the lease structure shows that WMATA may not have been able to strike a favorable deal for its constituents. First, the minimum guaranteed lease revenue ($1.6 million) is not inflation-adjusted. For a long-term lease (a 50-year term followed by an option for another 49-year term), this results in progressively declining lease revenue, in constant dollars. Moreover, apart from the minimum guaranteed revenue, WMATA shares BMJD revenues only when the annual gross revenue exceeds $31 million. For several years in the 1980s and 1990s, the gross revenue fell well short of $31 million (for some years, it was as low as $17 million). In those years WMATA had to settle for the minimum guaranteed revenue of $1.6 million. In hindsight, setting an inflation-adjusted minimum-gross-revenue target might have been to WMATA's advantage.

Stakeholder support

It is difficult to ascertain from primary sources whether the joint development encountered community or political opposition when it was developed. An in-depth search for newspaper articles did not reveal stakeholder opposition. In fact, a March 6, 1980, Washington Post article titled "Hotel, Commercial Complex Planned Atop Bethesda Metro Station" reports widespread support for the project, saying that it "won almost universal praise from county officials, business people and Bethesda residents, a surprise to many planners accustomed to hearing citizens oppose high-rise development near their homes." The article also cites the large buffer zone between the joint development project and the residential areas as key to the resident support (Hodge, 1980).

Revenue yield, stability, and growth

The revenue yield from the BMJD is stable and substantial, as WMATA is guaranteed minimum revenue of $1.6 million. However, the upside revenue potential is limited because WMATA shares only 7.5 percent of annual gross revenue in excess of $31 million, and this revenue sharing has occurred only sporadically over the last 30 years.

Dadeland South Joint Development, Miami, FL

Overview of Miami-Dade Transit

Miami-Dade Transit (MDT) provides transit service to Miami-Dade County, FL. Serving a population of nearly a quarter million people, MDT is the 15th-largest transit provider in the country and the largest in Florida. It operates four transit services: Metrobus; a downtown Miami people-mover system; Metromover (an automated fixed-guideway system); a paratransit service; and Metrorail (MDT, n.d.a; MDT, 2009).

The Metrorail is a 25-mile-long, dual track, elevated rapid-transit heavy-rail system with 23 stations (see Figure 6.1, p. 114). Metromover is a 4.4-mile-long elevated system that serves the downtown Miami area. Metrobus has more than 90 routes, including seven routes serving the South Miami-Dade Busway, which is a fully separated bus rapid-transit (BRT) system running along US Highway 1. In FY 2012, system ridership totaled over 107 million boardings (MDT, n.d.a; MDT, n.d.b; MDT staff email communication, May 14, 2013).

Overview of Dadeland South Station

Opened for service in 1984, the Dadeland South Metrorail Station (hereafter called Dadeland South) is at the southern terminus of the Metrorail system (MDT, n.d.c). In addition to Metrorail, numerous bus lines serve Dadeland South (MDT, n.d.d).

Details of the Joint Development

The Dadeland South joint development was MDT's first joint development project. It includes office, retail, and hotel space, along with a shared parking garage that includes 1,100 parking spaces for Metrorail riders. The project broke ground in 1982 and was built in four phases. The construction schedule is shown in Table 6.3 (p. 115) (MDT, n.d.d).

The Dadeland South joint development began as a public-private venture between the Green Company and MDT. The Green Company owned a six acre parcel of property adjacent to the southern end of the Metrorail right-of-way. At the time, MDT was planning to acquire the property for the purpose of constructing a parking garage. Recognizing the significant land-development potential, the developer approached MDT with a joint development proposal. The developer proposed to transfer ownership of the six acre parcel of property to MDT in return for the development rights on the property. This arrangement benefitted both MDT and the Green Company. The Green Company retained the development rights on the property without the requirement to pay property taxes on the land since it was now owned by MDT (a department of the county government), and MDT was provided with a substantial, long-term source of revenue (MDT staff email communication, May 14, 2013).

Figure 6.1   Miami-Dade Transit Metrorail system map
Source: Miami-Dade Transit.

Under the terms of the agreement, the air rights are to be maintained by a 99.5-year lease which began in 1982—a 55.5-year lease followed by the option to renew for an additional 44 years (MDT, n.d.e). As part of the lease terms, MDT annually receives the greater of $400,000 or a percentage of gross revenue specified as follows: 4 percent of the gross revenue from Phases I and III, 2 percent from Phase II, 1.5 percent from Phase IV A, and 1 percent from Phase IV B (DCTA, 1982).

Table 6.3   Phases of the Dadeland South Station joint development

Phase	Year opened	Type of development
Phase I and III	1984	Datran Center I & II—Class A Office buildings with 476,000 rentable square feet, 35,000 square feet of retail space (511,000 square feet total) and 3,5000 parking spaces, 1,100 designated as Park and Ride
Phase II	1984	Miami Marriott Dadeland Hotel and Conference Center with 302 luxury hotel rooms
Phase IV A	2005	Dadeland Centre I—18-story 152,014 square feet Class A office building (8 floors offices, 9 floors parking)
Phase IV B	2008	Dadeland Centre II—15-story, 119,516 square feet, Class A office building with 8 floors of office space, 6 floors of parking and ground floor retail

Source: MDT, "Joint Development Projects," Available at: http://www.miamidade.gov [accessed: 12.5.11].

Table 6.4   Participation rent payments from the Dadeland South Station joint development, 2000–2010

	2000	2001	2002	2003	2004	2005	2005	2007	2008	2009	2010
Lease revenue ($1000s)	833	887	832	859	925		995	1086	977	939	894

Source: Abel Lera (Miami-Dade Transit), interview with Shishir Mathur, October 4, 2011.

In addition to the lease revenue, the county receives substantial property-tax revenue levied on the improvements that have been constructed on the property (Evans and Roth, 1998). The annual-lease-revenue data for 2000–2010 are shown in Table 6.4 (above).

In addition to the revenue sharing, both parties entered into cost-sharing agreements, which included (1) sharing the excavation costs and the cost of constructing the station's foundation; (2) sharing the cost of the parking garage; and (3) sharing some of the parking garage operating costs. The parking garage and some of the development's buildings also share a common ventilation system and auxiliary generators. The county attributes $4 million in savings to the cost-sharing measures (Cervero, et al., 2004).

Case Analysis

Enabling environment
In 1978, six years before the Metrorail System became operational, the Miami-Dade Board of County Commissioners recognized coordination of land use and transportation as vital to a viable rail system. Therefore, it adopted Ordinance No. 78–74 (Fixed-Guideway Rapid Transit System—Development Zone) in 1978 (MDT, n.d.d). Seeking to develop a cohesive transit-conducive zone along the heavy-rail corridors, the ordinance states: "The Board of County Commissioners for Miami-Dade County, Florida, hereby declares and finds that the uncoordinated use of lands within the County threatens the orderly development and the health, safety, order, convenience, prosperity and welfare of the present and future citizens of this County" (MDC, 1978). In areas where the Rapid-Transit Zone (RTZ) is located within a municipality, the ordinance requires the County and municipality to jointly adopt development standards that are acceptable to both the County and the municipality. This policy framework called for a series of studies called the Station Area Design and Development (SADD) studies. Conducted during the planning of the Metrorail system, the SADD studies were undertaken collaboratively by the county, MDT, and local municipalities (MDT staff email communication, May 14, 2013). The studies set up guidelines for future development and inventoried existing uses around station areas (MDT, n.d.d). To date, development standards have been adopted for those stations located within the boundaries of the City of Miami (MDT staff email communication, May 14, 2013).

The county's Comprehensive Plan also provides incentives to the private sector to pursue joint development opportunities and maximizes the potential of joint development to provide an important revenue source for MDT. Furthermore, it calls for locating transit corridors and stations in areas conducive to joint development, stating "In the siting of transit stations in future rapid transit corridors, major consideration will be given to the opportunities for joint development and/or redevelopment of prospective stations sites, and adjacent neighborhoods, offered by property owners and prospective developers" (MDC, 2010).

In spite of the clear policy direction, the next wave of joint developments did not occur until more than a decade later. There were differing opinions within the County on what direction transit joint development should take. Some factions felt that transit property should be used for social purposes, such as affordable housing, while others believed that the land should be used to provide the best possible stream of revenue to MDT. Over time, the County has come to realize that joint development can be used both as a means of providing much needed revenue to MDT and as a means of providing needed affordable housing. MDT currently has a mix of various types of joint developments at eight Metrorail stations. These developments include commercial office buildings, government office buildings, a hotel, retail development, market rate residential development and affordable residential development. Additionally, there are developments in various stages of planning at five other stations (Albert Hernandez and Froilan Baez, MDT, interviewed by Shishir Mathur, June 30, 2011, MDT staff email communication, May 14, 2013).

Institutional capacity
MDT's joint development program requires significant institutional capacity. The county set up a special office of leasing to conduct the SADD studies and to manage and market the development sites (Evans and Roth, 1998). Furthermore, the agency continues to employ staff to identify, negotiate, and manage joint development projects. However, as a result of financial constraints, staffing has been reduced in recent years (MDT staff email communication, May 14, 2013).

Horizontal and vertical equity
The equity concern for the joint development projects primarily revolves around whether the joint development agreement benefits the involved parties in proportion to their stake and risk in the development (horizontal equity). Of particular concern is whether the interests of the public sector agency, in this case MDT, have been protected.

Analysis of the lease structure of Dadeland South shows that MDT has been able to strike a favorable deal for its constituents. The minimum guaranteed lease revenue ($400,000) is inflation-adjusted, and for a long-term lease (55.5 years followed by renewal option for another 44 years). This results in progressively increasing lease revenue in nominal dollar terms. Moreover, MDT has the opportunity to share joint development profits. It gets the higher of the inflation-adjusted $400,000 or a percentage of the gross revenue (Participation Rent). As shown in Table 6.4 (p. 115), the Participation Rent payments were significantly higher than the minimum guaranteed revenue between 2000 and 2010.

However, the joint development agreement has some weaknesses. First, it does not give MDT the power to penalize the Green Company for construction delays. In fact, the entire joint development took well over two decades (1984 to 2008). Second, the developer sold development rights to a third party for a much higher value, and the agreement did not require the Green Company to share the sale profits with MDT. These weaknesses were rectified by MDT in subsequent joint development leases (Smith, 2008).

Stakeholder support
The developer gained from the joint development agreement in two ways: It retained the development rights to property that MDT was planning to acquire, and though there are property taxes levied on the developer's improvements, there are no property taxes levied on the land itself since the ownership of the land is retained by the County. Thus, the developer supported the joint development, and there is no evidence that the other major stakeholders—the local community and other public agencies—opposed the development.

Revenue yield, stability, and growth

Lease revenues for 2000–2010, though stable, were moderately impacted by the economic and real estate market downturn. The revenues peaked in 2007 at $1.1 million and then dropped to a little less than $1 million in 2008, before further declining to a little below $900,000 in 2010. However, the revenues are still above their 2004 levels. In addition to the lease revenues, the county receives property- and sales-tax revenues from this development.

Resurgens Plaza, Atlanta, GA

MARTA provides regional and local transit in the Atlanta metropolitan area. It, along with others, operates a heavy-rail regional subway system that serves about 260,000 weekday passengers and a bus system that serves about 220,000 (Ferreira, n.d.).

The MARTA rail system has four lines: Red Line, Gold Line, Blue Line, and Green Line (see Figure 6.2, p. 119). The system opened in 1979, with lines running east-west. Two years later, a north-south line opened, followed by additional lines that opened in 1992, 1996, and 2000. Lenox Station, on the Gold Line, opened in 1984 and is the site of Resurgens Plaza (Ferreira, n.d.).

Overview

Completed in 1988, Resurgens Plaza is a 27-story Class A office building located in the dense business district within Atlanta's upscale Buckhead district. The building's north side is at street grade, and its south side is connected to the Lenox MARTA Station, with access from the building's third floor. While MARTA's current parking policy seeks to limit parking in its new TODs, Resurgens Plaza predates this policy.

The building's first 10 floors are parking decks. A lobby on the third floor connects the building to the Lenox Station, while the remaining 17 floors contain offices. The building was 95 percent occupied until 2010, when it lost one of its major tenants, the law firm of Fisher & Philips. After that, default was imminent, and the building's $82 million loan was transferred to a special servicer (Citybiz Real Estate, n.d.).[1]

Overview of MARTA's TOD Policy

MARTA has a policy of promoting smart growth and TOD, in part because the transit system is expected to expand dramatically in the near future, with new

---

1   A special servicer specializes in dealing with loans that are already in default or are at risk of default.

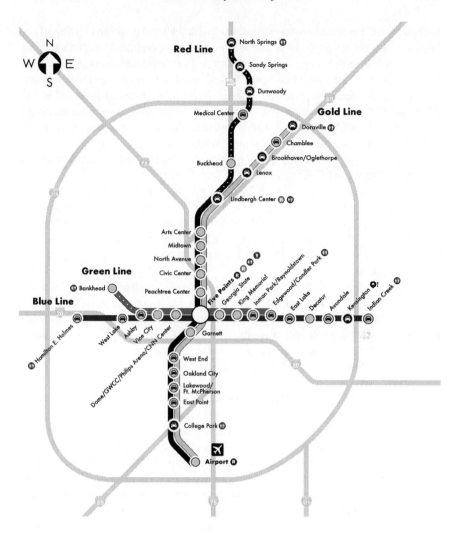

Figure 6.2   MARTA rail map
Note: The full map can be downloaded from http://www.itsmarta.com.
Source: Metropolitan Atlanta Rapid Transit Authority.

streetcar, commuter-rail, light-rail, and BRT lines. The opportunities for TODs will therefore greatly expand (MARTA, 2010).

In 2010, the agency formalized its plan to develop areas near stations in order to take advantage of these TOD opportunities. The process of implementing a joint development starts with an evaluation of the potential opportunities in the agency's inventory of station properties. When a potential development site has been chosen, MARTA staff meet with the local municipality and county officials to determine if the development is consistent with the local plans and zoning. If the finding is affirmative, MARTA commissions property appraisal, taking into account any restrictions on the property. After the property is appraised, the agency selects a developer by issuing an RFQ. An RFP is released once qualified developers are chosen through the RFQ process. If more than one property is included in the RFQ, qualified developers can be awarded more than one development site. In some cases, MARTA will also consider unsolicited development proposals. It also has special provisions for working on proposals from other government agencies whereby it may bypass a competitive bidding process and work directly with the government agency (MARTA, 2010).

Once the developer is selected, MARTA and the developer negotiate a joint development agreement (JDA). The JDA "governs the legal and business" relationship between the agency and the developer and must be approved by the MARTA board. MARTA retains ownership of its joint development properties but may make exceptions for projects that cannot move forward without property sale (MARTA, 2010).

MARTA also has policy guidelines intended to create socially and environmentally responsible joint developments. For example, MARTA requires 20 percent of the joint development to consist of affordable housing in its RFPs for housing developments with more than 10 units. The agency places low priority on planning for automobile access to its stations, limits parking, and encourages sustainable building practices (MARTA, 2010).

Overview of MARTA's Office Dealing with TODs

The Office of Transit Oriented Development & Real Estate is the arm responsible for overseeing MARTA's joint development projects. The goals of the TOD program include (1) increased revenue and ridership for MARTA; (2) acting as a catalyst for new development; (3) reducing dependence on automobiles; and (4) providing new services and amenities for customers. The agency seeks to develop high-quality, compact, viable, and sustainable development within one-quarter to one-half mile of the transit stations. MARTA has developed five successful joint development projects, including Lindbergh City Center, Resurgens Plaza, and St. Joseph's Doctor Building (MARTA, n.d.).

Air-rights details

The deal between the developer of Resurgens Plaza, Resurgens Plaza South Associates, and MARTA provides MARTA with $120,000 annually, with increases based on the CPI. In exchange, the developer obtained the right to build over the station (Cervero, et al., 2004). By 2001, the air-rights lease totaled $177,000; it is currently estimated to be close to $200,000. The lease was signed for 50 years, with an option for 50 additional years, and includes only development rights over the station (Cervero, Hall and Landis, 1992, Ted Tarantino and Jason Ward, MARTA, interview by Shishir Mathur, December 6, 2011).

Factors Supporting Air-rights Development

The real estate market in Atlanta was booming during the 1980s, and the Atlanta metropolitan area added some 400,000 jobs between 1980 and 1988. Developers had many opportunities for less-costly development in the suburbs, which did not give MARTA much leverage in negotiating development deals. Other types of less-costly development on MARTA property, such as ground development, were not allowed by the agency's charter, which states that the agency cannot purchase land for non-transit-related purposes. This is why MARTA has pursued primarily air-rights joint developments (Cervero, Hall and Landis, 1992).

More Effective Air-rights Development

MARTA has learned some lessons as it has gained experience with joint developments. Its policy on parking and automobile access has shifted since the booming real estate market period of the 1980s. Resurgens Plaza, while located on a transit station, devotes 10 floors of the building to parking. Such a generous parking provision reduces building tenants' incentive to use transit, and increases project cost. MARTA has taken steps to correct this problem with its new TOD policy.

Case Analysis

Enabling environment
MARTA's charter provides very strict joint development rules. It prohibits MARTA from using its condemnation powers to purchase property for anything other than transit-related purposes. In practice, the agency cannot pursue joint developments when land has to be purchased. Because the agency is new and does not own large tracts of undeveloped land, air-rights development over stations is the only type of joint development it can pursue (Cervero, Hall and Landis, 1992).

Institutional capacity
By devoting an entire office to joint development, MARTA has shown its commitment toward building significant institutional capacity to undertake such development.

Horizontal and vertical equity
The air-rights lease revenue ($120,000 annually) seems low for a project the size of Resurgens Plaza. Furthermore, unlike MDT (in the case of Dadeland South),

MARTA does not share joint development gross revenue. On a positive note, the lease revenues are CPI-adjusted.

It is important to note that the rail system was new and had low operations and maintenance costs at the time the lease agreement was negotiated. The low cost of running the transit system allowed MARTA to lease air rights at a low price (Cervero, Hall and Landis, 1992).

Stakeholder support
There is no evidence of stakeholder opposition to the construction of Resurgens Plaza.

Revenue yield, stability, and growth
The MARTA staff believed that the revenue yield, although small (approximately $200,000 in 2010), would be stable and would grow with the CPI, even if the building went into foreclosure (Ted Tarantino and Jason Ward). The building indeed went into foreclosure on December 6, 2011 (Sams, 2011).

Concluding Remarks

Joint developments are likely to succeed in the presence of supportive land use and zoning. For example, Miami-Dade County, FL, used its land use and zoning powers and created a new, Rapid Transit Zone (RTZ) to encourage joint development along rapid transit lines. The RTZ seeks to lessen private developer risk by standardizing the zoning ordinance among all municipalities within the County's RTZ. Conversely, WMATA, which operates in several jurisdictions, does not control the local zoning ordinances. Therefore, WMATA is only able to engage in joint development with local zoning support.

In addition to transportation accessibility, the zoning relaxation/change that often accompanies joint development projects may create at least some value for project developers. Therefore, it is difficult, if not impossible, to tease out the property value effect of transportation accessibility from zoning change. Furthermore, it is possible that the zoning change was only possible due to the availability of the transit service, in which case the availability of transit would be the primary cause of zoning change and subsequent property value increase. It is also possible that the zoning would have been changed irrespective of transit availability.

Joint developments fall under the larger umbrella of public-private partnerships (PPPs). Research on PPP notes that the public sector needs a clear understanding of the role that the private sector should play in a PPP project (Flyvbjerg, Bruzelius and Rothengatter, 2003). MDT's joint development experience speaks to the need for such clarity of vision and direction.

References

Bethesda Metro Joint Development, Bethesda, MD

Cervero, Robert, et al. 2004. *Transit-Oriented Development in the United States: Experiences, Challenges, and Prospects.* TCRP Report 102. Washington, DC: Transportation Research Board [Online: Transportation Research Board]. Available at: onlinepubs.trb.org/onlinepubs/tcrp/tcrp_rpt_102.pdf [accessed: October 15, 2011].

Hodge, P. 1980. Hotel, Commercial Complex Planned Atop Bethesda Metro Station, *The Washington Post*, March 6, 1980 [Online: LexisNexis] [accessed: October 16, 2011].

Malasky, G. 2010. *Joint Development to Spur Economic Growth.* Japan International Transport Institute USA, Washington, DC, October 20, 2010 [Online: Japan International Transport Institute, USA]. Available at: http://www.japantransport.com/seminar/WMATA.pdf [accessed: December 2, 2011].

Meridian Group. n.d. *Bethesda Metro Center—Bethesda, MD* [Online: The Meridian Group]. Available at: http://www.meridiangroupinc.com/site/project detail.asp?IdProject=7 [accessed: October 16, 2011].

Metropolitan Washington Council of Governments (MWCOG). n.d. *WMATA Vision and Need for Dedicated Funding* [Online: Metropolitan Washington Council of Governments]. Available at: http://www.mwcog.org/uploads/committee-documents/s11XVlY20041130072828.pdf [accessed: October 16, 2011].

Schumin Web Transit Center. n.d. *Bethesda.* Available at: http://transit.schuminweb. com/transit/wmata/red-line.php?station=A09[accessed: October 16, 2011].

SEC Info. 1999. *Capital Income Properties C Limited Partnership, SEC File 0–14513* [Online: SEC Info]. Available at: http://www.secinfo.com/dNQ1j.6a.htm [accessed: October 16, 2011].

Washington Metropolitan Area Transit Authority (WMATA). 2008. *WMATA Joint Development Policies and Guidelines* [Online: Washington Metropolitan Area Transit Authority]. Available at: http://www.wmata.com/pdfs/business/Guidelines%20Revision11–20–08.pdf [accessed: October 16, 2011].

Dadeland South Joint Development, Miami, FL

Cervero, R., et al. 2004. *Transit-Oriented Development in the United States: Experiences, Challenges, and Prospects.* TCRP Report 102. Washington, DC: Transportation Research Board [Online: Transportation Research Board]. Available at: onlinepubs.trb.org/onlinepubs/tcrp/tcrp_rpt_102.pdf [accessed: October 15, 2011].

Dade County Transportation Administration (DCTA). 1982. *Dadeland South Joint Development Land Lease.*Miami, FL: Metro-Dade Transportation Administration.

Evans, H. and Roth, D. 1988. *Funding Strategies for Public Transportation, Volume 2, Casebook Part E*. Washington, DC: National Academy Press.

Miami-Dade County (MDC). 2010. *Comprehensive Development Master Plan, Transportation Element*. Available at: http://www.miamidade.gov/planzone/cdmp/plan/CDMPTransportationElement2.pdf [accessed: December 5, 2011].

Miami-Dade County (MDC). 1978. *Fixed-Guideway Rapid Transit System—Development Zone, Miami-Dade County Code of Ordinances, Ord. No. 78–74, § 1, 10–17–78, Chapter 33C*. Available at: http://search.municode.com/html/10620/level2/PTIIICOOR_CH33CFIIDRATRSYEVZO.html [accessed: December 5, 2011].

Miami-Dade Transit (MDT). n.d.a. *MDT Facts* [Online: Miami-Dade County—Miami-Dade Transit]. Available at: http://www.miamidade.gov/transit/about_facts.asp [accessed: December 4, 2011].

Miami-Dade Transit. n.d.b. *Metrobus Facts* [Online: Miami-Dade County—Miami-Dade Transit]. Available at: http://www.miamidade.gov/transit/about_metro bus.asp [accessed: December 4, 2011].

Miami-Dade Transit (MDT). 2009. *Existing Services* [Online: Miami-Dade County—Miami-Dade Transit]. Available at: http://www.miamidade.gov/transit/library/10_year_plan/3.0_existing_services.pdf [accessed: December 4, 2011].

Miami-Dade Transit.n.d.c. *Faster and Easier Connection* [Online: Miami-Dade County—Miami-Dade Transit]. Available at: transit/improve_signage.asp [accessed: December 5, 2011].

Miami-Dade Transit. n.d.d. *Dadeland South Metrorail Station* [Online: Miami-Dade County—Miami-Dade Transit]. Available at: http://www.miamidade.gov/transit/rail_dadeland_south.asp [accessed: December 4, 2011].

Miami-Dade Transit. n.d.e. *Joint Development Project—Dadeland South* [Online: Miami-Dade County—Miami-Dade Transit]. Available at: http://www.mia midade.gov/transit/about_joint_dadeland_south.asp [accessed: December 4, 2011].

Smith, G.C. 2008. *Use of Fees or Alternatives to Fund Transit*. Legal Research Digest 28. Washington DC: Transportation Research Board [Online: Transportation Research Board]. Available at: http://onlinepubs.trb.org/onlinepubs/tcrp/tcrp_lrd_28.pdf [accessed: October 30, 2011].

Resurgens Plaza

Cervero, R., et al. 2004. *Transit-Oriented Development in the United States: Experiences, Challenges, and Prospects*. TCRP Report 102. Washington, DC: Transportation Research Board [Online: Transportation Research Board]. Available at: onlinepubs.trb.org/onlinepubs/tcrp/tcrp_rpt_102.pdf [accessed: October 15, 2011].

Cervero, R, Hall, P. and Landis, J. 1992. *Transit Joint Development in the United States*. Berkeley, CA: Institute of Urban and Economic Development, University of California, Berkeley.

Citybiz Real Estate. n.d. *$82M Loan on Resurgens Plaza in Atlanta Transferred to Special Servicer* [Online: citybizlist]. Available at: http://atlantarealestate. citybizlist.com/3/2011/4/27/82M-Loan-on-Resurgens-Plaza-in-Atlanta-Transferred-to-Special-Servicer.aspx [accessed: August 31, 2011].

Ferreira, R. n.d. *Atlanta, Georgia.* Available at: http://world.nycsubway.org/us/atlanta/ [accessed: August 31, 2011].

Metropolitan Atlanta Rapid Transit Authority (MARTA). 2010. *Policies for Implementing MARTA's TOD Guidelines* [Online: MARTA—Metropolitan Atlanta Rapid Transit Authority]. Available at: http://www.itsmarta.com/ TOD%20Guidelines%202010-11.pdf [accessed: August 31, 2011].

MARTA. n.d. *Transit Oriented Development* [Online: MARTA—Metropolitan Atlanta Rapid Transit Authority]. Available at: http://www.itsmarta.com/TOD. aspx [accessed: August 31, 2011].

Sams, D. 2011. CW Capital Forecloses on Resurgens Plaza. *Atlanta Business Chronicle*, December 30, 2011. Available at: http://www.bizjournals.com/ atlanta/print-edition/2011/12/30/cw-capitalforecloses-on-resurgens.html [accessed: January 7, 2013].

Concluding Remarks

Flyvbjerg, B., Bruzelius, N. and Rothengatter, W. 2003. *Megaprojects and Risk: An Anatomy of Ambition.* Cambridge, UK: Cambridge University Press.

Chapter 7
Tax Increment Financing

Three TIF-funded public transportation projects are examined in this chapter. These are: Contra Costa Centre Transit Village, Contra Costa County, CA; Wilson Yard Station, Chicago, IL; and Portland Streetcar, Portland, OR. These projects were chosen on the basis of the following criteria: First, TIF must be used specifically to fund transit projects, such as stations or transit infrastructure, as opposed to funding only TODs. Second, the West and Midwest, especially California and Illinois, are the regions with the most TIF use. Therefore, deliberate efforts were made to include cases from these regions. Third, the TIF districts must have already been formed, and, finally, data must be available.

Contra Costa Centre Transit Village, Contra Costa County, CA

The BART's Pleasant Hill Station is located in Contra Costa County, CA. The station is the site of a mixed-use TOD called the Contra Costa Centre (CCC) transit village. The TOD was financed through a variety of funding mechanisms, including TIF and cost-sharing agreements between the public agencies and private developers, under a PPP framework. The TOD facilities are all within one-quarter mile of the BART station fare gates and include the following land uses (Kennedy, 2008): 422 residential apartments (including 85 affordable units); 100 for-sale condominiums (planned but not yet built); 35,590 square feet of local-resident-serving retail space; 19,400 square feet of business conference center space (planned but not yet built); 270,000 square feet of office space (planned but not yet built); and a 1,550-space parking garage (TIF-funded replacement parking for BART).

BART Overview

BART is a heavy-rail-based transit system that began operating in 1972. Consisting of five lines that serve 44 stations, BART provides regional transit for San Francisco Bay Area residents and connects San Francisco with the cities to the east and south. With an average weekday ridership of more than 300,000, BART is one of the nation's highest ridership rapid-transit systems (BART, n.d.a). The Pleasant Hill Station is near the end of the Pittsburgh/Bay Point—SFO-Millbrae Line in the East Bay (a map of the BART system is at http://www.bart.gov/stations).

PPP Overview

The TOD is a product of a partnership between the Contra Costa County, the Contra Costa County Redevelopment Agency (RDA), BART, Avalon Bay Communities, Inc., and Millennium Partners (Kennedy, 2008). A joint powers authority (JPA) was created to manage the property, with representatives from Contra Costa County, the Contra Costa County RDA, and BART on the board of directors. The JPA is called the Pleasant Hill BART Leasing Authority. BART has leased the property in the station area to the JPA, which in turn has subleased it to the developers—Millennium Partners and Avalon Bay Communities—for 100 years. The ground-lease payments made by the developers to the JPA are shared by BART (25 percent) and the county (75 percent) (Kennedy, 2008). The lease revenues over the 100-year lease period are estimated to be from approximately $700 million to $1 billion (Kennedy and Litten, 2010).

All property in the TOD is BART-owned except the for-sale condominiums (yet to be built). The land is leased to the developers, and three agencies have agreed to finance different portions of the project (Kennedy, 2008). The county issued $135 million in bonds to finance the residential portion. The RDA contributed $59.5 million toward the parking garage, station infrastructure, and various other improvements. The developers contributed $3.9 million toward the parking garage, $11.9 million toward the residential development, and $131 million toward the office space (Kennedy, 2008). The finance plan is summarized in Table 7.1 (p. 129).

The TOD design is the result of a charrette process that began in 2001. The charrette involved the local community members, the county, BART, and Millennium Partners. It was an important part of the development process, as previous development efforts had failed to gain stakeholder acceptance. Championed by one redevelopment agency board member as a tool for creating a development proposal, the six-day design charrette produced the concept, design guidelines, and attendant zoning framework for the village (James Kennedy, Redevelopment Director, Contra Costa County Redevelopment Agency, interviewed by Shishir Mathur, May 6, 2011). The plan was approved by the County Planning Commission in 2005.

The TOD is being built in three phases. Developed in 2006–2008, the Phase I included the replacement BART parking garage. Residential and retail was developed during Phase II (2008–2011). Finally, the offices are planned for the yet to be developed Phase III.

Phase I is complete, and Phase II is partially complete. The rental residential units and retail space are complete, while the for-sale condominiums have not been built. Ground has not yet been broken for two blocks of office space scheduled to be built in Phase III.

Phases II and III are victims of unfortunate timing. Housing bonds totaling $125 million were sold by the county in mid-July 2008 to pay for Phase II.

Table 7.1   Finance plan for the CCC transit village

Funding Source	Amount of Funding ($ millions)			
	Phase I (Garage)	Phase II (Residential/ retail)	Phase III (Office)	Total
Public				*59.5*
RDA– BART parking	45.3			
RDA– backbone infrastructure		2.7		
RDA–place-making		9.0		
RDA– housing		2.5		
Public/private				*135.0*
Tax-exempt housing bonds		135.0		
Private				*171.8*
Backbone infrastructure	3.9	11.9	131.0	
Total	49.2	186.1	131.0	366.3

Source: James Kennedy, "Building a Heart at Contra Costa Centre: Practices and Perspectives," Summer 2008, p. 12, http://centrepoints.org [accessed: 12.10.11].

However, the real estate market downturn halted the development of the 100 condominiums and the Phase III office space (James Kennedy).

In spite of the downturn, the developed portions of the TOD have done reasonably well. The TOD accommodates more than 2,300 residents, 5,000 employees, and 6,000 BART riders per day. Although the retail space has not done very well, the rental residential units are fully occupied. The TOD is projected to generate $8 million in revenue annually (James Kennedy).

Station-area Development Funds

The Contra Costa County RDA contributed TIF funds for the construction of the transit village. The largest share of the RDA funds was spent on the parking garage that was constructed to replace the surface parking lot that was displaced by the development.

Additional TIF funds were used for infrastructure development (James Kennedy). The TIF revenues came from the Contra Costa Centre redevelopment area—one of five redevelopment areas in Contra Costa County.[1] The other four areas are the Bay Point redevelopment area, the North Richmond redevelopment area, the Rodeo redevelopment area, and Montalvin Manor.

---

1   Originally called the Pleasant Hill BART Redevelopment Area, the RDA renamed the TIF district the Contra Costa Centre Redevelopment Area.

Contra Costa Centre Redevelopment Area

Located along the I-680 corridor and the BART line, the Contra Costa Centre Redevelopment Area includes 125 acres surrounding the Pleasant Hill BART Station. Created in 1984, the redevelopment area was planned to operate for 40 years, until 2024. The RDA was authorized to collect up to $90 million in tax increment, at which point it was required to either stop collecting the tax increment or amend the terms of the redevelopment-area formation through further legislation (CCCRA, 1984). Tax increment from the redevelopment area rose steadily between 1986 and 2011 (see Figure 7.1, p. 131).[2]

Historically, the redevelopment area was agricultural. However, rapid low-density suburban residential development followed soon after the beginning of BART service in 1973. Higher-density land uses started replacing single-family homes near the station in the late 1970s to take advantage of BART access (BART, n.d.a). A 1975 plan sought to bring some order and cohesion to the station-area development, which had been a medley of low- and high-density developments. The plan established a three-acre minimum parcel size, but several forces worked against it, including private-developer opposition and local transportation circulation problems. Therefore, the plan was scrapped, and an amended plan was agreed upon by Contra Costa County, BART, the city of Pleasant Hill, and the city of Walnut Creek. The plan was later re-examined and updated and was approved by the County Board of Supervisors in 1998 (CCC, n.d.a).

The updated plan's overall goals are: to (1) allow high-intensity land uses with the station area as a focal point; (2) develop higher-density housing in the area north of the station (north of Las Juntas); and (3) maintain low-intensity uses in the Buskirk frontage area, which has access limitations (see Figure 7.2, p. 132). The plan seeks to redevelop the areas within three main categories: land use and development, transportation and circulation, and urban design. Some of the main goals and objectives for each category are listed below (CCC, n.d.a):

1. Land use and development: increase the density of office, retail, housing, and institutional uses; integrate housing into the station area; develop retail, commercial, and other public services in the station area and nearby; provide opportunities for mixed land uses; prohibit low-density development where inappropriate; and develop cooperatively with BART and the private sector to maximize station-area resources.
2. Transportation and circulation: maximize the use of public transit for residents and businesses; improve local transit service to and from the station area, including automobile access; improve bicycle and pedestrian

---

2	Effective February 1, 2012, RDAs were dissolved in California. The RDAs were in charge of TIF. Interestingly, they were charged with siphoning off property-tax revenue from other taxing agencies such as school districts and counties.

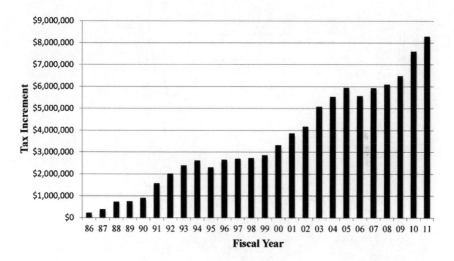

Figure 7.1   Annual tax increment collected from the Contra Costa Centre redevelopment area

amenities and safety; and replace parking that is displaced by the station-area development.
3. Urban design: create a positive station appearance and an image with local identity; protect native oaks and incorporate them into the design; provide a network of open spaces; promote good design for functionality and personal safety; and create a pedestrian-friendly environment through good design features.

Details of TIF for the TOD

Garage construction was one of the obstacles to the BART-station-area development because of BART's one-to-one parking replacement policy, which effectively requires that any development that displaces BART parking must replace it with an equal amount of parking. This policy often requires construction of very expensive structured parking, that is, a garage (CCC, 2001). The requirement came about after a 2002 decision by BART board to provide paid parking for commuters (BART, 2002). Thus, the parking garage was a prerequisite for the development of the CCC Transit Village.

The RDA originally agreed to pay $27 million for the parking garage (Kennedy, 2006). Construction began in 2006 at an estimated cost of $35 million (CCCRA, n.d.). By the time the garage was completed in 2008, the cost had escalated to $52 million. The RDA increased its contribution to $47 million (Kennedy, 2006; James Kennedy). Construction of the CCC Transit Centre began soon after the completion of the garage (BART, n.d.b; CCC, n.d.a).

Figure 7.2   Pleasant Hill BART Station redevelopment area
Source: Contra Costa Centre.

Additional RDA funds paid for the backbone infrastructure, beautification, and place-making around the station (James Kennedy), including $2.5 million for the backbone infrastructure, $4 million for beautification of the station to match the colors and accents of the transit village, and $9 million for place-making projects, such as the plaza, street furniture, and public art.

Case Analysis

Enabling legal environment for TIF use
California redevelopment law allowed the use of TIF funds for station-area development (CDFA, 2007). Redevelopment in California began after the passage of the California Community Redevelopment Act of 1945, which was intended to help cities and counties ameliorate urban blight, and was shaped by a series of laws passed in the next few years, including a 1951 amendment to the tax code that laid the groundwork for TIF by allowing future taxes to pay for redevelopment projects. In 1952, the California Community Redevelopment Law was enacted, allowing the distribution of tax increment to agencies, making California the first state to allow TIF (A History of California Redevelopment, 2011).

There were 397 active RDAs in California in 2011 (CRA, n.d.). However, effective February 1, 2012, the RDAs were dissolved. Successor agencies are managing the RDAs' liabilities and disposing off their assets.

Typical redevelopment projects include affordable housing; roads, water and drainage systems, and public works and infrastructure; community centers, parks, libraries, public-safety buildings, and other community facilities; investment in small businesses and revitalization of downtown shopping districts; revitalization of run-down, blighted neighborhoods to reduce crime; and landscaping, street improvements, and greenbelt creation (CRA, n.d.).

Enabling environment for joint development
A disposition and development agreement (DDA) and the JPA created the enabling framework for the CCC Transit Centre joint development. California state law Chapter 5, Division 7, Title 1 allows for the creation of JPAs and also allows multiple agencies to act as a single entity with a single board of directors (California State Code, section 6500). The JPA manages the transit village and distributes revenues between its partners according to the terms of the DDA.

Stakeholder support
Garnering stakeholder support, especially from the community, was critical for the joint development construction. Previous attempts to develop the property had failed to gain community support. For example, one proposal for high-density office space around the station was swiftly rejected by the community, as well as by BART and developers (James Kennedy). Community involvement in the CCC transit village design ensured that the local community was satisfied.

The project has attracted some community opposition, although not very significant. Citing RDA indebtedness and opposition from neighborhood residents as the primary reasons, a 2002–2003 Grand Jury report recommended that the RDA not get involved in the project. The Grand Jury noted that the RDA is interpreting its powers "liberally" by working with BART to pay for the garage (CCC, n.d.b).

Revenue yield, stability, and growth
The strength of the real estate market has influenced this development. Its plans were amended or delayed because of economic slowdowns at several points in its 40-year history. As of 2011, the real estate market was sluggish in the San Francisco Bay Area, especially in outlying areas, such as Walnut Creek and Pleasant Hill (Lazo, 2010). This softness in real estate demand, especially office-space demand, has delayed Phase III of the development (James Kennedy). The Phase II construction of 100 condominiums is also delayed because of poor housing demand.

Despite these shortcomings, the TOD is a stable investment for the county, the RDA, and BART. TIF revenues have increased from $6 million in 2007, before the village was built, to more than $8 million in 2011 (see Figure 7.1). The county expects to receive a 7 percent return on its investment in the long term. Guaranteed to receive 25 percent of the lease payments, a new garage, and increased revenue from additional farebox collection, BART has found a stable revenue source without taking significant risk.

The lease payments allow the public agencies (the county and BART) to share future profits. These include minimum guaranteed rent (a fixed annual rent), percentage rent (a proportion of the adjusted gross income [AGI]), bonus rent (a proportion of the AGI, after the AGI reaches a minimum threshold), and participation rent—a portion of the net proceeds from the sale of condominiums (Kennedy and Litten, 2010).

Institutional capacity
The significant institutional capacity needed to set up and administer a TIF district is likely to be a major factor in a jurisdiction's ability to use TIF funding for transportation projects. The administrative costs for the CCC Redevelopment Area were about $0.5 million annually between FY 2005 and FY 2010 (see Table 7.2, p. 135). Contra Costa County already had an RDA to form and administer the TIF district, but jurisdictions that do not have such an agency may need additional staff and resources.

In addition to the administrative capacity needed for the TIF district, the joint-development portion of the project also required considerable administrative capacity to form the JPA and develop and administer the DDA.

Horizontal and vertical equity
Overall, the TOD has been horizontally equitable for the parties involved. The RDA receives 75 percent of the lease revenue, and BART receives the other 25 percent, along with other benefits, including increased transit ridership. Additionally, BART retains land ownership. While the county's large share of the lease revenue may seem inequitable, it is fair because the county took all of the initial financial risk. Between 2008 and 2011, the county received around $1.8 million in lease revenue (Kennedy and Litten, 2010) and will continue to receive revenue over the entire course of the lease period.

Table 7.2   Administrative costs for the CCC Redevelopment Area, FY 2005 to FY 2010

	Fiscal year					
	FY 05	FY 06	FY 07	FY 08	FY 09	FY 10
Administrative expenditures ($)	443,070	542,895	451,059	524,537	510,753	407,340

Source: Contra Costa County Redevelopment Agency, RDA Expenditures 2005–2010.

The RDA benefits from the dramatically increased tax increment. As shown in Figure 7.1, the revenues have increased to more than $8 million annually. This number will only go up with the development of the rest of the village. Furthermore, the development has been equitable for the community residents as well. Finally, the CCC Transit Village Centre is vertically equitable for the community, as 20 percent of the condominiums would be affordable-housing units, a proportion secured by the RDA in its negotiations with the developers.

Wilson Yard Station, Chicago, IL

Overview

Illinois is one of the nation's leading users of TIF. Its TIF-enabling legislation, called the Illinois Tax Increment Allocation Redevelopment Act, was passed in January 1977. As of 2006, there were nearly a thousand TIF districts in the state, about 16 percent of them in Chicago (ITIA, 2007).

Several conditions must be met in order to create a TIF district in Illinois. Blight-related requirements must be met, or the area must be designated as a conservation area (for buildings over 35 years old) or an industrial park conservation area. The presence of certain land uses, such as mines and quarries, may also qualify an area for TIF. The "but for test" must also be met—the municipality must demonstrate that the conditions would not improve without the creation of a TIF district (ITIA, 2007).

Once the requirements are met, a detailed project-area redevelopment plan must be prepared and made available for public input. Finally, the TIF proposal must be approved by the City Council or the relevant governing body (ITIA, 2007).

TIF Funding for Public Transportation

Illinois does not specifically prohibit the use of TIF for public transportation. Although the list of eligible uses does not include public transportation, funds have been used for transit station redevelopment, but not for the rolling stock. Eligible uses of TIF include property acquisition, rehabilitation or renovation of existing public or private buildings; construction of public works or improvements; job retraining programs; relocation; financing costs, including interest assistance; studies, surveys, and plans; professional services such as architectural, engineering, legal, property marketing; financial planning; demolition and site preparation; and day-care services (ITIA, 2007).

TIF in Chicago

TIF has been used extensively in Chicago, where there were 166 active TIF areas as of June, 2011. Chicago is subdivided into seven districts, each with several TIF areas. These TIF areas cover a large proportion of the land within the districts (some cover more than half of the district area). The Housing and Economic Development Department is in charge of overseeing TIF in the city (City of Chicago, n.d.).

Chicago's long history of successful TIF implementation includes working with local industries to create jobs. In fact, the Housing and Economic Development Department's stated objective is to "help local companies expand and create employment opportunities for Chicago residents" (City of Chicago, n.d.). Several TIF-funded programs—including TIF works and the Small Business Improvement Fund—have provided non-repayable grants for local businesses to train employees, create new jobs, and improve buildings. Recently, the city worked with a local business, Accretive Health, to create 650 new entry-level jobs in addition to retaining 175 current positions in exchange for $6 million in TIF funds. The funds were used to refurbish the company's headquarters. Without them, the company might have relocated its headquarters elsewhere (City of Chicago, n.d.).

Public Transit in Chicago, the Red Line, and Wilson Station

The Chicago Transit Authority (CTA) operates the second-largest public transportation system in the United States. The system serves the city of Chicago and 40 surrounding suburbs (CTA, n.d.).

Chicago is famous for its L, or elevated trains, which have been in operation since the late nineteenth century. The L is a heavy-rail system that runs partly on elevated tracks and partly underground. The L system was formerly run by several competing private companies, which unified in 1924 but remained privately run. In 1947, the CTA took over operation of the L system. It then consolidated the system and streamlined its operations in order to make the system competitive with the automobile (Chicago "L."org, n.d.a)

The CTA's costs rose rapidly throughout the 1970s. The task of providing transit became increasingly difficult with rapid auto-dependent, low-density suburbanization. The CTA system ridership was at its lowest level in the 1980s and 1990s, and service was cut drastically. Several new efficiencies were introduced in the late 1990s, including the use of magnetic swipe cards and one-person train operations. These efficiencies reduced costs significantly, leading to a fiscal surplus for the first time in decades. As a result, the CTA restarted previously cut services, including night and weekend services, on some lines (Chicago "L."org, n.d.a).

Today, with 140 bus routes and eight rail lines, the CTA is the dominant bus and rapid-transit service operator in the greater Chicago area. It has one of the highest overall riderships in the country, with about 1 million daily weekday bus riders and almost 700,000 weekday rail riders, for a combined weekday ridership of 1.7 million (Chicago "L."org, n.d.a).

The Red Line

Running North-South through the greater Chicago area, the Red Line is the Chicago's main and busiest transit line. Serving 167,000 customers on weekdays and approximately 130,000 on Saturdays, the Red Line connects several popular destinations, including the major universities, sports stadiums, and the downtown loop area (Chicago "L."org, n.d.b).

Wilson Station

Wilson Station is on the Chicago L Red Line. In addition to serving the Red Line, it serves four bus connections (Chicago "L."org, n.d.c). Constructed in 1900, the station over time earned a notorious reputation as one of the worst CTA-run rail stations. A 2009 article gave Wilson Station the dubious distinction of being Chicago's "crustiest and most rotten" station (O'Neil, 2009). Undoubtedly, it was in dire need of redevelopment.

Wilson Yard TIF District

Authorized for 25 years, the Wilson Yard TIF district was created in 2001. A 144-acre site located in the Uptown neighborhood, the area is a mix of commercial, institutional (Truman College and the CTA-owned Wilson Yard), and residential uses (City of Chicago, 2000).

The Uptown neighborhood is home to several ethnic groups who moved in the 1970s and 1980s. By 1990, about one-third of the residents were foreign-born and low-income (City of Chicago, 2000). The 1990 median family income (MFI) was about half the citywide average. However, in recent years, the neighborhood has gentrified, and real estate prices have risen.

Redeveloping the Wilson Yard site is one of the TIF district's primary goals. The district suffered from deteriorating buildings and traffic congestion (City of Chicago, 2000), and the site was used by the CTA for maintenance purposes. Part of the redevelopment plan for the TIF district involves moving Wilson Station from its original location north of Wilson Avenue to the Wilson Yard site.

A study in 2000 found the Wilson Yard area eligible for TIF funding. Eighty-five percent of the 289 buildings in the area were more than 35 years old. The study found that several buildings were dilapidated, were below code standards, had inadequate facilities, and lacked property-value growth (City of Chicago, 2000).

The redevelopment-plan objectives included the preservation of existing cultural diversity, residences, and businesses; facilitation of development of vacant and underutilized land; redevelopment of the Wilson Yard site in a way that enhances the neighborhood's attractiveness; support for Wilson Station relocation; improvements to major thoroughfares' physical condition (i.e., building conditions, streetscaping, and walkability); preservation and encouragement of retail, commercial, and institutional uses and historically significant buildings; creation of distinctive streetscaping and landscaping that creates a cohesive neighborhood feel and support improvements in accessibility for persons with disabilities; and encouragement of opportunities for women and minority-owned businesses; and support locally owned businesses and jobs and training programs (City of Chicago, 2000).

Totaling close to $7 million in 2010, the TIF revenues are substantial and have funded several projects in the district.

After earlier attempts to renovate the station had failed, TIF funds maintenance and improvements were authorized in February 2010 through an intergovernmental agreement between the CTA and the city of Chicago. The main improvements to the station are interior and exterior repairs to the Gerber building, which houses the station and the retail concession area (City of Chicago, 2010). Other improvements include replacing the roof on the Gerber building, the electrical system, the plumbing, and the heating and cooling system (O'Neil, 2009). Additional improvements include asbestos and lead-paint remediation, relocation of the customer assistance booth and turnstiles from the mezzanine to a first-floor location closer to the station entrance, addition of new turnstiles, light-emitting diode (LED) illumination on the exterior of the station building, new floor tiles, and walls and passageway clean-up.

The total TIF funding for these improvements cannot exceed $3 million (City of Chicago, 2010). The renovations began in 2010 and are currently under way (Mark Segun, Fiscal Administrator, City of Chicago, Department of Housing and Economic Development, interview by Shishir Mathur, October 7, 2011). An additional $6 million in federal funds was granted in October 2011 for exterior rehabilitation and installation of a new elevator (Chicago "L."org, n.d.c).

Case Analysis

Enabling environment
The Illinois Redevelopment Act does not prohibit TIF funding for transit projects. Wilson Station was clearly eligible for TIF funding because it was blighted and a conservation site.

Institutional capacity

Significant institutional capacity is needed to form and administer a TIF district. $96,500 is projected to be spent to administer the district in 2011 (City of Chicago, 2009). While this amount may seem small compared to the TIF district's annual revenue, the amount would probably be much higher for a city that lacks Chicago's experience, ability to realize economy of scale, and qualified personnel to administer the TIF.

Stakeholder support

The city is divided into 50 wards, each represented by one alderman. The past and present aldermen and the CTA approached the city with the station redevelopment proposal. There was no significant public opposition to using TIF for station redevelopment (Mark Segun).

Horizontal and vertical equity

Wilson Station is an important feature of the Wilson Yard TIF district. Since TIF funds were clearly needed to refurbish the station, their use was equitable and probably welcomed by most residents and stakeholders in the neighborhood. Furthermore, use of TIF revenues for public transportation is horizontally equitable, as it improves accessibility for all neighborhood residents. By improving access to the neighborhood and by providing more transportation options, the refurbished Wilson Station has helped other groups as well. For example, businesses should benefit from the increased foot traffic, and the college students and faculty benefit from safe and improved access to their campuses. These indirect benefits are in addition to the direct benefits that automobile users and pedestrians will receive from the improved TIF-funded roadways and streetscapes.

The use of TIF to fund public transportation is also vertically equitable to the extent that low-income people with lower ability to own an automobile are more likely to be dependent on public transportation.

Revenue yield, stability, and growth

The Wilson Yard TIF district has generated substantial revenues. The impact of the economic and real estate downturn has been minimal, with slight revenue dips in 2007 and 2009 (see Table 7.3, p. 140). Overall, annual revenues have grown more than two-fold, from approximately $3 million in 2002 to $7 million in 2010.

Central Streetcar Project, Portland, OR

Overview

Planned and built in the 1990s and 2000s, the Portland Streetcar Project was intended to link Portland's neighborhoods with quality transportation and to spur development along the streetcar lines. Four streetcar lines were built on the west

Table 7.3   Annual revenues from the Wilson Yard TIF District

	Year								
	2002	2003	2004	2005	2006	2007	2008	2009	2010
Revenue ($ million)	3.1	2.4	4.7	5.2	6.2	5.8	6.8	6.1	7.0
Year-to-Year change (%)		-25[a]	98	11	24	-8	18	-11	15

Note: [a] The decrease in revenue is due to the fall in total assessed value of the property. The value decreased as a result of land acquisition and the removal of dilapidated structures.
Source: Data for 2002–2008 are from 2002–2008 Wilson Yard TIF Annual Reports, http://www.aldermanshiller.com. Data for 2009–2010 are from the 2010 Annual Report, http://www.cityofchicago.org.

side of the Willamette River in the 2000s in the Central Streetcar Project, which includes 46 stops in an eight-mile continuous loop (PSI, n.d.). The streetcar lines were funded with a combination of funds, including TIF and SADs (PSI 2010).

This case study discusses the use of both TIF (through the urban renewal areas, or URAs) and local improvement districts, or LIDs (SADs are called LIDs in Oregon), to fund this project.

Tax Increment Financing

History of urban renewal and TIF in Portland
A 1951 state law authorized urban renewal in Oregon. The legislation authorizes cities to use federal funding and TIF revenues to revitalize inner-city areas. In 1958, Portland residents voted to create an urban renewal agency called the Portland Development Commission, PDC (PDC, 2003).

Creation of URAs
In Portland, URAs are created when community organizations and the PDC recognize that an area is in need of improvements. Furthermore, the state requires a finding of blight, and the residents and the PDC must come to an agreement on the URA boundaries, taking into consideration ways to "maximize the effectiveness of planned projects and programs" as well as "economic, legal, and political considerations" (PDC, 2003). Next, the financial plans are developed for the URA, legal analysis is conducted, and community input is considered before the City Council approves the urban-renewal plans (PDC, 2003).

Funding for URAs has completely changed since they were first created after World War II. URAs today are funded through TIF, after federal funding for urban renewal was cut in the 1970s (Marks, 2005). At that time, the Oregon legislature increased the applicability of URAs by expanding the definition of blight. However, funding was restricted two decades later, in 1991, when Oregon passed legislation that capped the property-tax rate. Measure 5, which places a tax ceiling of one percent of real market value, required many URAs to reduce tax rates (PDC, 2003).

The URAs are created for a finite period, after which they expire and normal taxing rules apply. For example, the North Macadam URA was created in 1999 and will expire in 2020. Since its creation in 1958 up until 2011, the PDC created 20 URAs, 11 of which were active as of 2011 (PDC, n.d.a).

Enabling legislation

Oregon's legislation allows TIF to be used for transportation capital investments, enabling Portland to fund a significant portion of its streetcar lines with it. Other Oregon cities have taken advantage of this legal provision as well—for example, Eugene used TIF to construct a transit center (Johnson and Tashman, 2002). The TIF funds must be used only for capital expenditures and are prohibited from funding operations and maintenance. The following uses are permissible under the Oregon law: permanent public improvements such as transportation facilities, lighting, trees, parks, and utilities; financial and technical assistance for private reinvestment, including storefront grants, home repairs and improvements, and commercial rehabilitation incentives; funding partnerships for new housing and mixed-use developments; land acquisition (typically for key redevelopment sites or public projects); planning of capital projects (including development of urban-renewal plans); and general administrative costs related to the activities of the URA (City of Hillsboro, n.d.).

URA funding of the Central Streetcar Project

Three URAs funded the Central Streetcar Project: North Macadam, South Park Blocks, and River District. Funding for initial capital expenditure came from TIF-backed bonds, which were paid back with revenue collected from the three URAs (Lisa Abouf, Central City Manager, Urban Development Department, PDC, interview by Shishir Mathur, March 4, 2011)

The North Macadam URA was created in 1999. At that time, the North Macadam area was largely under-utilized and vacant, with some brown-field developments. It also lacked transportation access. Since then, North Macadam has turned around and has become a central city hub with new employment centers, housing, parks, and transportation options. A new biosciences facility currently in the planning stage is expected to bring new jobs. The area's successful transportation improvements have helped improve accessibility and spur growth (PDC, n.d.b).

Created in 1985, the South Park Blocks area consists of several neighborhoods. Some of the major development goals for the area include supporting and expanding the downtown retail area, assisting the advancement of Portland State University, and preserving the West End mixed-income neighborhood (PDC, n.d.c).

Created in 1988, the River District includes what is known as the Pearl District (the former location of the Burlington Northern rail yards), Old Town, Chinatown neighborhoods, and the Union Station area. The district has sought to create a new neighborhood at the site of the former rail yard, connect neighborhoods to the waterfront, and develop infrastructure, such as parks, the streetcar, and parking. The district is intended to be a "24-hour," dense, urban area with a mix of residential and commercial uses oriented toward the Willamette River (PDC, n.d.d).

Annual TIF revenues dedicated to the Central Streetcar Project
The Central Streetcar Project was developed in four phases and opened throughout the 2000s. TIF revenues were a major funding source (PSI, 2010). Details of the four lines are listed in Table 7.4 (p. 143).

Proportion of TIF revenues expended on the Central Streetcar Project
For the North Macadam URA, the percentage of the total revenue expended on the streetcar was highest in FY 2002 through FY 2005, when the streetcar expenditures accounted for more than half of the URA budget (PDC, n.d.e). See Table 7.5 (p. 143).

South Park Blocks URA revenues funded the streetcar line from Legacy Good Samaritan Hospital to Portland State University from 1998 through 2002. The funds spent per year are summarized in Table 7.6 (p. 144).

Legal challenges to TIF
The use of URA funds for the Portland Streetcar Project has not encountered legal challenges to date. URA funds were previously used for other transit projects in the city, such as light-rail lines, so any legal challenges to the use of URA funds for transit were probably resolved in those projects (Lisa Abouf). Additionally, the enabling legislation clearly allows the use of TIF revenue for transportation capital expenditures.

It is important to note that URA funds have not been used to purchase rolling stock (rail cars). Since rolling stock is not used exclusively within a specific URA, the use of URA funds to purchase it was considered a legal grey area (Lisa Abouf).

Local Improvement Districts

Overview
Portland has used LIDs as funding sources to help finance all phases of the Central Streetcar Project. A new LID was created for each phase, sometimes using many different assessment methodologies (Vicky Diede, Portland Street Car Project Manager, City of Portland, interview by Shishir Mathur, February 22, 2011). The

Table 7.4   URA funding of Portland Central Streetcar Project capital cost

Streetcar line	Legacy Good Samaritan Hospital to Portland State University (Phase I and II)	Portland State University to RiverPlace (Phase 3a)	RiverPlace to SW Gibbs Street (Phase 3b)	SW Moody and Gibbs to SW Lowell (Phase 3c)
Length/type of track	2.4 miles of double track	0.6 miles of double track	0.6 miles of single track	0.4 miles of double track
Service began	July 20, 2001	March 11, 2005	October 20, 2006	August 17, 2007
Capital budget ($ millions)	56.9	16.0	15.8	14.45
Funds from URA ($ millions)	7.5	8.4	3.8	1.8
Percent of capital budget from URA	13.18	52.50	24.05	12.46
URA involved	South Park Blocks	North Macadam	North Macadam	North Macadam

Source: Portland Streetcar, Inc., Portland Streetcar Capital and Operations Funding (September 2010).

Table 7.5   Percentage of North Macadam URA expenditures on Portland Central Streetcar Project

	FY 2000–01 Actual	FY 2001–02 Actual	FY 2002–03 Actual	FY 2003–04 Actual	FY 2004–05 Actual	FY 2005–06 Revised
Total expenditure on streetcar ($)	23,387	28,726	1,301,113	4,512,619	6,559,490	184,949
Total project expenditures ($)	2,040,059	1,683,925	2,503,041	6,382,047	8,500,280	14,871,392
Percent of total expenditure on streetcar	1.15	1.71	51.98	70.71	77.17	1.24

Source: PDC, Adopted Fiscal Year Budgets (2000 to 2006), http://www.pdc.us [accessed: 7.16.11].

LIDs are regulated by state and city laws. Formed by City Council resolution, LIDs are initiated by the property owners, one of the city's bureaus, or the City Council (City of Portland, Ordinance 177124). LIDs were approved for the Central Streetcar Project in 2000. The contributions of LID funds for the various phases of the project are detailed in Table 7.7 (p. 144).

Table 7.6   Percentage of South Park Blocks URA expenditures on Portland Central Streetcar Project

	FY 1998–99	FY 1999–2000	FY 2000–01	FY 2001–02
Total expenditure on streetcar ($)	163,671	7,915,850	8,866	196,319
Total revenue generated in the URA ($)	12,780,443	11,587,773	1,907,910	13,948,340
Total expenditure on streetcar as a percent of total revenue generated in the URA	1.28	68.31	0.46	1.41

Source: PDC, Adopted Fiscal Year Budgets (1998 to 2002), http://www.pdc.us [accessed: 7.16.11].

Table 7.7   Total costs of the Central Streetcar Project funded by LIDs

Phase	Total cost ($ millions)	LID total ($ millions)	Percent LID funded
Phase 1 & 2	56.9	9.6	17
Phase 3a	14.4	3.0	21
Phase 3b	15.8	2.0	13
Phase 3c	13.4	4.8	36
All phases combined	100.5	19.4	19

Source: E.D. Hovee & Company LLC, "Streetcar-Development Linkage: The Portland Streetcar Loop," Prepared for City of Portland Office of Transportation (February 2008), p. 11, http://www.edhovee.com [accessed: 12.10.11].

Assessment calculation methodology

The various phases of the Portland Central Streetcar project used the methodologies outlined in Table 7.8 (p. 145) to calculate the assessments. The methodology adopted for a particular phase depends on a number of factors, including local circumstances and the types of properties within the LID.

The LIDs for Phases 1 and 2 contain a large number of owner-occupied residential properties, which increased the probability of property-owner opposition. Balancing the revenue loss and the possibility of such opposition, the city decided to exempt owner-occupied residential properties from paying assessments (Vicky Diede). The decision was mainly political.

As defined in the Phase 1 and 2 LID petition memos, the LIDs extend 550 to 780 feet from the street abutting the streetcar line (hereafter called the streetcar street) (Vicky Diede). The LIDs are divided into two zones. The first zone includes all properties within 200 feet of the streetcar street. Properties that abut the streetcar street are assumed to be zero feet away and are the properties deemed

Table 7.8   LID assessment methodology for Portland Central Streetcar project

Phase	Assessment methodology
Phase 1 and 2	$30 per foot of frontage + rate x property value; 2 zones; rate varies by land use and zone
Phase 3a	Larger of: $6/$1,000 property value x total property value "or" $0.90/sq. ft. x land area; 2 zones; rate varies by zone
Phase 3b	$1.35 per square foot x land area x distance factor
Phase 3c	$3.23 per square foot x land area x distance factor

Source: LID Petitions (Vicky Diede, Portland Street Car Project Manager, City of Portland, interview by Shishir Mathur, July 18, 2011).

to benefit from the streetcar frontage. For these properties, the assessment is a sum of $30 times the linear feet of the property fronting on the streetcar street and property value times a base rate. The base rate varies by the principal land use of the property and the zone in which the parcel is located.

For example, an apartment complex in the first zone with a 100-foot streetcar street frontage and a value of $1 million will be assessed $8,500 ($30 x 100, or $3000, plus a $5.50 base rate x $1 million ÷ $1,000, which equals $5,500). A similarly valued apartment complex in the second zone will be assessed only $2,750 ($2.75 base rate x $1 million ÷ $1,000) because it does not enjoy streetcar street frontage and is further away than the apartment complex in the first zone.

As defined in the Phase 3a LID petition memo, the LID extends up to 720 feet (one-eighth of a mile) from the streetcar street. The properties pay assessments equal to a distance factor (a number that is inversely proportional to the quotient obtained by dividing the distance from a streetcar street by 720 feet) times the larger of (a) property value times $6 per $1,000 of property value and (b) the parcel area of the property times $0.90 per square foot of parcel area.

For example, the assessments for a property with a value of $2 million and a land area of 10,000 square feet that is 100 feet from a streetcar street is $10,320, computed as follows: value method: $6.00 ÷ $1,000 x $2,000,000 = $12,000; land-area method = $0.90 per square foot x 10,000 square feet = $9,000; distance factor = 1 − (100 ÷ 720) = 0.86. In this case, the value method applies, and the assessment = $12,000 x 0.86 = $10,320.

As defined in the Phases 3b and 3c LID petition memos, the LIDs extend up to 1,320 feet (one-quarter of a mile) from the streetcar street. The properties are charged assessments equal to the land area times a base rate ($1.35 per square foot for Phase 3b and $3.23 per square foot for Phase 3c) times a distance factor (a number that is inversely proportional to the ratio resulting from dividing the distance from a streetcar street by 1,320 feet).

For example, the assessment for a Phase 3b property with a value of $2 million and a land area of 10,000 square feet that is 100 feet from a streetcar street is

$2,484, computed as follows: $1.35 ÷ $1,000 x $2,000,000 = $2,700, distance factor = 1 – (100 ÷ 1320) = 0.92. In this case, the estimated assessment = $2,700 x 0.92 = $2,484.

The assessment for a similar property in Phase 3c is $5,943, computed as follows: $3.23 ÷ $1,000 x $2,000,000 = $6,460, distance factor = 1 – (100 ÷ 1320) = 0.92. In this case, the estimated assessment = $6,460 x 0.92 = $5,943.

In Phases 3a, 3b, and 3c, all residential properties within the LID were assessed charges (Vicky Diede). For phase 3c, Portland State University was charged a lump sum of $500,000.

Use of assessments to fund the Central Streetcar Project
The city issued and sold assessment-backed bonds to pay for the construction of the streetcar. According to the Oregon state law, assessments cannot be levied until the project is substantially complete. Furthermore, the property owners have the option of paying the assessments in full or over a 5-, 10-, or 20-year period. Therefore, the assessment funds are typically not available during the construction phase. The city issued assessment-backed bonds for the streetcar project to address this revenue-expenditure mismatch. The bonds were backed by the citywide LID construction fund (Vicky Diede).

Legal challenges to LIDs
Majority property owners supported the LIDs, as they believed that the streetcar would directly benefit their property (Vicky Diede). This support is evidenced by the fact that the LIDs were approved for all the phases of the Central Streetcar Project and later for the Eastside Streetcar Project (Hovee and Jordan, 2008). Furthermore, the PDC deliberately minimized the potential for legal challenges by exempting owner-occupied residential properties from paying assessments in several LIDs.

TIF and LIDs: Major revenue sources for the Central Streetcar Project
Portland has used TIF and LIDs to fund a large portion of the Central Streetcar Project. Funds from TIF and LIDs combined were used for 30 percent to 71 percent of the total capital costs of the project (see Table 7.9, p. 147). The LID funding demonstrated the local community support, which has been effective in leveraging federal and state investments. The project received significant federal and state funding from the US Department of Housing and Urban Development, the Federal Transportation Fund, and Connect Oregon (PSI, 2010).

Portland cites three main success factors in the development of the Central Streetcar Project. These include: the city documented the positive impacts of the streetcar and its philosophy of development-oriented transit; development within one block of the streetcar increased rapidly after it was built, leading to developer and resident support for the project. The city interviewed developers and found them confident that investment in the streetcar would attract new development;

Table 7.9   Percentages of Portland Central Streetcar capital expenditure funded with TIF and LID revenues

	Legacy Good Samaritan Hospital to Portland State University (Phase I and II)	Portland State University to RiverPlace (Phase 3a)	RiverPlace to SW Gibbs Street (Phase 3b)	SW Moody and Gibbs to SW Lowell (Phase 3c)
Percent funded with TIF and LID revenues	30.05	71.25	36.71	45.67

Source: Portland Streetcar, Inc., "Portland Streetcar Capital and Operations Funding (September 2010)," http://www.portlandstreetcar.org [accessed: 7.16.11].

and the LID revenues helped fund 10 percent of the streetcar—property owners believed that the streetcar increases property value and were therefore willing to back it financially (Hovee and Jordan, 2008).

The LIDs used a relatively fair methodology for calculating the assessment charges. For most of the phases, the city calculated the assessment charge based on a parcel's distance from the streetcar, as well as on the size or value of the property. This assessment methodology allows for lower-value properties to pay less (enhancing vertical equity) and also charges a lower rate to those further away from the streetcar line (enhancing horizontal equity) (Hovee and Jordan, 2008).

Case Analysis

Enabling legal environment
The state-level enabling legislation for both URAs and LIDs facilitated the use of TIF and LIDs. Oregon state law clearly identifies the potential uses for URA funds and allows LID formation through City Council resolution, among other mechanisms.

Stakeholder support
Portland received broad-based stakeholder support for URA and LID formation. The city was able to work with the stakeholders to find solutions when problems arose. For example, those living outside the underdeveloped North Macadam URA were initially concerned that their funds would be used to subsidize it. The city addressed this concern by creating the North Macadam Overlay, which helped specify the geography where the URA funds would be expended.

The city consulted with the stakeholders prior to the LID formation, thereby securing their strong support throughout the project. The city also revised assessments whenever mistakes were detected in the assessment calculation process (Vicky Diede). Finally, the city was strategic. In the Phase 1 and 2 LIDs, the city averted a potentially contentious political battle by exempting owner-occupied residential properties from paying assessments.

Institutional capacity

LIDs and URAs both require significant institutional capacity. The bond issuance, preliminary studies, fee assessment, public relations management, and other activities involved in administering LIDs and URAs demand significant staff time and resources. The PDC is especially geared toward creating and administering URAs. As discussed earlier, cities that do not have an established and experienced redevelopment agency might find TIF time-consuming and taxing on the staff. Even greater institutional capacity could be needed if the TIF districts or LIDs are legally challenged. For Portland, the institutional capacity to administer the URAs and LIDs was in place.

Horizontal and vertical equity

Several steps were taken to make the LID assessment methodology vertically and horizontally equitable. Basing assessments on the size or value of the parcel advanced vertical equity. Distance and use-based charges advanced horizontal equity.

The use of TIF funds for transit advanced horizontal equity, as the funds generated by a URA were used to fund capital expenditure within that URA. Furthermore, to the extent that lower-income people benefit more from transit than higher-income people, TIF funding for the Central Streetcar Project enhanced vertical equity as well.

Revenue yield, stability, and growth

URAs involved in funding the streetcar were impacted by the housing market downturn. This is especially true for URAs such as the North Macadam and River District URAs, where condominiums constitute a large portion of the new development. TIF revenues in these areas have decreased as a result of the weakened owner-occupied residential real estate market.

In the case of LIDs, revenue is typically very stable and predictable. However, since not all the revenue is collected up front, there is always a possibility that property owners may petition for a downward revision of assessments during bad economic times.

Concluding Remarks

Surprisingly, the use of TIF to fund public transportation is rare. The extant literature notes that transportation infrastructure accrue significant benefits at the local level. Many of these benefits are capitalized into property values. Further, TIF heavily relies on property value increases to generate revenues. Therefore, the use of TIF revenues to fund public transportation should be very common. What is the reason for this anomaly?

In my opinion, there are two major reasons. First, TIF in the US is often used to fight blight. The public agencies in charge of fighting blight and redeveloping an area often look at small scale, quick ways to increase the blighted area's property values, including, financial incentives to entice hotels, offices, and other tax generating uses in the redevelopment area. Second, a redeveloping area may not demonstrate a clear demand for a fixed right-of-way public transportation system such as a streetcar or a light or heavy rail. Further, even though a redevelopment area might need bus service, the Portland streetcar example shows that public agencies might consider TIF revenue funding of buses and other rolling stock to be a legal grey area and not use TIF revenues to provide bus service.[3]

The TIF revenues are highly dependent on the real estate market and often rely on the construction and performance of a few large projects. Therefore, such revenues can decline with the real estate market downturn or if large TIF-revenue-generating projects are delayed, scaled back, or fail to develop. The CCC Transit Village provides an example of all the above possibilities. The project was delayed for almost two decades. When the project was mid-way through construction, the real estate market downturn led to the completion of only two of the three phases. While this scaled down project accrues significant revenues to the public agencies (the county and BART), the revenues are arguably lower than what they would have been had the project been fully developed and not delayed.

Finally, the TIF-affected rise in property values has a downside. Rising rents and property taxes could financially burden low-income residents who are often minorities in the US. These residents may be forced to move out of their homes to make way for higher-income "gentry" during a process called gentrification. Therefore, the use of TIF should be complemented with strategies to minimize negative impacts on low-income residents. Such strategies could include using a portion of TIF revenues to provide housing or economic development opportunities for low-income residents.[4]

---

3   In several cases, the TIF-enabling legislation might completely prohibit the use of TIF for public transportation or selectively prohibit the use of TIF for purchase of rolling stock, such as buses and train cars.

4   As per the California redevelopment law, at least 20 percent of TIF revenues should be spent on affordable housing.

References

Contra Costa Centre Transit Village, Contra Costa County, CA

A History of California Redevelopment. 2011. *Signal Tribune*, January 21, 2011. Available at: http://www.signaltribunenewspaper.com/?p=8989 [accessed: January 8, 2013].

Bay Area Rapid Transit (BART). 2002. *Pleasant Hill BART Station Access Plan* [Online: BART—Bay Area Rapid Transit]. Available at: http://www.bart.gov/docs/planning/Pleasant_Hill_Access_Plan.pdf [accessed: December 2, 2011].

Bay Area Rapid Transit. n.d.a. *BART Chronology* [Online: BART—Bay Area Rapid Transit]. Available at: www.bart.gov/docs/BARThistory.pdf [accessed: July 23, 2011].

Bay Area Rapid Transit. n.d.b. *BART Breaks Ground for Transit Village at Pleasant Hill Station* [Online: BART—Bay Area Rapid Transit]. Available at: http://www.bart.gov/news/articles/2008/news20080717.aspx [accessed: July 23, 2011].

California Redevelopment Association (CRA). n.d. *Frequently Asked Questions About Redevelopment in California.* Available at: www.el-cerrito.org/redev/pdf/redev_faq.pdf [accessed: July 23, 2011].

California State Code, section 6500. Available at: http://www.leginfo.ca.gov/cgi-bin/displaycode?section=gov&group=06001–07000&file=6500-6536 [accessed: July 23, 2011].

Contra Costa County (CCC). 2001. *Pleasant Hill BART Property Charrette Response to Questions* [Online: Contra Costa County, CA Official Website]. Available at: http://www.co.contra-costa.ca.us/depart/cd/charrette/outcome/response_questions.htm#i [accessed: July 23, 2011].

Contra Costa County (CCC). n.d.a. *Pleasant Hill BART Transit Village Final Development Plan* [Online: Contra Costa County Redevelopment]. Available at: http://www.ccreach.org/ccc_redevelopment/ph_finaldp.cfm [accessed: July 23, 2011].

Contra Costa County (CCC). n.d.b. *Contra Costa County Grand Jury Report No. 0306.* Available at: http://www.saveelsobrante.com/GrandJurytimetore directredev0306rpt.htm [accessed: July 23, 2011].

Contra Costa County Redevelopment Agency (CCCRA). 1984. *Pleasant Hill BART Station Area Redevelopment Plan.*

Council of Development Finance Agencies (CDFA). 2007. *Tax Increment Finance Best Practices Reference Guide* [Online: International Council of Shopping Centers]. Available at: www.icsc.org/government/CDFA.pdf [accessed: November 12, 2011).

Kennedy, J. 2006. Patient Capital, TOD, and Public Real Estate Asset Management: Pleasant Hill BART at Contra Costa Centre, Rail-Volution, Chicago, IL, November 6, 2006. Available at: http://www.railvolution.org/rv2006_pdfs/rv 2006_104a.pdf [accessed: December 2, 2011].

Kennedy, J. 2008. *"Building a Heart at Contra Costa Centre." Practices and Perspectives* [Online: Contra Costa Center Transit Village]. Available at: http://centrepoints.org/pdf/BuildingAHeart.pdf [accessed: December 2, 2011].

Kennedy, J. and Litten, J. 2010. *Building a Heart at Contra Costa Centre–The Power of Partnering*, at the Urban Land Institute meeting titled Public Finance for Private Development, January 20, 2010.

Lazo, A. 2010. Bay Area Housing Market Slow in February. *Los Angeles Times*, March 17, 2010 [Online: Los Angeles Times]. Available at: http://latimesblogs.latimes.com/money_co/2011/03/bay-areas-housing-market-slow-infebruary.html [accessed: July 23, 2011].

Wilson Yard Station, Chicago, IL

Chicago "L."org. n.d.a. *"L" System History* [Online: Chicago "L.'org]. Available at: http://www.chicago-l.org/history/index.html [accessed: August 14, 2011].

Chicago "L."org. n.d.b. *Red Line* [Online: Chicago "L.'org]. Available at: http://www.chicago-l.org/operations/lines/red.html [accessed: August 14, 2011].

Chicago "L."org. n.d.c. *Wilson Station* [Online: Chicago "L.'org]. Available at: http://www.chicago-l.org/stations/wilson.html [accessed: August 14, 2011].

Chicago Transit Authority (CTA). n.d. *CTA Overview* [Online: Chicago Transit Authority]. Available at: http://www.transitchicago.com/about/overview.aspx [accessed: January 8, 2013].

City of Chicago. 2010. *Ordinance No. 010–20* [Online: Chicago Transit Authority]. Available at: http://www.transitchicago.com/assets/1/ordinances/010–020WilsonYard.pdf [accessed: December 2, 2011].

City of Chicago. 2009. *Projected TIF Balances 2009–2011* [Online: City of Chicago]. Available at: http://www.cityofchicago.org/content/dam/city/depts/dcd/general/ProjectedTIFFundBalances2009_2011.pdf [accessed: December 10, 2011].

City of Chicago. 2000. *Wilson Yard Redevelopment Project Area: Tax Increment financing District Eligibility Project and Plan* [Online: City of Chicago]. Available at: http://www.cityofchicago.org/dam/city/depts/dcd/tif/plans/T_110_WilsonYardRDP.pdf [accessed: January 8, 2013].

City of Chicago. n.d. *Tax Increment Financing (TIF)* [Online: City of Chicago]. Available at: http://www.cityofchicago.org/city/en/depts/dcd/provdrs/tif.html [accessed: August 14, 2011].

Illinois Tax Increment Association (ITIA). 2007. *What Communities in Illinois Use TIF?* [Online: The Illinois Tax Increment Association]. Available at: http://www.illinois-tif.com/FAQ5.asp [accessed: August 6, 2011].

O'Neil, K. 2009. Wilson Station and #156 LaSalle Bus: Redeye's Crustiest and Most Rotten, *Chicago Now*, August 11, Available at: http://www.chicagonow.com/ctatattler/2009/08/wilson-station-and-156-lasalle-bus-redeyes-crustiest-and-mostrotten/ [accessed: August 14, 2011].

Central Streetcar Project, Portland, OR

City of Hillsboro. n.d. *Urban Renewal* [Online: Hillsboro, Oregon]. Available at: http://www.ci.hillsboro.or.us/economicdevelopment/DowntownByDesign/ FAQ.aspx#What_is_UR [accessed: July 17, 2011].

City of Portland, Ordinance 177124, Portland, OR

Hovee, E. and Jordan, T. 2008. *Streetcar-Development Linkage: The Portland Streetcar Loop.* Vancouver, WA: E.D. Hovee & Company LLC [Online: Reconnecting America]. Available at: http://www.reconnectingamerica.org/ assets/Hovee-Report-Eastside-2008.pdf [accessed: May 10, 2013].
Johnson, N. and Tashman, J. 2002. *Urban Renewal in Oregon: History, Case Studies, Policy Issues, and Latest Developments.* Portland, OR: Tashman and Johnson LLC.
Portland Development Commission (PDC). 2003. *Urban Renewal: Its Role in Shaping Portland's Future* [Online: Portland Development Commission]. Available at: http://www.pdc.us/pdf/about/%20oregon_urban_renewal_history. pdf [accessed: July 17, 2011].
Portland Development Commission (PDC). n.d.a. *Current Projects* [Online: Portland Development Commission]. Available at: http://www.pdc.us/ currentwork/default.asp [accessed: July 17, 2011].
Portland Development Commission (PDC). n.d.b. *North Macadam URA* [Online: Portland Development Commission].Available at: http://www.pdc.us/ura/ sowa_n-macadam.asp [accessed: July 17, 2011].
Portland Development Commission (PDC). n.d.c. *South Park Blocks URA* [Online: Portland Development Commission]. Available at: http://www.pdc. us/ura/south-park-blocks/south_park_blocks.asp [accessed: July 17, 2011].
Portland Development Commission (PDC). n.d.d. *River District URA* [Online: Portland Development Commission]. Available at: http://www.pdc.us/ura/ river.asp [accessed: July 17, 2011].
Portland Development Commission (PDC). n.d.e. *Adopted Fiscal Year Budgets (2000 to 2006)* [Online: Portland Development Commission]. Available at: http://www.pdc.us/budget/default.asp [accessed: July 17, 2011].
Portland Streetcar, Inc. (PSI) 2010. *Portland Streetcar Capital and Operations Funding* [Online: Portland Streetcar]. Available at: http://www.portland streetcar.org/pdf/%20capital_and_operations_detail_20100908.pdf [accessed: July 17, 2011].
Portland Streetcar, Inc (PSI). n.d. *Streetcar History* [Online: Portland Streetcar]. Available at: http://www.portlandstreetcar.org/node/33 [accessed: July 17, 2011].

Chapter 8
Transit Impact Fees

While impact fees are widely used to fund automobile-related transportation projects, there are few instances of transit impact fees. This paucity of cases made the case study selection process rather simple. Recent research documents five major instances of transit impact fees (or variants of them): Portland, OR (transportation system development charge); Broward County, FL (concurrency fee); Aventura, FL (transportation mitigation impact fee); San Francisco, CA (transportation impact development fee); and Seattle, WA (transportation-mitigation payment) (Smith, 2008; Nelson, Nicholas and Juergensmeyer, 2009). Seattle's program is voluntary, and thus it is farthest removed from a traditional impact fee. Furthermore, Aventura's impact fee program is very new, adopted in 2009, and impact fee has been charged only once. Hence, the remaining three examples are selected as transit-impact-fee case studies.

Transportation System Development Charge, Portland, OR

Overview

Portland's transportation system development charge (TSDC) is levied on new developments and on property-use changes (City of Portland Office of Transportation, n.d.a). The fee helps mitigate the transportation impacts of new developments or property use by augmenting the transportation-system capacity (City of Portland Office of the City Auditor, n.d.a), and is due at the time a building permit is issued (City of Portland Bureau of Transportation, n.d.a).

The TSDC is used to fund a variety of transportation projects, including transit projects. However, the TSDC may be used only for capital expenditures, not for ongoing operation and maintenance expenses (City of Portland Office of Transportation, n.d.a). The city is required to spend TSDC revenues within 10 years (City of Portland Office of the City Auditor, n.d.b).

TSDC Time Line

Several small cities in Oregon and other states began charging transportation impact fees in the 1990s. This trend led Portland to follow suit. While other cities charge the fees for roads, Portland is probably the first city in the country to charge a multimodal fee (Kathryn Levine, Projects Control Manager, Portland Bureau of Transportation, interview by Shishir Mathur, February, 18, 2011). The city built public support for the TSDC by including residents and business leaders in the early stages of fee development. Stakeholder interviews were conducted, and business leaders and interest-group representatives were appointed to the Policy Advisory Committee. The city also held community meetings to explain the TSDC, answer questions, and address residents' concerns (City of Portland Office of Transportation, n.d.b). The Policy Advisory Committee was committed to equity with regard to funding multiple transportation modes and to ensuring that all areas within the city would benefit from the charges (Kathryn Levine). The fee was implemented in 1997 (Samdahl, 2008).

Organizations Involved in Approving the Fee and its Revisions

The TSDC is one of four system-development charges (SDCs)—transportation, water and sewer, drainage, and parks and recreation—levied by the city. The Portland Bureau of Development Services assesses the fee at the time a building permit is granted. The rates charged for all SDCs must be approved by the City Council. Fee revenues are used by four city bureaus—Environmental Services, Parks and Recreation, Water, and Transportation—to fund projects under their purview.

Revenues collected from the TSDC are placed in an SDC account and are used only for qualified projects that are in the city's Capital Improvement Plan (CIP). The Portland Bureau of Transportation (PBOT) uses TSDC funds to finance transportation projects included in the CIP (City of Portland Bureau of Development Services, n.d.).

What are the Current Charges?

The current TSDC rate varies by development type and also by the number of dwelling units (or beds for nursing homes), the square feet of floor area, the number of rooms for hotels, and such other criteria. The rate list and the units of measure are shown in Table 8.1 (p. 155) (City of Portland Bureau of Transportation, n.d.b).

TSDC-funded Projects

Oregon's SDC legislation and Portland's laws require that SDCs be used only for projects that are included in a CIP and that "increase the capacity of the city's transportation system" (City of Portland Office of the City Auditor, n.d.c). The several purposes listed in the TSDC Code as eligible uses for TSDC funds include the project development, design and construction plan preparation; right-of-way acquisition, including any costs of acquisition or condemnation; construction of roads, turn lanes, bridges, drainage and storm water treatment facilities, bicycle facilities, pedestrian connections, walkways, curbs, medians, and shoulders. Other permissible projects include purchase and installation of traffic signs and signals, relocation of utilities to accommodate new roadway construction, surveying and

**Table 8.1   Selected Portland's citywide TSDC rates:
July 10, 2010–June 30, 2011**

Type of development	Unit of measure	TSDC per unit ($)
Residential (single-family; multi-family; rowhouse/townhouse/condo)		2,566; 1,836; 1,604
Commercial–services		
Bank; Library; Post Office	sq. ft./GFA	22.21; 8.24; 15.86
Day care	student	227
Hotel/motel	room	2,355
Movie theater	screen	28,635
Carwash	wash stall	13,442
Marina	Acre	671
Commercial–institutional		
School, K-12; University/college	Student	265; 530
Church	sq. ft./GFA	2.39
Hospital	sq. ft./GFA	4.61
Park	Acre	444
Commercial-restaurant (restaurant; drive-through)	sq. ft./GFA	17.81; 41.20
Commercial–retail		
Miscellaneous retail	sq. ft./GFA	4.33
Shopping center	sq. ft./GFA	5.45
Supermarket	sq. ft./GFA	12.99
Convenience market	sq. ft./GFA	46.33
Free-standing discount store	sq. ft./GFA	8.48
Car sales new/used	sq. ft./GFA	8.33
Commercial-office (Administrative office; Medical office/clinic)	sq. ft./GFA	3.30; 8.69
Industrial (light industrial, warehousing, self-storage)	sq. ft./GFA	0.79 to 2.08
Truck terminal	Acre	27,244

Source: Adapted from Portland Bureau of Transportation, http://www.portlandonline.com [accessed: 4.4.11].

soils and material testing, and landscaping. The permissible public transportation projects include bus pullouts, transit shelters, fixed-rail transit systems, and appurtenances (City of Portland Office of the City Auditor, n.d.c)

The prohibited uses include any expenditure that would be classified as a maintenance or repair expense; costs associated with the construction of administrative office facilities that are more than an incidental part of other capital improvements; and costs associated with acquisition or maintenance of rolling stock (City of Portland Office of the City Auditor, n.d.c).

Revenue Raised from the TSDC

Gross revenues of more than $66 million have been raised since the TSDC's inception in 1997. Annual revenues reached a maximum of a little over $9 million in 2006–2007 (just before the economic recession) before falling to $2.5 million in 2009–2010. See Table 8.2 (p. 157) for the annual revenue yield.

Between 1999 and 2007, a total of 37 transportation projects were partially funded by the TSDC (City of Portland Bureau of Transportation, n.d.c). About 25 percent of the cost of the projects on the current CIP list is expected to be funded by the TSDC (City of Portland Bureau of Transportation, n.d.d), along with 100 percent of cost attributed to new growth (City of Portland Bureau of Transportation, n.d.e). TSDC funds have also been used to leverage federal, state, and other funding (City of Portland Office of Transportation, n.d.a).

The TSDC is not the main funding source for Portland's public-transportation capital expenditures. Rather, it is used to fill the gaps that remain after securing funds from the federal and state governments and from the assessment districts. For example, the TSDC funded only about 4 percent of the Eastside Portland Streetcar Loop Project (funding sources for the projects are listed in Table 8.3, p. 157). Similarly, the TSDC funded a little more than 3.5 percent, or $2 million, of the $55 million Central City Streetcar Project. The proportion of funding for the city's light-rail projects has also been small, with a little more than 3.5 percent, or $55 million, earmarked for the $1.49 billion projects (Kathryn Levine).

Who Pays the Fee?

Application of the TSDC is simple. The fee is charged on all new developments and property-use changes within the city, with a few exceptions, including affordable residential housing developments, which are exempted to facilitate the availability of affordable housing. However, the housing developments must meet the following criteria to qualify for exemption (City of Portland Office of the City Auditor, n.d.d):

> For affordable rental projects, the developments must serve households earning at or below 60 percent of the MFI adjusted for household size with a maximum debt burden of 30 percent for a 60-year period. Moreover, if a proposed rental housing development has units that do not meet the above requirements or include a commercial component, the actual exemptions will be prorated as applicable to the residential portion of the development subject to the affordable-housing restrictions.

> For affordable homeownership projects, the developments must serve households at or below 100 percent of the MFI for a family of four—$71,200 in 2011 and adjusted annually. This limit is adjusted upward for households of more than four people. Furthermore, the units must sell for less than the price cap—$275,000 as

Table 8.2   Annual gross TSDC revenues, 1997–2010

Fiscal Year	Annual gross TSDC revenues ($)
Original 10-year rate study and project list	
1997–1999	5,263,262
1999–2000	3,870,427
2000–2001	4,892,759
2001–2002	4,395,590
2002–2003	5,197,901
2003–2004	5,284,517
2004–2005	5,052,866
2005–2006	6,209,059
2006–2007	9,582,352
2007–2008	5,661,570
Renewed 10-year rate study and project list	
2007–2008	2,542,883
2008–2009	5,690,991
2009–2010	2,537,101
Total Gross revenue 1997–2010	66,181,278

Source: Katherine Levine, Project Controls Manager, email communication, February 18, 2011.

Table 8.3   Funding sources for Eastside Portland Streetcar Loop extension

Funding source	Amount of funding ($ millions)
Federal Transit Administration	75.00
Local improvement district	15.50
Portland Development Commission	27.68
Regional funds	3.62
SDC/other city funds	6.11
Stimulus funds	0.36
Total federal project	128.27
Vehicles from state of Oregon	20.00
Total project cost	148.27

Source: The Portland Streetcar Loop: Facts at a Glance, http://www.portlandstreetcar.org [accessed: 8.4.11].

of 2011, and the units must be sold to homebuyers who will occupy the homes as the initial occupants. Finally, properties receiving homeownership exemptions may not be rented.

Other exemptions include the following: temporary uses, which are fully exempt as long as the use or structure proposed in the new development is not used more than 180 days in a single calendar year; and new development that will not generate more than 15 percent more vehicle trips than the previous use. An exemption for transit-oriented development was phased out at the end of 2010 and is no longer on the list of exempted land uses (City of Portland Office of the City Auditor, n.d.d).

How is the Fee Calculated?

Three transportation modes are considered in TSDC calculations: motorized, transit, and non-motorized (Samdahl, 2008). The TSDC rate for each transportation mode is based on (1) the cost per trip—the amount of money the city needs to expend over the next 10 years to build transportation-system capacity to accommodate the new-growth-related trips—and (2) the number of trips generated by the new development—the projected amount of growth in households and employment over the next 10 years (City of Portland Bureau of Transportation, n.d.d).

To determine the fee for each project, the TSDC rate is multiplied by the number of trips a proposed land use generates, based on nationally compiled statistics from the Institute of Transportation Engineers' Trip Generation 7th Edition (City of Portland Bureau of Transportation, n.d.d). The trip-generation rates for the existing and proposed uses are added together. The TSDC is not charged if the use generated by the proposed new development is within 15 percent (above or below) of the previous use of the property. However, if the TSDC for the new development is more than 115 percent of the previous property use, the applicant must pay the difference between the new TSDC and the previous TSDC. The applicant is eligible for reimbursement if the difference is less than 85 percent (City of Portland Office of the City Auditor, n.d.e). In such a case, the applicant must formally request the refund within 180 days of issuance of the building permit. The refund is granted promptly once the request is approved (City of Portland Bureau of Transportation, n.d.a).

Credits can be given for projects whose developer has contributed to a project that meets certain criteria for improving the transportation system (City of Portland Office of the City Auditor, n.d.f). Additionally, an alternative methodology can be proposed if an applicant disagrees with the trip-generation rates proposed by the city. If the city accepts the new methodology, the revised trip-generation rates are applied to the project (City of Portland Office of the City Auditor, n.d.g).

Every two years, the Bureau of Transportation reviews the amount of TSDC money collected and used. On the basis of this review, the city determines whether sufficient funds are available to finance the projects that would increase transportation capacity, and the rates are adjusted if needed. The new rates must be adopted by the City Council (City of Portland Office of the City Auditor, n.d.h).

Refinements Made to the TSDC

The city has refined the TSDC a few times. For example, small neighborhood restaurants are a "hot button" issue in Portland. Because the fee tended to place a significant burden on small restaurants, all restaurants with areas of less than 3,000 square feet were treated as retail, effectively reducing the fee rate from $17.81 per square foot of gross leasable area (GLA) to $4.33. Affordable-housing exemptions were also refined, placing closer scrutiny on the buyer and builder qualifications (Kathryn Levine).

The addition of the North Macadam Transportation System Development Charge Overlay Program was another significant change. Effective in 2009 (City of Portland Bureau of Transportation, 2009), the Overlay Program allowed an additional fee to be charged in the North Macadam urban renewal area (URA).

A former central city industrial area, the North Macadam URA is in need of substantial investment (Kathryn Levine). The Overlay Program was created to address concerns that the city would use a disproportionately large amount of the TSDC revenues there, essentially requiring the entire city to pay for investments in one specific neighborhood. An additional fee was placed on the North Macadam URA to address this potential horizontal inequity. Funds from the overlay fee can be used only within the URA. Thus, the program secures needed investments without draining funds from the other parts of the city.

Case Analysis

Enabling legal environment
Oregon's impact-fee-enabling legislation is one of the key contributors to the success of the TSDC. The legislation clearly allows the TSDC to be used for public transportation, putting Portland on solid legal ground to charge the fee. Specifically, the Oregon legislation for SDCs has a clear purpose statement of intent to facilitate growth. It reads, "The purpose of ORS 223.297 to 223.314 [the code on system development charges] is to provide a uniform framework for the imposition of system development charges by local governments, to provide equitable funding for orderly growth and development in Oregon's communities and to establish that the charges may be used only for capital improvements"(State of Oregon, 2009). The legislation goes on to define capital improvements, including public transportation, as uses eligible for SDC funds (State of Oregon, 2009).

Stakeholder support
Community participation also played a key role in the success of the TSDC. The city consulted the community, business leaders, and interest groups while developing it, and this broad-based community participation incorporated and balanced the

interests of a large variety of stakeholder groups and improved geographical and modal equity making funding for each mode equitable (Kathryn Levine).

Institutional capacity
On a day-to-day basis, the fee does not require additional administrative and technical capacity. However, significant resources were required when the fee was first implemented and again in 2007, when it was revised (Kathryn Levine).

Horizontal and vertical equity
The TSDC design is sensitive to equity issues. Addressing vertical equity (ATP concerns), the fee allows exemptions for affordable housing. It not only accommodates low-income residents but makes exemptions for middle-income households as well. For example, a homeownership project qualifies for an exemption if it serves those at or below the MFI, which was $71,200 for a family of four in 2011 (City of Portland Office of the City Auditor, n.d.d).

The fee seems to be horizontally equitable as well. It is charged throughout the city rather than only in specific sections. Moreover, almost all property types pay it. The fee amount is reasonable—impact fees in other states, such as California, are considerably higher. Finally, the fee treats developers fairly. It allows for credits when the developers contribute to transportation-related projects.

The TSDC could be made more equitable for residential properties if it were charged on a per-bedroom basis rather than on a per-unit basis. Currently, all residential units are charged at the same rate regardless of size or the number of residents. The fee structure unfairly impacts smaller homes with few residents by charging them the same rate as larger homes that may have many residents.

Revenue yield, stability, and growth
As discussed earlier, the revenue from the fee declined significantly in recent years because of the economic recession's negative impact on real estate development. The decline shows that the yield and growth of TSDC revenues are dependent upon real estate market conditions. Furthermore, used primarily as a gap financing tool, the fee funds only a small portion of total project costs, although it covers all of the costs associated with new growth.

Transit Concurrency Fee, Broward County, FL

Overview

Florida state law requires the provision of a basic level of service and facilities "concurrent" with growth (Broward County, n.d.a). Amendments to the law in 2011 made transportation concurrency optional; before that, transportation was one of the services that had to be concurrently provided in order for municipalities or counties to approve new development (Broward County, n.d.a; Florida Department of Economic Opportunity, n.d.).

Broward County charges a transit concurrency fee to mitigate the impact of new developments on its transit system. Most of the county roads are built out, and very little unused land is available for new construction. Therefore, the fee is transit-focused. It was adopted by the County Commission in 2005 as a way for new developments to pay their "fair share" (Broward County, n.d.b). Fee revenues are used to pay for capital expenses and for three years of operating costs of transit projects within a new development's local district (Broward County, n.d.b). The county is divided into 10 districts, which fall into two categories—standard concurrency districts and transit-oriented concurrency districts (State of Florida Department of Community Affairs, 2006)

Standard concurrency districts include areas that lack significant transit infrastructure. Roads are the dominant form of transportation in these districts, and roadway improvements are the main form of concurrency-revenue-funded improvements. Two of the 10 districts are in this category.

Transit-oriented concurrency districts include parts of the county characterized as "compact geographic area(s) with an existing network of roads where multiple, viable alternative travel paths or modes are available for common trips" (State of Florida Department of Community Affairs, 2006). Eight of the 10 districts are classified as transit-oriented.

For transit-oriented concurrency districts, revenues from the fee are used to ensure that the desired transit level of service is maintained. The county enhances the level of service by reducing transit headways, developing neighborhood transit centers, and adding new bus routes (State of Florida Department of Community Affairs, 2006).

Organizations Involved in Levying the Fee

The Development Management Division of Broward County assesses the concurrency fee at the beginning of the development process. Broward County Transit (BCT) spends most of the fee revenue. The fee is levied before the jurisdictions within the county can begin processing building-permit applications. An applicant must receive a Transportation Concurrency Satisfaction Certificate from the Broward County Development Management Division to move forward with the permitting process (Broward County, n.d.c; State of Florida Department of Community Affairs, 2006).

Who Pays the Fee?

Any development within the eight transit-oriented concurrency districts that is new, changes use, or changes floor area is required to pay the fee (Broward County, n.d.c). Since the fee is due at the beginning of the development process, the property developer has the legal obligation to pay it. The eight districts cover all parts of the county except the two standard districts.

No land uses within the transit-oriented districts are exempt from paying the fee (State of Florida Department of Community Affairs, 2006). Current fee amount varies, based on land use and development size. Residential uses are charged on per-dwelling-unit basis. The fee varies from $129 to $482 per unit. Other uses, including commercial uses, are charged on per-square-foot basis. The fees range from $521 to $1,636 per 1,000 square feet.

How is the Fee Determined?

The fee is calculated as "total peak-hour trip generation of the proposed development, multiplied by a constant (for each year) dollar figure for each district that represents the cost per trip of all the enhancements in that district listed in the County Transit Program" (State of Florida Department of Community Affairs, 2006). These enhancements include the construction of bus bays, the purchase of buses, and pedestrian improvements near the transit stations. The funds are spent within the district on projects included in the County Transit Program (State of Florida Department of Community Affairs, 2006).

How Has the Fee Changed Over Time?

Fee collection began in April 2005. More than $28 million was collected between April 2005 and January 2011 (Martin Berger, Planning Section Manager, Broward County, FL, Environmental Protection and Growth Management Department, email communication, March 1, 2011). As shown in Figure 8.1 (p. 163), the fee revenue has decreased dramatically since its peak in fiscal year (FY) 2007 (note that FY 2005 includes only six months). This revenue decline resulted from the decrease in new projects due to the housing and economic crisis.

Between 2005 and 2010, a substantial portion of the concurrency fee was spent on operating expenses in newly growing areas with low transit ridership. This focus on newly developing areas strained the county financially, as fare-box revenues were very low in these areas. Going forward, the county will expend transit-concurrency-fee revenues primarily on the existing transit system by funding capital facilities, such as buses, bus stops, and transit-station improvements (Martin Berger).

Use of the Fee to Fund Transit Projects

The majority of the concurrency fee is spent in two areas: capital improvements and operations (Broward County, n.d.b). For FY 2011, BCT expected that $4.9 million would be transferred from the concurrency fund to the capital budget. This represents about 17 percent of BCT's FY 2011 capital budget. The agency expects to use only $604,000 of the concurrency-fee revenue for its operating

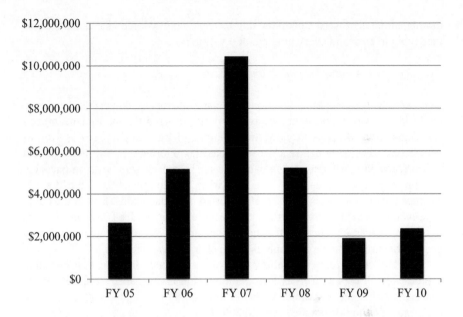

Figure 8.1   Broward County, FL, Transit Concurrency Fee revenue from April 2005 to January 2011

Source: Broward County, FL.

budget; the concurrency-fund contribution is approximately 0.5 percent of that budget (Broward County Transit, n.d.).

Between 2006 and 2010, the fee helped fund numerous capital projects and BCT operations throughout the county, including the following: upgrade of 125 bus stops, purchase of 10 small buses, three neighborhood transit centers, pedestrian improvements near transit stations, 40 bus bays, operating costs to reduce headways along numerous routes, expansion of several routes, and administrative and management expenses (Broward County, n.d.b).

Legal Basis for Charging the Fee

In 1985, Florida passed statewide growth management legislation called the Local Government Comprehensive Planning and Land Development Regulation Act. This legislation laid the foundation for Broward County's transit concurrency fee. The Act mandated infrastructure concurrency, requiring services to be provided concurrently with development (Chapin and Connerly, 2004).

In 1974, Broward County residents granted land use authority to the county. Under its charter, the Broward County Council is the authority responsible for local land use planning and traffic-way plans (Broward County Planning Services Division, n.d.). Unlike many counties, where land use decisions rest with individual municipalities, Broward County is able to make county-wide land use decisions that apply to each and every municipality within it.

Concurrency Fees as a Variant of Impact Fees

Concurrency fees essentially function in the same manner as impact fees. However, in Florida, the legislation authorizing concurrency fees is different from the impact-fees legislation. Broward County, for example, charges impact fees as well as concurrency fees. Its concurrency fees are based on Florida's growth-management concurrency law, whereas the impact fees are based on state-level impact-fee-enabling legislation. Because of their similarity, "transit impact fees" and "transit-oriented concurrency fees" are sometimes used interchangeably. Broward County has several impact fees but does not charge a transit impact fee (Broward County, n.d.d). Moreover, jurisdictions that fall in the concurrency exception areas cannot charge concurrency fees, although they can charge impact fees.

Florida's concurrency law allows use of concurrency fees for transportation capital expenditures as well as for operations and maintenance expenses. Many states allow such fees for capital expenses only, but Florida, along with California, is an exception to this practice (Smith, 2008).

Case Analysis

Enabling legal environment
Florida's growth management act provides the legal framework for Broward County's transit concurrency fee. Furthermore, the county government has land use authority over the entire county area. This authority enables the county to implement the fee without going through the arduous process of seeking each municipality's formal approval.

Stakeholder support
Stakeholder support was not a concern for Broward County. In fact, developers have welcomed the fee, which is transparent and known ahead of time (Martin Berger).

Institutional capacity
Until the 2011 amendments, Florida's concurrency requirements essentially forced the imposition of transportation concurrency fees. The institutional capacity to charge the fees was thus in place—the county was already charging a variety of concurrency fees.

Horizontal and vertical equity
The concurrency fee enhances vertical equity to the extent that transit users have lower income than automobile users (Ferrell and Mathur, 2012).

The fee also promotes horizontal equity. The revenue from it must be spent within a localized area, so those who pay the fee benefit from it. The county did not impose it on the two districts where transit was deemed unsuitable. However, the fee assessment methodology could be made more equitable. While other uses are assessed a fee based on their square footage, number of acres, or beds, all residential uses are assessed the concurrency fee on a per-unit basis. Although those uses are broken down into different types that have some correspondence with their size and households' ability to pay the fee,[1] e.g., apartments or mobile homes, a more equitable assessment methodology would base the fee on square footage or number of bedrooms.

Revenue yield, stability, and growth
The economic recession and real estate downturn caused the transit concurrency fee to run into trouble shortly after its 2005 inception. Broward County faced a $40 million to $110 million budget shortfall (Broward Metropolitan Planning Organization, n.d.). As revenue from the fee and the fare-box fell, the county had to find other revenue sources to keep the transit system running. It is now using a more strategic approach wherein the fee dollars are used in the areas that have higher ridership and that can generate more fare-box revenue (Martin Berger).

Transit Impact Development Fee, San Francisco, CA

Overview

A transit impact development fee (TIDF) is levied by the city and county of San Francisco to help mitigate the impacts of new non-residential developments on the city's public transportation system (Price Waterhouse, 1998). The TIDF was initially established in 1981 in response to a significant rise in downtown office development in the 1970s. This office growth was expected to increase the demand for transportation, necessitating greater emphasis on alternatives to automobile travel. It was estimated that this shift in travel behavior would put substantial new demand on the public transportation system (City of San Francisco, n.d.; Price Waterhouse, 1998), and the TIDF would help finance the increase in capacity required to meet this demand. While the initial TIDF accommodated some growth, it was strictly limited to financing peak-hour growth in transit demand on the transit lines passing through the downtown district.

While San Francisco usually pays for its transit from the city's general fund, providing transit to accommodate the new buildings would have exhausted the funds and strained taxpayers. The city therefore looked to alternative mechanisms to fund transit (Price Waterhouse, 1998). The TIDF was retroactively applied to

---

1   The fees are paid by the developers, often at the time of building-permit issuance. However, several empirical studies have found that developers are able to pass the fee on to the households that purchase the home from them. Therefore, these households bear the actual burden of the fees.

include office developments built after 1979. It was expanded after a 2001 study concluded that developments outside of the original downtown district required the municipal railway, called Muni, to maintain and expand service; purchase, maintain, and repair rolling stock; install new lines; and service existing lines (City of San Francisco, n.d.).

All impact fees in San Francisco are collected by the Department of Building Inspection before building permits are issued (City of San Francisco, n.d.). The San Francisco Municipal Transportation Agency (SFMTA) manages and spends the TIDF revenue (SFMTA, n.d.a).

With more than 5,000 employees, the SFMTA is the seventh largest transit system in the United States. It is responsible for overseeing all forms of surface transportation, as well as parking and taxi regulation, in San Francisco. Formed in 1912, Muni is run under the authority of the SFMTA. It serves the city and county of San Francisco, with 63 bus routes, seven light-rail lines, the historic streetcar F Line, and three cable car lines (SFMTA, n.d.b).

What is the Fee Used For?

The TIDF is intended to meet "a portion of the demand for additional Muni service and capital improvements for the city caused by new non-residential development" (City of San Francisco, n.d.). Toward that aim, the fee can be used for capital and operating expenses as the SFMTA deems fit to maintain the base level of service. The official ordinance lists the following permitted uses (the list is not exhaustive, and other uses, such as payment of salaries, may also be permitted: (City of San Francisco, n.d) "Capital costs associated with establishing new transit routes, expanding transit routes, and increasing service on existing transit routes, including, but not limited to procurement of related items such as rolling stock; design and construction of bus shelters, stations, tracks, and overhead wires; operation and maintenance of rolling stock associated with new or expanded transit routes or increases in service on existing routes; and capital or operating costs required to add revenue service hours to existing routes, and related overhead costs."

Who Pays the Fee?

The TIDF is assessed on all new non-residential land uses within San Francisco with areas of more than 3,000 square feet. It is computed and charged prior to the issuance of the building or site permit for any new development and is paid before the permits are issued or, with the inclusion of a surcharge, at the time a certificate of occupancy is issued (City of San Francisco, n.d.).

Effective through June 2013, a fee deferral program was set up in 2010 in response to the economic recession to help development continue through hard times. The deferral allows developers to defer 80 percent of the fee until just prior to the issuance of a certificate of occupancy, an estimated delay of 10 to 30 months (City of San Francisco, n.d.).

Payment of the TIDF is not required for property owned by the city, the state, or the federal government or their agencies, or for any development in parts of the city where the TIDF is inconsistent with the redevelopment plan, including Mission Bay North or South (City of San Francisco, n.d.). In addition, the following non-residential uses do not have to pay the TIDF (City of San Francisco, n.d.): public facilities/utilities; open recreation/horticulture, including private non-commercial recreation use; vehicle storage and access; automotive services; and wholesale storage of materials and equipment.

What is the Current Fee?

The assessed fee, depending on the type of land use, was $8 to $10 per gross square foot in 2010 (City of San Francisco, n.d.). The land uses and corresponding fees are listed in Table 8.4 (p. 168).

How is the Fee Calculated?

Before the adoption of the TIDF in 1981, the city's Public Utilities Commission conducted a study to demonstrate the cost of providing transit for a new office development. The study found that the cost was $9.18 per square foot of new office space. In 1983, a private accounting firm conducted a cost analysis to defend the ordinance from a legal challenge and found that the cost of providing the service was $8.36 per square foot. A study conducted in 2001 by the city-hired private transportation-planning firm Nelson/Nygaard (with substantial input from the city agencies) to determine whether the fee overage should be expanded from the downtown area to the entire city concluded that new and future non-residential uses would have enough impact on the transit system to warrant citywide application of the TIDF (City of San Francisco, n.d.).

While the original TIDF was assessed only for office space, the new TIDF was expanded to include all non-residential land uses (with the exception of those mentioned earlier). The TIDF is based on the number of square feet of a new development. "Whenever any new development or series of new developments cumulatively creates more than 3,000 gross square feet of covered use within a structure, the TIDF shall be imposed on every square foot of such covered use (including any portion that was part of prior new development below the 3,000-square-foot threshold)" (City of San Francisco, n.d.).

After extensive research and discussion, it was agreed that the $8-per-square-foot fee would adequately cover land uses generating 6.60 trips per 1,000 square feet, and the $10-per-square-foot fee would cover land uses generating 8.25 trips per 1,000 square feet. Figure 8.2 (p. 168) outlines the methodology used to arrive at the $10 fee. The principal steps in this process are the following: First, the total daily unlinked auto and transit trips are calculated from a travel demand model. Next, the total daily hours of transit service and the daily cost of providing transit are identified. Thereafter, the total daily trips divided by the total cost of the trip

Table 8.4   TIDF charge based on land use as of 2010

Economic activity category	TIDF per gross square foot of development ($)
Cultural/institution/education	10
Management, information, and professional services	10
Medical and health services	10
Production/distribution/repair	8
Retail/entertainment	10
Visitor services	8

Source: City of San Francisco, Ordinance 108–10: Development Impact and In-Lieu Fees (May 3, 2010): 59.

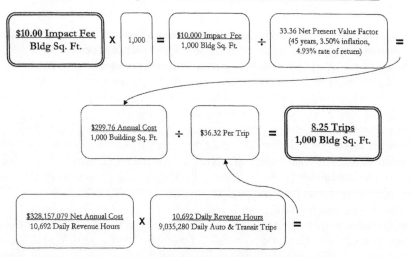

Figure 8.2   Illustrative calculation of the Transit Impact Fee
Note: Formula calculates the trip rate associated with a given fee amount.
Source: San Francisco Municipal Transportation Agency.

provide the annual cost per trip ($36.32 per trip). Then, the $10-per-square-foot fee is estimated to correspond to a 45-year annuity of $299.76 (using 3.5-percent inflation and a 4.93-percent rate of return). The 45-year term corresponds to the useful life of the non-residential development that pays the fee. Next, the $299.76 annuity divided by the annual cost per trip ($36.32) yields 8.25 daily trips. Finally, the trips generated by various land uses are estimated. Uses expected to generate at least 8.25 trips are assessed a fee of $10 per square foot.

The fee is adjusted annually by the two-year-average change in the consumer price index (CPI) for the San Francisco/San José Primary Metropolitan Statistical Area (PMSA). Additionally, every five years, the Director of Transportation at the SFMTA, in coordination with the Director of Planning, is required to prepare a report detailing whether the TIDF should be adjusted for each economic activity. The Director of Transportation must also update other information pertinent to calculating the fee, such as the base service standard, cost per revenue service hour, and placement of particular land uses in economic-activity categories. The report is subject to public hearings (City of San Francisco, n.d.).

The amount collected by the TIDF cannot exceed the capital and operating costs required to maintain the base level of service over the 45-year useful life of the development. The funds are placed in a trust overseen by the Treasurer and are used for a variety of capital and operating expenses (City of San Francisco, n.d.).

How Has the Fee Changed Over Time?

The TIDF has gone through significant changes in its 30-year history. It has expanded to include the participation of more agencies and has become more comprehensive in size and scope (SFCTA, 2009). The original fee, which was implemented in May 1981, was $5 per square foot of office space, was charged only for a small downtown district, and was assessed only for office buildings (Brisson, 2008).

Twenty years after the TIDF was established, a study conducted to explore the possibility of expanding its size and scope found that new developments throughout the city had significant impacts on the transit system and should therefore be incorporated. In 2004, the citywide TIDF was approved by the San Francisco Board of Supervisors and went into effect for new non-residential uses (with some exclusions) (Brisson, 2008).

In 2009, four agencies—the San Francisco County Transportation Authority, the San Francisco Planning Department, the Office of Economic and Workforce Development, and the San Francisco County Transportation Authority—entered into a memorandum of understanding (MOU) to expand the scope of the fee. A new nexus study was commissioned to expand the TIDF into the Comprehensive Transportation Impact Development Fee (CTIDF). The nexus study comprises three parts, as defined in a memorandum from the San Francisco County Transportation Authority: "Part One of the Study would develop a legal basis for continued collection of the existing TIDF and would be managed and funded solely by the MTA [Metropolitan Transportation Authority]. Part Two of the Study would develop a legal basis for the potential future adoption of a new CTIDF that would expand upon the existing TIDF to address the effects of new development on the entire City transportation system. This part of the Study would be jointly reviewed by all four parties to this agreement but funded entirely by the MTA. Part Three of the Study would develop a legal basis for the potential adoption of a new auto trip mitigation fee that would mitigate significant transportation-related environmental effects identified pursuant to the California Environmental Quality

Act. This part of the study would be jointly reviewed by all four parties to the agreement and funded by all four agencies pursuant to the cost sharing provisions described in the MOU" (SFCTA, 2009).

Case Analysis

Enabling legal environment

California's impact-fee-enabling legislation, called the California Mitigation Fee Act, was passed in 1989, several years after San Francisco's TIDF was implemented (Mullen, 2011). The legislation was passed with the intention of codifying existing "constitutional and decisional law" regarding impact fees and exactions, meaning that it codified previous court decisions that had already shaped California law (City and County of San Francisco, 2008). The legislation is broad in its language, allowing for impact fees to be used on projects that are reasonably related to increased demand for facilities. It also specifically allows the use of impact fees for transit- and transportation-related improvements, consistent with the San Francisco TIDF (Mullen, 2011).

The TIDF was originally enabled by a local ordinance passed by the San Francisco County Board of Supervisors. The ordinance is now covered in Article 4 of the San Francisco Planning Code (SFMTA, n.d.a). It passed without the benefit of the state-level enabling legislation and was therefore vulnerable to legal challenges. The challenge described below came shortly after it was passed. The ordinance was successfully defended, and the courts upheld the fee.

The legal basis for charging the TIDF hinges on the fee's classification as an impact fee rather than a tax. To be classified as a fee, the TIDF must pass the rational nexus test, meaning there must be a rational nexus, or link, between the fee and the service provided. In 1981, a class action lawsuit entitled Russ Building Partnership v. City and County of San Francisco was filed against the city for imposing the fee. The Court of Appeals and the Supreme Court of California upheld the TIDF, noting that it is not a tax but a legitimate development fee, and that there is in fact a rational nexus for it (Russ Building Partnership v. City and County of San Francisco, 1987).

The plaintiff argued that the $5-per-square-foot fee was unreasonable and exceeded the cost of increased transit service, hence was a "special tax," subject to two-thirds vote, and that it violated California's Constitution articles XIII A or XIII B which place restrictions upon the imposition of such taxes. The plaintiff further argued that the fee unfairly burdened office buildings built after 1979, while exempting retail stores, claiming that differential treatment of new office buildings was a violation of the equal-protection clause. It was additionally alleged that the methods used and the assumptions made to arrive at the fee amount were unsound. Another plaintiff in the case argued that the retroactive application of the fee was illegal and alleged that the fee violated the city charter (Russ Building Partnership v. City and County of San Francisco, 1987).

The courts, however, disagreed with all of these opinions and found the fee legal. They sided with the city on all counts and stated in their findings, "In summary, we hold that the transit fee was a lawful development fee which is not governed by California Constitution articles XIII A or XIII B, and it does not interfere with plaintiffs' due process and equal protection rights. The fee is not a double tax and does not violate section 3.598 of the city's charter. Any error in calculating the fee was harmless, and the judgment in favor of the city and against Russ Building plaintiff is affirmed" (Russ Building Partnership v. City and County of San Francisco, 1987). The argument about the exemption of retail stores was rejected on the ground that retail uses do not exert added strain on the transit system during peak traffic hours, while the offices do. Therefore, office developments require Muni to provide additional service (Russ Building Partnership v. City and County of San Francisco, 1987).

Stakeholder support
Apart from the earlier challenges to the legality of the fee and continued rumblings from the developer community, stakeholder support for the TIDF is strong within the city's political leadership and staff. This support is evidenced by the fee expansion in 2004 and by recent discussions regarding its further expansion. San Francisco adopted the fee deferral program in 2010 to ease the fee's impact on the developers.

Institutional capacity
The TIDF requires significant administrative and technical capacity—it has placed added administrative burden on the SFMTA and added costs for consultants and attorneys. Consulting firms were hired to conduct nexus studies, and the SFMTA presumably hired attorneys to defend the TIDF during the 1981 lawsuit.

Horizontal and vertical equity
The fee is fairly equitable for all parties involved. The transportation system in San Francisco is such that large new developments' transportation needs can be met only with public transit. Many of San Francisco's transit lines run at capacity during the peak commuting hours, requiring expanded service during those times.

The fee is also horizontally equitable. It is applied to all non-residential developments of over 3,000 square feet. Furthermore, there is some variation in the fee, depending on the amount of transit service needed by the type of land use. Smaller developments, which place fewer burdens on the transit system and are also less likely to afford the fee, are excluded.

Revenue yield, stability, and growth
Despite the relative strength of the San Francisco real estate market (Cummins, 2011), the recent downturn impacted fee revenues, which declined from a traditional annual average of between $4 million and $5 million to $2 million (Jay Reyes,

Table 8.5   TIDF revenues in 2004–2009

	Fiscal year					
	FY 04	**FY 05**	**FY 06**	**FY 07**	**FY 08**	**FY 09**
Revenue from TIDF ($ millions)	9.88	12.80	10.19 (approved)	10.16 (proposed)	8.4	10.34

Source: SFMTA, Adopted Budgets FY 2004–2010. http://www.sfmta.com [accessed: 12.18.2011].

TIDF Administrator, SFMTA, San Francisco, CA, interview by Shishir Mathur, December 15, 2011). On a positive note, the TIDF has built-in stability measures. The fee is CPI-adjusted, which keeps it abreast with inflation. Finally, the fee may be reviewed and revised every five years.

The TIDF represents a small but significant component of the SFMTA revenues (see Table 8.5, above). For example, for FY 2007, the SFMTA budgeted $10.16 million of its revenue to come from the TIDF. This was 1.5 percent of the entire $678.68 million budget (SFMTA, 2006). While a small percentage of the entire budget, the TIDF provides a much-needed stream of revenue. The percentage is likely to be higher if the transit costs associated with only new growth are considered.

Concluding Remarks

Although impact fees nation-wide are primarily used to fund capital expenses, three of the four case study jurisdictions use the fee to fund capital expenses in addition to operating, maintenance, and administrative expenses. In fact, local level enabling statutes explicitly allow the use of the fee revenues for such purposes. Furthermore, clear language concerning the uses eligible for impact fee funding should provide robust legal protection if the fee is challenged in court. Because operations, maintenance, and administrative expenses are a significant fiscal burden for transit providers, the permissive use of fee revenues towards these expenses greatly increases the usefulness of the transit impact fee.

Horizontal inequities can occur through exemptions for certain types of properties, crude fee rates, and geographically imbalanced spending. The San Francisco TIDF was challenged in court because the fee was only charged to office uses, leaving most properties exempt. Likewise, exemptions have created some degree of inequity in Broward County. Crude fee rates, such as charging a fee for residential uses on a per-unit rather than per-square-foot or per-bedroom basis have negatively impacted equity in Broward County and Portland. Finally, spatial inequity may result when only certain areas receive benefits from the fee. Portland mitigated this spatial inequity with the use of the overlay programs, which charge higher rates for the districts that receive disproportionately large transportation investments. Broward County addresses this problem by delineating districts in which fees must be locally spent.

Finally, the "nexus" and "rough proportionality" requirements ensure that the fee creates minimal horizontal inequities. However, no such legal requirements exist regarding the fee's vertical equity impacts. This lack of legal requirement is reflected in the uneven use of vertical inequity mitigation strategies adopted by the case study jurisdictions. Indeed, equity concerns motivate a large body of empirical literature to estimate the effect of impact fees on housing prices. This body of literature (see, e.g., Evans-Cowley, et al., 2009; Ihlanfeldt and Shaughnessy, 2004; Mathur, 2013; Mathur, 2007; Mathur, Waddell, and Blanco, 2004) generally finds that impact fees increase home prices and potentially reduce housing affordability. Therefore, jurisdictions planning on levying impact fees might consider the adoption of strategies that reduce the fees' negative impacts on low-income residents. For example, Portland and Broward County exempt affordable housing developments, while San Francisco exempts properties under 3,000 square feet (this only reduces vertical inequity to the extent that these property owners have low ATP). To the extent that people with low ATP are less likely to challenge impact fees on grounds of vertical inequities, local jurisdictions should be mindful of the fees' vertical equity impacts during the design and implementation of an impact fee program.

References

Case Study Selection Criteria

Nelson, A., Nicholas, J.C. and Julian C. Juergensmeyer. 2009. *Impact Fees: Principles and Practice of Proportionate-Share Development Fees*. Chicago, IL: American Planning Association.
Smith, G.C. 2008. *Use of Fees or Alternatives to Fund Transit*. Legal Research Digest 28, Transit Cooperative Research Program, Washington, DC: Transportation Research Board [Online: Transportation Research Board]. Available at: http://onlinepubs.trb.org/onlinepubs/tcrp/tcrp_lrd_28.pdf [accessed: October 30, 2011].

Transportation System Development Charge, Portland, OR

City of Portland Bureau of Development Services. n.d. *System Development Charges* [Online: City of Portland, Oregon]. Available at: http://www.portlandonline.com/bds/index.cfm?c=34186 [accessed: March 11, 2011].

City of Portland Bureau of Transportation. 2009. *Annual Report 2008–09* [Online: City of Portland, Oregon]. Available at: http://www.portlandoregon.gov/transportation/article/271668 [accessed: January 9, 2013].

City of Portland Bureau of Transportation. n.d.a. *Administrative Procedures for System Development Charges* [Online: City of Portland, Oregon]. Available at: www.portlandonline.com/auditor/index.cfm?&a=180518&c=31884 [accessed: March 6, 2012].

City of Portland Bureau of Transportation. n.d.b. *TSDC City Wide Rates: July 1, 2010–June 30, 2011* [Online: City of Portland, Oregon]. Available at: http://www.portlandonline.com/transportation/index.cfm?c=46210&a=295763 [accessed: March 11, 2011].

City of Portland Bureau of Transportation. n.d.c. *Transportation System Development Charges 1999–2007 Project List* [Online: City of Portland, Oregon]. Available at: http://www.portlandonline.com/transportation/index.cfm?c=46210&a=179039 [accessed: March 11, 2011].

City of Portland Bureau of Transportation. n.d.d. *Transportation System Development Charges Frequently Asked Questions* [Online: City of Portland, Oregon]. Available at: http://www.portlandonline.com/transportation/index.cfm?c=46210&a=295488 [accessed: March 11, 2011].

City of Portland Bureau of Transportation. n.d.e. *FAQs—Frequently Asked Questions* [Online: City of Portland, Oregon]. Available at: http://www.portlandonline.com/transportation/index.cfm?print=1&a=295488&c=46210 [accessed: December 17, 2011].

City of Portland Office of the City Auditor. n.d.a. *Chapter 17.15.010 Transportation System Development Charge, Scope and Purposes* [Online: City of Portland, Oregon]. Available at: http://www.portlandonline.com/auditor/index.cfm?c=28848#cid_242165 [accessed: March 11, 2011].

City of Portland Office of the City Auditor. n.d.b. *Chapter 17.15.130 Transportation System Development Charge, Time Limit on Expenditure of SDCs* [Online: City of Portland, Oregon]. Available at: http://www.portlandonline.com/auditor/index.cfm?c=28848#cid_242165 [accessed: March 11, 2011].

City of Portland Office of the City Auditor. n.d.c. *Chapter 17.15.100 Transportation System Development Charge, Dedicated Account and Appropriate Use of Account* [Online: City of Portland, Oregon]. Available at: http://www.portlandonline.com/auditor/index.cfm?c=28848#cid_242165 [accessed: March 11, 2011].

City of Portland Office of the City Auditor. n.d.d. *Chapter 17.15.050 Transportation System Development Charge, Partial and Full Exemptions* [Online: City of Portland, Oregon]. Available at: http://www.portlandonline.com/auditor/index.cfm?c=28848#cid_242165 [accessed: March 11, 2011].

City of Portland Office of the City Auditor. n.d.e. *Chapter 17.15.040.A Transportation System Development Charge, Application* [Online: City of Portland, Oregon]. Available at: http://www.portlandonline.com/auditor/index.cfm?c=28848#cid_242165 [accessed: March 11, 2011].

City of Portland Office of the City Auditor. n.d.f. *Chapter 17.15.020.FF Transportation System Development Charge, Definitions* [Online: City of Portland, Oregon]. Available at: http://www.portlandonline.com/auditor/index. cfm?c=28848#cid_242165 [accessed: March 11, 2011].

City of Portland Office of the City Auditor. n.d.g. *Chapter 17.15.070 Transportation System Development Charge, Alternative Calculation for SDC Rate, Credit or Exemption* [Online: City of Portland, Oregon]. Available at: http://www. portlandonline.com/auditor/index.cfm?c=28848#cid_242165 [accessed: March 11, 2011].

City of Portland Office of the City Auditor. n.d.h. *Chapter 17.15.120 Transportation System Development Charge, City Review of SDC* [Online: City of Portland, Oregon]. Available at: http://www.portlandonline.com/auditor/index.cfm?c= 28848#cid_242165 [accessed: March 11, 2011].

City of Portland Office of Transportation. n.d.a. *Transportation SDC Fact Sheet* [Online: Portland Transport]. Available at: http://portlandtransport.com/ documents/tsdc_fact_sheet.pdf, p. 1 [accessed: March 11, 2011].

City of Portland Office of Transportation. n.d.b. *Update of Transportation System Development Charges* [Online: City of Portland, Oregon]. Available at: http:// www.portlandonline.com/transportation/index.cfm?c=46210&a=313028 [accessed: March 11, 2011].

Samdahl, D. 2008. *Multi-Modal Impact Fees*, ITE 2008 Annual Meeting and Exhibit. Compendium of Technical Papers [Online: ITE Western District]. Available at: http://www.westernite.org/Sections/washington/newsletters/Sam dahl%20multimodal%20impact%20fees.pdf [accessed: March 11, 2011].

State of Oregon. 2009. *State code § 223.297* [Online: Oregon State Legislature]. Available at: http://www.leg.state.or.us/ors/223.html [accessed: March 11, 2011].

Transit Concurrency Fee, Broward County, FL

Broward County. n.d.a. *Traffic Concurrency* [Online: Welcome to Broward County]. Available at: http://www.broward.org/Regulation/Development/ Pages/TrafficConcurrency.aspx [accessed: March 24, 2011].

Broward County. n.d.b. *2006–2010 Broward County Capital Budget* [Online: Welcome to Broward County]. Available at: http://www.co.broward.fl.us/ Budget/2006/Documents/Adopted/05otherfundtransitprojects.pdf [accessed: March 24, 2011].

Broward County. n.d.c. *Transit Concurrency System* [Online: Welcome to Broward County]. Available at: http://www.broward.org/Regulation/Development/ Documents/dmi00158.pdf [accessed: March 24, 2011].

Broward County. n.d.d. *Impact Fees* [Online: Welcome to Broward County]. Available at: http://www.broward.org/Regulation/Development/Pages/impact fees.aspx [accessed: March 24, 2011].

Broward County Planning Services Division. n.d. *Transit Oriented Development: The Broward County Experience* [Online: Florida Transit-Oriented Development]. Available at: http://www.floridatod.com/docs/Workshops/080328_FtLauderdale/TODBrowardExp.pdf [accessed: March 24, 2011].

Broward County Transit. n.d. *Broward County Transit FY 2011 Transit Development Plan (TDP) Annual Update* [Online: Welcome to Broward County]. Available at: http://www.broward.org/BCT/Documents/BCTFY2011.pdf [accessed: March 24, 2011].

Broward Metropolitan Planning Organization. n.d. *Transportation Concurrency – Broward County, Florida* [Online: Florida Department of Economic Opportunity]. Available at: http://www.dca.state.fl.us/fdcp/dcp/gmw/2009/StuartTransportation.pdf [accessed: March 24, 2011].

Ferrell, C. and Mathur, S. 2012. *The Influence of Neighborhood Crime on Mode Choice.* Transportation Research Record, 2320: 55–63.

Florida Department of Economic Opportunity. n.d. *Transportation Planning.* http://www.floridajobs.org/community-planning-and-development/programs/technical-assistance/planning-initiatives/infrastructure-planning/transportation-planning [accessed: January 9, 2013].

Smith, G.C. 2008. *Legal Research Digest 28: Use of Fees or Alternatives to Fund Transit.* Washington, DC: Transportation Research Board [Online: Transportation Research Board]. Available at: http://onlinepubs.trb.org/onlinepubs/tcrp/tcrp_lrd_28.pdf [accessed: January 9, 2013].

State of Florida Department of Community Affairs. 2006. *Transportation Concurrency Requirements and Best Practices: Guidelines for Developing and Maintaining an Effective Transportation Concurrency Management System* [Online: CUTR—Center for Urban Transportation Research]. Available at: http://www.cutr.usf.edu/pdf/TCBP%20Final%20Report.pdf [accessed: March 24, 2011].

Transit Impact Development Fee, San Francisco, CA

Brisson, L. 2008. *A Local Funding Mechanism For Chapel Hill: Transit Impact Fees* [Online: Carolina Digital Repository]. Available at: https://cdr.lib.unc.edu/record;jsessionid=BEC314EF688A9F60B7767856EE60EA0B?id=uuid%3A7d621ae5-c78b-4ee1-a0f8-70b3483e7a20 [accessed: December 20, 2011].

City and County of San Francisco. 2008. *Citywide Development Impact Fee Study* [Online: City & County of San Francisco Office of the Controller]. Available at: http://www.sfcontroller.org/ftp/uploadedfiles/controller/Final_Full_Report.pdf [accessed: December 21, 2011].

City of San Francisco. n.d. *San Francisco Planning Code Article 4: Development Impact Fees and Project Requirements that Authorize the Payments of In-lieu Fees* [Online: American Legal Publishing Corporation]. http://www.amlegal.com/

nxt/gateway.dll?f=templates&fn=default.htm&vid=amlegal:sanfrancisco_ca [accessed: December 17, 2011].

Cummins, C. Strong Demand for Office Sector. *The Sydney Morning Herald*, September 14, 2011. Available at: http://www.smh.com.au/business/strong-demand-for-officesector-20110913–1k7j2.html [accessed: September 18, 2011].

Mullen, C. 2011. *State Impact Fee Enabling Acts.* Austin, TX: Duncan Associates [Online: impact fees.com]. Available at: http://www.impactfees.com/public ations%20pdf/state_enabling_acts.pdf [accessed: September 25, 2011].

Price Waterhouse. 1998. *Funding Strategies for Public Transportation, Volume 2 Casebook*. Transit Cooperative Research Program, Report 31, Washington DC: Transportation Research Board National Academy Press [Online: Reconnecting America]. Available at: http://www.reconnectingame rica.org/assets/Uploads/bestpractice093.pdf [accessed: January 9, 2013].

Russ Building Partnership v. City and County of San Francisco. 1987 [Online: impact fees.com]. Available at: http://www.impactfees.com/caselaw_pdf/ RUSS.pdf [accessed: September 11, 2011].

San Francisco County Transportation Authority (SFCTA). 2009. *Memorandum: Recommend Approval of the MOU for the Transportation Nexus Study* [Online: San Francisco County Transportation Authority]. Available at: http://www. sfcta.org/images/stories/Executive/Meetings/finance/2009/feb10/Nexus%20 Study%20Finance%20Memo.pdf [accessed: December 20, 2011].

San Francisco Municipal Transportation Agency (SFMTA). 2006. *FY2007 Proposed Budget* [Online: San Francisco Municipal Transportation Agency]. Available at: http://www.sfmta.com/cms/rbudget/documents/FY2007Approved BudgetBook_v6.pdf [accessed: January 9, 2013].

SFMTA. n.d.a. *Transit Impact Development Fee (TIDF) and Office Space Development Fee (OSDF)* [Online: San Francisco Municipal Transportation Agency]. Available at: http://www.sfmta.com/cms/aprocurement/tidfosdfindx. htm [accessed: September 11, 2011].

SFMTA. n.d.b. *About Us* [Online: San Francisco Municipal Transportation Agency]. Available at: http://www.sfmta.com/cms/ahome/indxabmu.htm [accessed: September 11, 2011].

Concluding Remarks

Evans-Cowley, J.S. et al. 2009. The Effect of Development Impact Fees on Housing Values. *Journal of Housing Research*, 18(2), 173–193.

Ihlanfeldt, K.R. and Shaughnessy, T.M. 2004. An Empirical Investigation of the Effect of Impact Fees on Housing and Land Markets. *Regional Science and Urban Economics*, 34, 639–661.

Mathur, S., Waddell, P. and Blanco, H. 2004. Effect of Impact Fees on Price of New Single Family Housing. *Urban Studies*, 41(7), 1303–1312.

Mathur, S. 2013. Do All Impact Fees Affect Housing Prices the Same? *Journal of Planning Education and Research*, 33(4), 442–455.

Mathur, S. 2007. Do Impact Fees Raise the Price of Existing Housing? *Housing Policy Debate*, 18(4), 635–659.

Chapter 9
Application of Case Study Findings

This chapter begins by briefly summarizing the key findings of chapters 5 through 8. Next, it presents a comparative assessment of the suitability of each of the four VC mechanisms with the aim of developing a decision-support matrix that can be used by public transportation policy makers and professionals as they deliberate the suitability of one or a combination of VC mechanisms to meet their project-specific needs. Finally, by developing realistic scenarios that simulate real-world legal, political, policy and project-specific contexts, the chapter operationalizes the decision-support matrix.

Key Findings from the Property Value Capture Case Studies

Impact Fees

Enabling environment
The impact-fees cases analyzed in this book (San Francisco TIDF, Broward County transit concurrency fee, and Portland TSDC) indicate the usefulness of state-level acts and local-level ordinances enabling the use of impact fees (the case-analysis findings are summarized in Table 9.1, p. 182). These acts and ordinances specify the projects and expense types eligible for impact-fees funding. Several states do not allow impact fees to fund transit, while some (such as Oregon) allow impact fees to fund only capital expenditures. Furthermore, strong and unambiguous legal provisions, accompanied by a robust nexus study, defend the fees in case of lawsuits. In summary, there is a strong need for an appropriate legal enabling environment.

Institutional capacity
All three cases demonstrate the need for moderate institutional capacity to design and charge impact fees. Institutional capacity is also frequently required to convince the political leadership and the community (especially the developer community) about the need for a transit impact fee.

Stakeholder support
Of the four major stakeholder groups—residents, the business community, developers, and public agencies—the developer community is most likely to be concerned about transit impact fees. This concern was evident in San Francisco, where in 2010, developers were allowed to defer impact-fee payments for three

years. In summary, local governments can expect a moderate level of stakeholder opposition to transit impact fees, primarily from the developer community.

Revenue yield
In Portland's TSDC—the best-case scenario—the fee is expected to fund 25 percent of all transit projects' capital cost over the next 10 years. This translates into funding 100 percent of the cost attributable to new growth. Broward County's transit concurrency fee is expected to fund 17 percent of the capital costs for FY 2011. This percentage would be even higher if only cost attributable to new growth is considered. In San Francisco, although the impact fee traditionally generates approximately $4 million to $5 million annually, it constitutes less than two percent of the transit-agency budget.

An impact-fee revenue yield is dependent upon its geographical and property-development base. For example, the San Francisco TIDF was initially charged only in the downtown area but was later expanded citywide. Currently, almost all property types pay impact fees in San Francisco, except for government-owned buildings and properties within specific redevelopment areas. Broward County goes one step further by not exempting any properties. Similarly, apart from a few exceptions (such as affordable-housing developments), all properties pay the fee in Portland.

In summary, transit impact fees meet varying proportions of transit-funding needs, from all (in the case of Portland and Broward County) to moderate (in the case of San Francisco).

Revenue stability
The revenues from impact fees are likely to grow under the following scenarios: (1) the fee rate increases; (2) the magnitude of property development/ redevelopment/expansion increases; and (3) the fee base (the geographical area or the fee-paying property-development types) increases. The case study findings show that real estate market conditions greatly affect the probability of realization of any of these scenarios or combinations of them.

In the cases of Broward County and Portland, the fee amount peaked at a little more than $10 million by the middle of the last decade before plummeting to $2 million by the end of the decade. The real estate downturn led San Francisco to institute a TIDF deferral program in 2010. Annual revenue fell from an average of between $4 million and $5 million to $2 million.

The case studies also suggest a few strategies to enable revenue growth. For example, San Francisco conducts periodic fee review to ascertain whether the fee meets the transit funding requirement. Its fee is also CPI-adjusted and therefore increases with inflation.

In summary, impact-fees revenues display low to moderate stability in the cases analyzed for this report. Jurisdictions with a consistently strong real estate market and ample greenfield or in-fill development opportunities are likely to see strong revenue growth and low volatility.

Potential for horizontal inequity

The potential for horizontally inequitable impact fees is low to moderate in all the cases analyzed. In Broward County, the fee is levied in the eight districts where transit is a viable transportation mode, while impact fees are charged citywide in San Francisco and Portland because the fee revenues fund transit service citywide.

In all the cases, the fee rate varies by property type. This variation reflects the properties' differing transit impacts. For example a 1,000-square-foot industrial warehouse is likely to generate fewer transit riders than a similar-sized office building.

Horizontal equity is negatively impacted in San Francisco, where residential developments are exempt from paying the fee. It is highly unlikely that residential developments do not generate any transit riders. In fact, recent efforts in the city are aimed at expanding the fee to include residential developments. Similarly, exempting public buildings from paying the fee (as is the case in Portland) also impacts horizontal equity.

Potential for vertical inequity

The ability-to-pay (ATP) principle operationalizes vertical equity. The potential for application of vertically inequitable impact fees is low to moderate in all four cases. Users with low ATP (such as Portland residents living in affordable housing developments and small-business owners in San Francisco) are exempt from paying the fee. However, Broward County does not provide such exemptions.

Finally, in two cases (Broward County and Portland), the fee paid by residential properties is charged on a per-housing-unit basis. Impact fees based on number of bedrooms or per square foot of living space would be more vertically equitable. The ATP of a household living in a one-bedroom condominium is clearly likely to be less than that of a household living in a five-bedroom mansion. The findings of the case analyses are summarized in Table 9.1 (p. 182).

Tax Increment Financing

Enabling environment

All the states except Arizona have TIF-enabling legislation.[1] Most states require the finding of "blight" for TIF use, although some interpret the condition more liberally than others. Vermont has the most liberal legislation, allowing TIF to be used for development, job creation, or even simply to increase tax revenue. However, the mere presence of state-enabling legislation is often not sufficient. Some legislation, like Oregon's, specify permissible uses for TIF funds. Therefore, the enabling legislation should be closely examined to ascertain whether such a list exists and, if so, whether transit is included.

---

1   Effective February 1, 2012, RDAs, the agencies in charge of TIF, were dissolved in California. The TIF legislation is still in place.

Innovation in Public Transport Finance

Table 9.1   Impact fees case-analyses findings

Cases	Case study comparison criteria	Existence of enabling env.	Existence of inst. capacity	Resident opposition	Business community opposition	Developer community opposition	Other public agency opposition	Revenue yield	Revenue stability	Potential for horizontal inequity	Potential for vertical inequity
San Francisco, CA		Black	Grey	White	White	Grey	White	Grey	Grey	Grey	White
Broward County, FL		Black	Grey	White	White	White	White	Black	White	White	Grey
Portland, OR		Black	Grey	White	White	Grey	White	Black	White	White	White

Note: Black = High; Grey = Moderate; White = Low/none.

Institutional capacity

All the cases of TIF use examined in this book (CCC Transit Village, Wilson Yard and Portland Streetcar) demonstrate the existence of and need for significant institutional capacity to plan and create a TIF district. Institutional capacity may also be required to garner the support of the community and public agencies at the time of TIF-district formation. Finally, institutional capacity is required to track TIF usage for legal-compliance purposes. For example, none of the three cases used TIF funds to purchase rolling stock, as it was unclear whether a capital expenditure for items that are mobile (and hence likely to cut across TIF district boundaries) would be permissible under the TIF-enabling regulations.

Ample institutional capacity exists in the case study cities and county. The Contra Costa County Redevelopment Agency is in charge of TIF in Contra Costa County, the PDC in Portland, and the Housing and Economic Development Department in Chicago.

Stakeholder support

Of the four major stakeholder groups, residents and other public agencies are most likely to oppose TIF. The surrounding community opposed TIF use in the CCC Transit Village and the Portland Streetcar Project. None of the cases faced opposition from other public agencies or local governments.

In the case of CCC Transit Village, a civil Grand Jury recommended that the redevelopment agency should not get involved with the project, citing agency indebtedness and opposition from neighborhood residents as the primary reasons. The Grand Jury noted that the redevelopment agency was interpreting its powers "liberally" by working with the transit agency (BART) to pay for construction of a garage (Contra Costa County, n.d.).

In Portland, residents living outside the underdeveloped North Macadam URA were initially concerned that their funds would be used to subsidize it. However, the city was able to address this concern by creating the North Macadam Overlay. The overlay helped specify the geography where the URA funds would be expended.

In summary, the local governments in the case studies were met with low to moderate stakeholder opposition to TIF.

Revenue yield

In the best-case scenario, the Portland Streetcar Project, more than half of the TIF districts' revenues were used. TIF funded approximately one-fifth of the total $103.5 million project cost. In the case of the CCC Transit Village, TIF funds ($60 million) constituted the entire public contribution and one-sixth of the entire $366 million project cost. Finally, TIF revenues of $3 million are earmarked for Wilson Yard Station renovation. In summary, TIF funded a moderate proportion of the case-study transit-project costs.

Revenue stability

TIF revenues depend upon property taxes, which in turn are impacted by real estate market conditions, the intensity of redevelopment of the TIF district, and the effectiveness of the redevelopment projects in improving the quality of the TIF district.

While the TIF revenues are very stable in the CCC Transit Village and Wilson Yard, the TIF districts involved in funding the Portland Streetcar have been impacted by the housing market downturn. This downturn is pronounced in the North Macadam and River districts, where condominiums constitute a large portion of the new development. In summary, TIF revenues in the case studies display a moderate to high degree of stability.

Potential for horizontal inequity

TIF can cause horizontal inequity in two ways. First, horizontal inequity can result if the TIF-funded improvements do not accrue benefits to property owners within the TIF district. The potential for horizontal inequity for this reason is low in all three case-study projects. All of the projects benefit the property owners within the districts, even the CCC Transit Village, where the benefits from the BART parking garage spill outside the district. In this case, creation of the parking garage was a prerequisite to the development of the village, which has benefited the surrounding property owners by providing much-needed vibrancy to the area (Kennedy, 2008). The surrounding community benefits from the TIF-funded renovation of the Wilson Yard Station as well.

Second, to the extent that property taxes would have increased even without the use of TIF, the capture of the full property-tax increment by the TIF district results in less tax revenues for other taxing agencies, such as the school district, county, or city. Thus, TIF can negatively impact other essential services. Although I do not have pre-TIF-district empirical data for the case-study projects, anecdotal evidence suggests that at least one project, the Portland Streetcar—was key to its district's revival. Therefore, it is highly unlikely that property taxes within this district would have increased without the use of TIF.

Potential for vertical inequity
TIF use for transit enhances vertical equity to the extent that the transit projects benefit lower-income people more than higher-income people. However, TIF can cause vertical inequity if housing prices in the TIF district rise as a result of TIF investment, pricing out residents with low ATP. Therefore, it is advisable to mitigate the housing price impacts on the existing residents. The TIF district for the CCC Transit Village addresses this potential vertical inequity be apportioning 20 percent of the TIF revenues for affordable housing.

The findings of the case analyses are summarized in Table 9.2 (p. 185).

Special Assessment Districts

Enabling legal environment
State-level SAD-enabling legislation exists in the cases of the Seattle Streetcar, Portland Streetcar, and Los Angeles Red Line. The powers granted by the state-level legislation are often operationalized through local ordinances. For example, in Seattle, the City Council passed a local ordinance (No. 122424) authorizing the activities required to finance, construct, and maintain the streetcar project. Similarly, the District of Columbia Home Rule Act provides the authority to levy special assessments. This authority is operationalized through the New York Avenue Metro Special Assessment Authorization Emergency Act of 2001. In summary, a robust legal enabling environment is required for SAD formation.

Institutional capacity
All the case studies demonstrate the need for significant institutional capacity to plan, form, and manage SADs and to garner community support. For example, Action 29 proactively advocated for the New York Avenue Metro Station. In addition to holding several community meetings, the group raised substantial funds. The city did not initially have adequate financial and analytical capacity, and as a result, when the landowners offered $25 million for station construction, the city was unable to recognize the possibility of negotiating a higher contribution. In summary, while the institutional capacity required to use SADs may not be as great as the capacity required to use TIF, it is still substantial.

Stakeholder support
Of the four major stakeholder groups, residents are most likely to oppose SADs. In principle, any property owner (residential or non-residential) could oppose SAD if

Table 9.2   TIF case-analyses findings

Cases	Case study comparison criteria	Existence of enabling env.	Existence of inst. capacity	Resident opposition	Business community opposition	Developer community opposition	Other public agency opposition	Revenue yield	Revenue stability	Potential for horizontal inequity	Potential for vertical inequity
Contra Costa Centre, CA		Black	Black	Grey	White	White	White	Grey	Black	Grey	White
Streetcar Project, Portland, OR		Black	Black	Grey	White	White	White	Grey	Grey	White	Grey
Wilson Station, Chicago, IL		Black	Black	Grey	White	White	White	Black	Grey	Grey	Grey

Note: Black = High; Grey = Moderate; White = Low/none.

s/he believes that the benefits from the transit project are less than the assessments charged. However, the case analyses show that non-residential property owners are likely to appreciate the benefits of transit projects. In fact, the owners of brown-field industrial land championed construction of the New York Avenue Metro Station, and the business community welcomed Portland Streetcar.

Some property owners initially opposed the SAD for the Seattle Streetcar Project, and several SADs formed to fund Portland Streetcar exempted residential property owners from paying assessments in order to preempt opposition from them.

Several states require majority property-owner vote for SAD formation. Therefore, local governments considering SAD as a transit funding source must first examine their state and local legislation, and if such a vote is required, they can decide to not use SAD in a largely residential neighborhood, to conduct extensive community outreach to sense the resident sentiment toward a SAD, or simply to exempt residential properties from paying assessments. However, equity considerations and project funding needs should weigh in the decision to exempt properties from paying assessments.

Revenue yield
SADs funded substantial project cost in all four cases analyzed here. The Seattle Streetcar SAD, estimated to generate $25.7 million, would fund more than half (51.71 percent) of the project. The SADs for the New York Avenue Metro Station

and Portland Streetcar would fund one-quarter and one-fifth of the project costs, respectively. Finally, although they funded only nine percent of the project cost, SADs for Los Angeles Red Line Segment 1 led all four cases in terms of actual revenue, generating $130 million.

In summary, a SAD can be expected to generate large sums of revenue for transit projects. However, as a proportion of project cost, SAD revenues might fund a small part of capital-intensive transit projects, such as heavy-rail projects.

Revenue stability

SAD revenues are highly stable. Usually determined at the time of the SAD formation, the assessments are either collected up front (as in the cases of Portland Streetcar and Seattle Streetcar and the Los Angeles Red Line) or collected annually (as in the case of the New York Avenue Metro Station).

In all four cases, the revenues have been collected according to the schedule. Indeed, the SADs for the Los Angeles Red Line were dissolved after they lasted their predetermined period and generated the required revenue. In cases where the assessments are to be paid over a long period (usually 15 to 30 years), property owners could advocate for lower assessments, thereby making revenue growth a little volatile.

Potential for horizontal inequity

The assessment-fee calculation and collection methodology needs to be carefully designed to reduce horizontal inequities. Of the cases examined for this report, Seattle's assessment calculation methodology ensures the greatest horizontal equity, as it bases assessments on the estimated benefit derived by each property. A less-sophisticated methodology was adopted in Portland, where gross indicators such as parcel size, value, property use, and proximity to transit are employed as proxies for the potential benefit derived by the properties. Still simpler methodologies are used for the Los Angeles Red Line and the New York Avenue Station. In the former, the parcel and building size are used to determine the benefit, and in the latter, the year 2000 assessed property value is used.

Apart from the SAD for Seattle Streetcar and a few SADs for Portland Streetcar, the SADs exempt residential properties from paying assessments. Moreover, public buildings are commonly exempt. To the extent that residential and public properties benefit from transit infrastructure, such exemptions cause horizontal inequities.

In summary, all properties that benefit from the transit infrastructure should, ideally, pay assessments, and the assessments should be based upon the benefit received by each property. Less-sophisticated methodologies leave room for horizontal inequities.

Potential for vertical inequity

The potential for vertical inequity is low to moderate in all the cases analyzed. In Seattle, users with low ATP, such as qualifying senior citizens, are exempt from

Table 9.3   SAD case-analyses findings

Cases	Case study comparison criteria	Existence of enabling env.	Existence of inst. capacity	Resident opposition	Business community opposition	Developer community opposition	Other public agency opposition	Revenue yield	Revenue stability	Potential for horizontal inequity	Potential for vertical inequity
Seattle Streetcar		Black	Grey	Grey	White	White	White	Black	Black	White	White
LA Metro Red Line		Grey	Grey	White	White	White	White	Black	Black	Grey	Grey
Portland Streetcar		Grey	Grey	White	White	White	White	Black	Black	Grey	Grey
NY Avenue Metro Station		Black	White	White	White	White	White	Black	Black	Grey	White

Note: Black = High; Grey = Moderate; White = Low/none.

paying assessments, and other qualifying low-income property owners can defer payments for four to five years. Similarly, in the cases of Portland Streetcar and the Los Angeles Red Line, property owners have the option of paying assessments over an extended period (5 or 17 years in the Los Angeles Red Line case, and 5-, 10-, or 20 years in the Portland Streetcar case) at a reasonable interest rate that often equals the rate of interest paid by the local government on long-term borrowing. Finally, exempting smaller properties enhances vertical equity to the extent that the owners are likely to have lower ATP than the owners of larger properties. In the case of the New York Avenue Station SAD, properties smaller than 10,000 square feet in area are exempt from paying assessments.

The findings of the case analyses are summarized in Table 9.3 (above).

Joint Development

Enabling legal environment
While state- or local-level enabling legislation may not be mandatory to undertake joint development, a clear policy framework is helpful. At the minimum, a DDA forms the legal basis for joint development. For example, a DDA and the creation of a JPA formed the enabling framework for the CCC Transit Village joint development. WMATA and MDT have a long history of coordinating frameworks to guide joint development. WMATA has developed joint development guidelines, whereas local ordinances and a county comprehensive plan provide the guiding framework for MDT. Recently developed TOD guidelines provide a similar policy framework for MARTA.

Institutional capacity

All the cases analyzed—WMATA's Bethesda Metro joint development, MDT's Dadeland South Station joint development, Contra Costa County's CCC Transit Village, and MARTA's Resurgens Plaza—demonstrate the need for significant local-government/transit-agency institutional capacity to conceptualize, plan, create, and manage joint developments. Except for some extent in the case of MARTA, the local governments in the cases had the requisite institutional capacity at the time of joint development construction. Furthermore, project finance and real estate development expertise are critical to negotiate joint development terms, especially the lease structure. The lack of such expertise in the case of MARTA led to simple lease structure that favors private developers.

Stakeholder support

Of the four major stakeholder groups, residents are most likely to oppose joint developments. They may fear that joint developments will increase traffic congestion and air/noise pollution and will change the character of the neighborhood.

Resident opposition is well-documented in the case of CCC Transit Village and suspected in the case of Resurgens Plaza. In fact, resident opposition held-up development of CCC Transit Village for nearly two decades before a design charrette process finally drew consensus among the community. The residential neighborhood to the south of Resurgens Plaza is suspected of having opposed the joint development (Ted Tarantino and Jason Ward, interview by Shishir Mathur, December 6, 2011).

Revenue yield and stability

The revenue yield from joint development projects can vary widely. For example, CCC Transit Village is estimated to yield approximately $700 million to $1 billion over 100 years, providing the local government a seven percent return on investment. Similarly, Bethesda generates $1.6 million annually for WMATA. However, the lease revenues from all WMATA joint developments (which totaled $10 million in 2010) constitute less than one percent of the agency's $1.4 billion annual operating budget.

In all cases, the public agency receives either minimum guaranteed revenue (Bethesda, Dadeland South, and CCC Transit Village) or CPI-adjusted fixed revenue (Resurgens Plaza). In two cases (Bethesda and Dadeland South), the transit agency also shares a percentage of the gross revenues. WMATA receives 7.5 percent of gross revenue when the annual revenue exceeds $31 million. MDT receives the higher of $300,000 (CPI-adjusted) or 4 percent of the gross revenue. Sharing of the gross revenues makes the lease revenue stream dependent upon economic conditions and therefore a little volatile. For example, the Dadeland South revenues peaked at $1.1 million in 2007 before falling to $900,000 in 2010.

In summary, transit agencies need to carefully analyze the magnitude of revenue sharing and minimum-guaranteed revenues before and during negotiating and structuring lease revenue agreements, and consideration should be given to other, non-fiscal policy objectives (such as revitalization of blighted neighborhoods and transit-ridership generation).

Potential for horizontal inequity
The horizontal-equity concern for joint development projects primarily revolves around whether the joint development agreement benefits the involved parties in proportion to their stake in the development and their risk. Viewed from this perspective, CCC Transit Village, Bethesda, and Dadeland South are highly equitable, while Resurgens Plaza does not seem to benefit the public agency in proportion to its stake in the development. However, it is important to note that the equity assessment should consider both fiscal (lease revenues) and non-fiscal (for example, neighborhood revitalization) benefits.

Potential for vertical inequity
The private developer is usually the entity that must either pay lease revenue to the public agency or share the construction and maintenance costs. Since the public agency and the private developer voluntarily agree to participate in the joint development process, they are unlikely to enter into a vertically inequitable agreement. Therefore, the potential for vertical inequity is low.

The findings of the case analyses are summarized in Table 9.4 (p. 190).

Key Case Study Findings

The key findings from this book's review of VC mechanisms-funded projects can be distilled into the following six: First, revenue yield from TIF and SADs is likely to be the highest among the four VC mechanisms reviewed in this book. Second, local governments often use a combination of two VC mechanisms—for example, TIF and SAD fund the Portland Central Streetcar Project; TIF and joint development fund CCC Transit Village. Third, the use of TIF requires significant institutional capacity, community support, and agreement among taxing agencies. Fourth, transit impact fees are rarely used. Their use benefits from state- and local-level enabling legislation, robust nexus studies, a strong real estate market, and developer support. Fifth, transit impact fees and SADs need to be carefully designed and implemented in order to minimize inequities. Finally, strong real estate markets, significant institutional capacity, and clear policy guidelines are needed to undertake joint development.

Decision-support Matrix

Table 9.5 (p. 191) codifies the findings from the cases analyzed and from the overview of VC. This information can provide some insights for decision makers who must choose one of the VC mechanisms or a combination of them.

In addition to the 10 comparison criteria discussed in tables 9.1 through 9.4, two criteria need to be considered when choosing a VC mechanism: (1) whether

Table 9.4   Joint development case-analyses findings

Cases	Case study comparison criteria	Existence of enabling env.	Existence of inst. capacity	Resident opposition	Business community opposition	Developer community opposition	Other public agency opposition	Revenue yield	Revenue stability	Potential for horizontal inequity	Potential for vertical inequity
Bethesda Metro Station joint dev'ment		■	■					▦	■		
Costa Contra Centre		■	■					■			
Dadeland South Station joint dev'ment		■	■					▦	▦		
Resurgens Plaza		■	▦	▦					■	▦	

Note: Black = High; Grey = Moderate; White = Low/none.

the transit infrastructure is to be provided in a new or an existing urban area and (2) the geographical size of the area that will benefit from the transit infrastructure. For example, while TIF is most commonly used to revitalize existing blighted urban areas (hence the "E" in column 3 of the TIF row in Table 9.5, p. 191), impact-fee revenues are expected to be substantial for newly urbanizing areas (hence the "N" in column 3 of the Impact-fees row).

The following simple scenarios illustrate application of the decision-support matrix.

Scenario 1: Light rail in inner-city
A city would like to develop a light-rail transit system to serve its automobile-oriented inner core. The inner core is largely non-residential and not blighted. The real estate market cannot be considered strong, although it is not very weak either. The state-level legislation allows TIF and impact-fee funding for transit. Furthermore, the city is making several efforts to retain existing office and commercial development in its inner core and is hesitant to put an additional financial burden on the non-residential property owners. The city does not have well-developed joint development guidelines but has undertaken a few such projects in the recent past.

Table 9.5   Decision-support matrix

Property value capture tool	New (N) or existing (E) development	Benefit area size	Existence of enabling env.	Existence of inst. capacity	Potential for resident opposition	Potential for business community opposition	Potential for developer community opposition	Potential for other public agency opposition	Revenue yield	Revenue stability	Potential for horizontal inequity	Potential for vertical inequity
Impact fees	N	M/L	Black	Grey	White	White	Black	White	Grey	Grey	Grey	Grey
TIF	E	M/L	Black	Black	Grey	White	White	Grey	Black	Black	White	Grey
SAD	N/E	M/L	Grey	Grey	Grey	White	White	White	Black	Black	Grey	Grey
Joint dev'ment	N/E	S/M/L	Grey	Black	Black	White	White	White	Grey	Black	Grey	White

Note: N = New; E = Existing; L = Large; M = Medium; S = Small; Black = High; Grey = Moderate; White = Low/none.

Application of decision support matrix

The legal environment and the large transit-benefit area allow use of all four VC mechanisms. However, the inner-core is already developed, the real estate market is not strong, and the city does not want to financially burden property owners. As a result, impact fees are neither likely to generate significant revenue nor to be politically feasible. Therefore, the city can choose one or a combination of the remaining mechanisms—TIF, SAD, and joint development. It might want to gauge property-owner support for SADs and TIF. If property owners are not opposed, then all the remaining VC mechanisms are available for use.

TIF and SADs are capable of generating revenues that can fund a moderate to large portion of the light-rail-system costs. Joint development can be used to generate additional revenue that can be used to fund station construction and increase station-area density. However, joint development alone cannot be a significant funding source for the entire transit system. The city might then want to assess whether other property-tax-supported agencies (such as the county government and the school district) are likely to oppose TIF. If strong opposition is likely, the city might want to go ahead with a SAD and joint development and air rights. However, if the opposition to TIF is weak or can be addressed (for example, by allowing other taxing governments a share of TIF revenue), then both TIF and SADs can be used as major funding sources (as was the case in the Portland Streetcar Project), with supplemental revenues generated from the joint development and air rights.

Scenario 2: Extension of the heavy rail line and construction of a transit station on undeveloped land at the periphery of an urban area

A regional transit agency would like to extend one of its five rail lines, called "orange line" and to construct a new station that would serve as the end-station for the orange line. The transit agency has no land use powers and has little influence over the station-area zoning. Ample undeveloped land is available and would be acquired for the construction of the rail line and the station. The state-level legislation allows TIF and impact-fee funding for transit. The TIF legislation requires the finding of blight. Further, the transit agency does not have well-developed joint development guidelines but has a large professional staff. The real estate market, though not very robust, is among the strongest in the region. Finally, although the surrounding area does not have large residential population, there are half a dozen large employers in the 1-mile radius of the station site.

Application of decision support matrix

The legal environment and the large transit-benefit area allow use of all four VC mechanisms. However, since the line and the station would be constructed on undeveloped land at the periphery of an urban area, the need for TIF to fight blight would be very difficult to establish. On the other hand, the need for transit impact fee can be easily established and the "rational nexus" and "rough proportionality" requirements can be met.

The transit agency would need to work closely with the city government under whose jurisdiction the rail line segment and the station fall. The close coordination with the city government would be required for the successful use of remaining three VC mechanisms, namely, for coordinating use of transit impact fee revenues for the rail line extension and station construction, delineating special assessment district, and joint development.

Concomitantly, the transit agency should open talks with the major employers around the proposed station to gauge their interest in contributing to the cost of the rail line and the station. If enough interest exists, the city and the transit agency should consider securing formal property owner approval for a SAD. Furthermore, the transit agency should consult with the city to re- and/or up-zone land around the proposed station. For example, land around quarter-mile of the station could be zoned for high-density mixed used (office, commercial and multi-family residential). This re-/up-zoning would help increase SAD and transit impact fee revenue, and stimulate developer interest in the station area. This developer interest could be harnessed to solicit joint development partners for the station construction. The joint development could include development of the station, the parking structure, retail and office space, and residential apartments. The retail should be carefully designed to attract the daily office commuters that would use the station. The apartments could be marketed to the employees working in the station-area vicinity, especially for the large employers in the 1-mile radius. These employees would gain from close proximity to work. The rail line would provide them access to the city.

Since a well-established real estate market does not exist in the station-area vicinity, while negotiating the parameters of the joint development agreement, the transit agency might have to bear substantial risk up-front, typically in the form of higher equity participation in the construction phase, and/or smaller minimum guaranteed lease revenue. In-lieu of higher up-front risk, the transit agency could negotiate a larger share of future lease revenue.

In summary, SAD and joint development could be major revenue sources with supplemental revenues generated from transit impact fees.

References

Contra Costa County (CCC). n.d. *Contra Costa County Grand Jury Report No. 0306*. Available at: http://www.saveelsobrante.com/GrandJurytimetore directredev0306rpt.htm [accessed: July 23, 2011].

Kennedy, J. 2008. *Building a Heart at Contra Costa Centre." Practices and Perspectives* [Online: Contra Costa Centre Transit Village]. Available at: http://centrepoints.org/pdf/BuildingAHeart.pdf [accessed: December 2, 2011].

Chapter 10

The Way Forward

In the US, the use of VC mechanisms to fund transit projects is currently limited by two major factors. First, it is difficult to determine which VC mechanism should be used for a particular transit project. Second, the use of VC mechanisms to fund transit projects is limited. For example, transit impact fees have been used rarely to fund transit projects.

The lack of precedence is a significant limitation because implementing certain VC mechanisms requires significant institutional capacity and a favorable enabling environment. For example, transit impact fees often require state- and local-level enabling legislation, robust nexus studies, a strong real estate market, and the support of real estate developers. The fees also must be carefully designed and implemented to minimize inequities. Because there is little history of using VC mechanisms to fund transit projects, a city that intends to charge transit impact fees might find very little guidance on how robust its nexus studies must be, or how it might garner the support of the real estate development community for the fees.

Below, we will first examine several ways to encourage the use of VC mechanisms to fund transit projects. Thereafter, we will conclude with a discussion of two key trends that should further incentivize use of VC mechanisms in the US in the long term.

Ways to Encourage Use of VC Mechanisms to Fund Transit Projects

First, there should be better information sharing about using VC mechanisms to fund transit projects (such as this book). The information sharing could occur at professional workshops and conferences, through internet-based media such as webinars and through conventional educational formats including professional degree programs that are likely to produce local government officials, such as programs in urban and regional planning, public affairs, and public administration.

Second, there should be a stronger consensus that VC mechanisms can be used to fund transit projects. For example, impact fees are not commonly used to fund public transportation, although they are used extensively for water, sewer, and automobile-related transportation projects such as roads, highways, and bridges (Nelson, Nicholas and Juergensmeyer, 2009; Smith, 2008). Indeed, a national review of transit impact fees shows that at least 14 states do not allow their usage, whereas 20 states have adopted legislation or have favorable court decisions to allow them. Of these 20 states, 15 allow transit impact fees through enabling statutes (Smith, 2008); in the remaining five states, courts have upheld the authorities of municipalities to charge impact fees, although, the courts have provided no opinion about the legality of their use specifically for transit projects in four of those cases. Similarly, although TIF has been used to fund several redevelopment and economic development projects across the US, its use to fund transit projects is not common. Finally, SADs have been used extensively to fund roads and could also be used to fund transit projects.

Third, institutional structures and incentives for local governments (city and county governments) must be developed to cooperate with the transit providers that are frequently regional agencies. This cooperation is critical because many VC mechanisms, such as TIF, joint development, impact fees, and assessment districts, are usually implemented by local governments. The local governments should pass on the revenues to transit agencies. Continuing with the impact fees example, these fees are paid by developers to local governments during the permit approval process. Moreover, local governments must approve the impact fee schedule. Therefore, although transit impact fee revenues must be used by the transit providers, the actual fee setting and collection are the responsibility of the local government. Therefore, unless the transit provider is a local government agency (for example a city's transportation department), institutional inertia must be overcome, and perhaps new cooperative arrangements must be devised to facilitate implementation of transit impact fees.

The level of coordination required for joint development is even higher because local governments are often required to coordinate their land use and zoning decisions with the provision of transit. For example, the area around transit stations, particularly within walking distance, should be zoned for higher density multi-family housing and office /commercial development to maximize transit ridership. Transit agencies typically do not have such land use and zoning powers, and, therefore, require local governments' cooperation to create transit-supportive incentives, land use, and zoning policies. Further, they rely on the local governments for incentives to stimulate private sector interest in real estate development in and around station areas. Such incentives might include density bonuses and expedited permit review process.

Fourth, local and regional governments in general, and transit agencies in particular, must develop a more inclusive view of transit provision. Such a view should consider property development in and around station areas as essential to the success of the transit system. Hong Kong's Rail+Property development model provides useful insights. However, developing such an inclusive view is not easy. One key reason is that real estate development in the US is largely the domain of private sector developers. Typically, local government and transit agency staff and elected officials do not see an active role for their organization in real estate development. Moreover, the government and transit agency staff are often torn between the social objectives and the purely economic/profit objectives of real estate development. A case in point is the Miami Dade County Board of Commissioners. Miami-Dade County, FL, recognized the need to coordinate land development and transit provision in the 1970s and implored their regional transit agency, MDT, to explore the use of joint development along transit lines. The county also allowed the transfer of zoning authority from the county to the MDT for land along transit lines (MDT, 1978). However, during the initial years, the County Commissioners were torn between whether the joint developments should be used for social purposes, such as affordable housing, or whether these projects should be developed to their highest and best use, which were typically office and commercial uses. I would argue that local governments need not see the joint development projects as a social obligation versus a pure profit maximization opportunity. Rather, they should use joint development projects as an opportunity to achieve both objectives; an option that over time Miami Dade County realized and acted upon. MDT currently has a mix of various types of joint developments at eight Metrorail stations. These developments include commercial office buildings, government office buildings, a hotel, retail development, market rate residential development and affordable residential development (MDT staff email communication, May 14, 2013). Furthermore, the joint development policy guidelines of the Metropolitan Atlanta Rapid Transit Authority's (MARTA) require 20 percent of development to consist of affordable housing for housing developments with more than 10 units (MARTA, 2010).

Fifth, local governments must view and use VC mechanisms as a way to leverage external funds. In the US, federal public transportation dollars often require cost sharing on a 60/40 or a 50/50 federal-local cost share basis. The application for seeking state and federal funds for a transportation project is stronger when evidence of local community support for the transportation project can be demonstrated. What better way to provide such evidence than by showing local support for the implementation of VC mechanisms to fund the transportation project? Indeed, the City of Portland, OR, used special assessments to fund a large portion of the Central Streetcar Project, and this revenue source demonstrated the local community support. This evidence of community support has been effective in leveraging federal and state investments (PDOT, 2006). The streetcar project received significant federal and state funding from the US Department of Housing and Urban Development, the Federal Transportation Fund, and Connect Oregon (PSI, 2010).

Sixth, local governments must harness existing institutional capacity to design and implement VC mechanisms. For example, a city's housing department staff examine income and cost proformas of proposed affordable housing developments and assess developers' capacity to undertake the projects as part of the feasibility analysis performed when proposed projects seek local government subsidies by means of grants and soft loan. Similarly, a city's economic development department might undertake a fiscal impact analysis to determine the level of incentives/subsidies that a city can afford to offer to attract private business. Furthermore, city staff would have the experience (and expertise) to negotiate with private developers and businesses, which are similar to the skills needed to design and implement VC mechanisms.

Next, I call for a more ambitious urban and regional development agenda, essentially a move from land use-transportation coordination to land development-transportation coordination. Whereas the present focus on land use-transportation coordination is a welcome advance over traditional planning systems in which transportation planning was often divorced entirely from land use planning, this advance does not go far enough.

For example, little actual benefit is realized if land zoned for multi-family housing and commercial use does not develop, or develops so much later or so much more slowly that the type of synergies envisioned through land use-transportation coordination do not materialize. For example, a city's land use plan might call for higher density uses along a transit corridor, but such density might take decades to develop in the absence of supporting policies. Meanwhile, in the absence of enough ridership, transit provision might be delayed, or the transit system might be severely under-utilized; such delays and under-utilization would also waste precious public transit dollars. Therefore, transit and land development need to be closely coordinated.

Finally, in the concluding section I note a couple of key trends that could further encourage the use of VC mechanisms in the US in the long term.

Key Trends that Favor Increased Use of VC Mechanisms in the Long Term

Two key trends favor increasing use of VC mechanisms to fund transit projects in the US. First, decreased federal funding and fiscal belt-tightening at all levels of government has required that transit agencies and municipalities aggressively explore alternative revenue sources to fund transit projects. Second, the increased emphasis on land use-transportation coordination—in particular the efforts to reduce VMT and thereby reduce GHG emissions—is likely to forge closer ties among transit agencies and local governments, and to further strengthen the link between federal transportation dollars and land use-transportation integration. Let's examine these two trends in greater detail.

Renewed Impetus to Identify New Revenue Sources for the Provision of Transit

The case studies reviewed for this book demonstrate that VC mechanisms may be able to provide significant revenues for transit projects that may otherwise lack funding in several cases. For example, SADs and TIF funded approximately 40 percent of Portland Streetcar and SADs alone funded more than half of Seattle Streetcar, and 17 percent of Broward County Transit's FY 2011 capital budget was funded by a transit concurrency fee (Broward County Transit, 2010). Finally, the use of SADs and joint development demonstrate the local interest in, and commitment to, transit projects that could help leverage other state and federal funds.

Buoyed by the promise of VC as a source of infrastructure finance, VC has increasingly caught the attention of transit providers and policy makers in the US and internationally over the last 5–10 years. At the national level, the United States Government Accountability Office (GAO) submitted a report in 2010 to the US House of Representatives Committee on Transportation and Infrastructure. This report documents the extent to which four VC mechanisms—joint development, special assessment districts, transit impact fees and tax increment financing—have assisted in funding transit projects across the US. The report also notes the barriers to the use of the VC mechanisms and suggests ways in which federal guidelines for joint development projects can be streamlined to allow federal aid for these projects (GAO, 2010). More recently, the Lincoln Institute of Land Policy, a Cambridge, MA-based research and advocacy organization, organized a conference in 2011 that explored the theoretical basis and practical applications of VC mechanisms in the US and internationally. Further, arguing for land value capture as the basis for "inclusionary housing," Mallach and Calavita (2010) note that governments help increase land values by zoning land for market-rate housing. Therefore, the governments should be able to recapture some of the land value increases by requiring the market-rate housing developments to provide a small percentage (usually 5 to 20 percent in the US) of housing units at below-market rate. Finally, paper and poster presentations and panel discussions in the 2012 annual conference of US-based urban and regional planning academicians, the Association of Collegiate Schools of Planning (ACSP) conference, significantly emphasized VC. Internationally, property value capture was recently discussed in many fora. These included the World Bank's 2012 annual conference on land and poverty and in the Bank's recent publications (for example, Dharmavaram, 2013).

A sprinkling of reports produced by university-based research organizations, consulting firms, and advocacy groups systematically explore the potential for VC mechanisms. For example, a 2009 report by the Center for Transportation Studies, University of Minnesota, surveys the potential of several VC mechanisms to fund infrastructure and services in Minnesota (Lari, et al. 2009). Similarly, a report by the Center for Transit-Oriented Development, an advocacy organization, provides a brief overview of use of TIF, SAD, joint development and impact fees to fund transit projects across the US (Fogarty, et al., 2008). Finally, a 2013 report by the US Environmental Protection Agency (EPA) offers case studies showing the use of VC mechanisms to fund transit-oriented developments (TODs) (EPA, 2013).

A few studies simulate the potential revenue yield from various VC mechanisms by focusing (typically) on a specific geography. For example, the Chicago Metropolitan Agency for Planning (CMAP) commissioned a study to explore VC funding for approximately 20 transit projects for which the agency was looking for new local revenue sources. The need for local revenue sources was reinforced by the Federal Transit Administration's (FTA) local match requirement for New Starts Funds. The FTA funds transit projects under this program; although the local match must be at least 20 percent, in practice, the local match needs to be 40–60 percent of the project cost to be nationally competitive. The study explored three VC funding options. The first option included the possibility of creating a transit special assessment district, the second included a TIF district, and the third included charging transit impact fees. The study simulations showed that a TIF district is likely to generate the most funds, followed by a SAD and the use of transit impact fee (CMAP, 2011).

Internationally, property value capture has been widely used as evidenced by the extensive use of land pooling and readjustment (LPR) in Europe and Asia, sale of development rights in Sao Paolo, Brazil, and Rail+Property development model to fund public transportation in Hong Kong (see Chapter 3 for a fuller discussion of these property value capture mechanisms). The interest in property value capture is increasing, buoyed by a large number of recent international empirical studies that find a positive property value impact of the accessibility provided by public transportation systems (for example, see Karanikolas and Louka, 2012; Ibeas, et al., 2012; Pagliara and Papa, 2011; Debrezion, Pels and Rietveld, 2011; Agostini and Palmucci, 2008).[1] Multilateral development agencies such as the World Bank are also helping. For example, transit agencies in India such as Hyderabad Metro Rail Limited (HMR) are exploring the use of property value capture tools to fund urban rail systems. HMR and the World Bank recently conducted a workshop to explore ways to use value capture to fund the Hyderabad metro rail (NewsWala, 2013). Similarly, the state of Gujarat is exploring the use of value capture, including levying assessment charges along the rail corridor, to fund a metro rail system in the Ahmedabad metropolitan region (GIDB, n.d.). Similar Chinese public agency interest in value capture is evidenced by the recent Nanchang Municipal Government and the World Bank joint workshop to discuss international best practices for the use of land value capture to fund transit (World Bank, 2013). Further, the United Nations Human Settlements Programme, UN-HABITAT, is promoting property value capture as a sustainable urban development finance mechanism. Through publications, workshops, and expert group meetings, UN-HABITAT is helping developing countries build capacity for using property value capture tools (for example, see UN-HABITAT, 2013). The interest in property value capture is likely to gain further momentum because many developing countries are currently in the process of improving their land and property records and levying property taxes, which are prerequisites for the use of sophisticated property value capture mechanisms such as tax increment financing.

Land Use–Transportation Integration

The earlier federal push for land use transportation integration—such as the federal transportation acts, including the ISTEA and TEA-21—was driven primarily by the desire to improve local air quality, provide multiple transportation options, and increase the vitality of inner cities; currently, climate change concerns have lent a new sense of urgency to the need for such integration.

1	See Chapter 2 for a fuller description of these studies.

As discussed in Chapter 1, the transportation sector is responsible for more than a quarter of the GHG emissions in the US and was responsible for almost half of the increase in such emissions between 1990 and 2010 (EPA, 2012). Carbon emissions from cars and light duty vehicles comprised 40 percent of all such transportation sector emissions globally in the year 2003 (Fung, Fung and Feng, 2006); the US contributed almost half of the global carbon emissions emanating from cars and light duty vehicles in that same year. Thus, the impact of vehicular emissions on local and regional air quality—and on global warming and climate change—has gained increased attention.

Among the states in the US, California has assumed a leadership role in reducing carbon emissions and is voluntarily developing initiatives to reduce GHG emissions. Specifically, the California Global Warming Solutions Act of 2006 (AB 32) seeks to reduce GHG emissions to 1990 levels by 2020 (CARB, 2009).

Mirroring national trends, the transportation sector in California is a major GHG emitter, accounting for 40 percent of all California's GHG emissions. Automobiles and light trucks contribute 75 percent of these emissions, or 30 percent of total GHG emissions (CSAC, 2009).

The state understands that its GHG reduction goals can only be met through significant reductions in vehicular GHG emissions. The state also realizes that VMT reduction through better land use-transportation integration is critical for meeting the GHG reduction goals of AB 32, although significant vehicular GHG reductions can be achieved through new vehicle technology and by the increased use of low carbon fuel, (SB 375, 2008). Therefore, in 2008 California passed Senate Bill 375 (SB 375), or the Sustainable Communities and Climate Protection Act of 2008. Using the authority granted under SB 375, the California Air Resource Board (CARB) has provided vehicular-GHG reduction targets to the state's 18 Metropolitan Planning Organizations (MPOs). For example, the San Francisco Bay Area region has been asked to reduce such emissions 7 percent by 2020 and 15 percent by 2035, relative to 2005 levels. Moreover, the region's MPO, the Metropolitan Transportation Commission (MTC) and its regional planning agency, the Association of Bay Area Governments (ABAG), have been assigned the joint responsibility of developing a long-range plan that integrates transportation and land-use/housing plans to meet state-wide vehicular GHG emissions reduction targets (OneBayArea, 2013a). In response, the MTC and ABAG—in partnership with the Bay Area Air Quality Management District (BAAQMD) and the Bay Conservation and Development Commission (BCDC)—have embarked on a joint initiative called One Bay Area and are in the process of developing a long range plan called Plan Bay Area. The draft plan that was released in March 2013 seeks to work with the region's counties and cities to promote compact mixed-use development and affordable housing near transit (OneBayArea, 2013b).

Pursuant to the One Bay Area initiative, jurisdictions may receive grants to incentivize development of housing near transit (OneBayArea, 2013c). To identify transit-proximate locations that are ideal for the provision of housing, Priority Development Areas (PDAs) have been identified throughout the region, and federal transportation dollars and other resources have been linked to the development of housing in the PDAs. Therefore, several cities in the region plan to develop (or are in the process of developing) TODs around transit stations in these PDAs. For example, San Jose, the largest city in the San Francisco Bay Area region, calls these developments "Urban Villages" and plans to develop several in its PDAs. To that end, the city is in the process of preparing master plans for several Urban Villages and is actively soliciting the interest of real estate developers in developing projects in the Urban Villages.

The above example from the San Francisco Bay Area region indicates that concerns about the impact of GHG emissions on climate change are incentivizing local governments in California to develop housing and mixed-use real estate development near and around transit stations; these same local governments are actively seeking private developers to undertake such projects. These concerns are also further encouraging MPOs to direct federal transportation dollars to transit and to link transit provision with the development of compact housing and mixed-use developments. Should these climate-change-led emerging trends from California spread to other parts of the country, we might expect a sharper focus on TODs and closer linkages between transit and property development; eventually, we might expect increased use of VC mechanisms to fund transit projects, such as joint development projects in and around transit station sites.

Conclusions

The increased federal interest in the development of transit is not matched by funding. Therefore, fiscally-constrained local governments are searching for additional sources to fund transit projects, including VC mechanisms. At present, VC mechanisms such as special assessment districts and impact fees are frequently used to fund road construction. However, they have not been employed frequently to fund transit projects for a variety of reasons discussed in this chapter and elsewhere in the book. I am cautiously optimistic that the increased focus on public transportation, combined with knowledge regarding the successful cases of VC-mechanism-funded transit projects, will encourage many more local jurisdictions to find ways to create legal, institutional, fiscal and physical environments that would support using VC mechanisms to fund transit projects.

References

Agostini, C.A. and Palmucci, G. A. 2008. The anticipated capitalisation effect of a new metro line on housing prices. *Fiscal Studies*, 29(2), 233–256.
Broward County Transit (BCT). 2010. *Broward County Transit FY 2011 Transit Development Plan* 15 *(TDP) Annual Update* [Online: Broward County].

Available at: http://www.broward.org/BCT/Documents/BCTFY2011.pdf [accessed: March 24, 2011].

California Air Resources Board (CARB). 2009. *Climate Change Scoping Plan: A Framework for Change*. Sacramento, CA: California Air Resources Board [Online: California Environmental Protection Agency: Air Resource Board]. Available at: http://www.arb.ca.gov/cc/scopingplan/document/adopted_scop ing_plan.pdf [accessed: August 29, 2012].

California State Association of Counties (CSAC). 2009. *SB 375 (Steinberg): Addressing Greenhouse Gas Emissions from the Transportation Sector via Regional Transportation Plans: CSAV Analysis*. Sacramento, CA: California State Association of Counties [Online: California Department of Transportation]. Available at: http://www.dot.ca.gov/hq/tpp/offices/orip/ sb375_files/csac.pdf [accessed: September 02, 2012].

Chicago Metropolitan Agency for Planning (CMAP). 2011. *Transportation Value Capture Analysis for the CMAP Region*. Chicago, IL: CMAP [Online: Chicago Metropolitan Agency for Planning]. Available at: http://www.cmap.illinois.gov /documents/20583/311292a4–4f6e-431e-b94e-032ff348ebe5 [accessed: April 3, 2013].

Debrezion, G., Pels, E. and Rietveld, P. 2011. The impact of rail transport on real estate prices: An empirical analysis of the Dutch housing market. *Urban Studies*, 48(5), 997–1015.

Dharmavaram, S. 2013. *Land value capture in urban DRM programs*. East Asia and the Pacific (EAP) Disaster Risk Management (DRM) knowledge notes working paper series; no. 26. Washington DC: World Bank [Online: World Bank]. Available at: http://documents.worldbank.org/curated/en/2013/07/18136410/ land-value-capture-urban-drm-programs [accessed: September 13, 2013].

Fogarty, N. et al. 2008. *Capturing the Value of Transit*. Center for Transit-Oriented Development. Available at: http://www.reconnectingamerica.org/assets/Up loads/ctodvalcapture110508v2.pdf [accessed: April 03, 2013].

Fung, J.D., Fung, F., and Feng, A. 2006. *Global Warming on the Road: The Climate Impact of America's Automobiles* [Online: Environmental Defense Fund]. Available at: http://www.edf.org/sites/default/files/5301_ Globalwarmingontheroad_0.pdf [accessed: September 1, 2012].

Gujarat Industrial Development Board (GIDB). n.d. *DPR for Ahemdabad Metro*. Available at: http://www.gidb.org/downloads/sectors/studyreports/urban/ah dmetro/14_Ch10b_Property_Dev.pdf [Online: Gujarat Industrial Develop ment Board]. [accessed: August 23, 2013].

Ibeas, A. et al. 2012. Modelling transport and real-estate values interactions in urban systems. *Journal of Transport Geography*, 24, 370–382.

Karanikolas, N. and Louka, E. 2012. The effects of metro station on commercial values of residential properties: The case study of Thessaloniki, Greece before the completion of the metro project constriction. *International Journal of Academic Research*, 4(2), 136–143.

Lari, A., et al. 2009. *Value Capture for Transportation Finance: Technical Research Report*. Minneapolis, MN: Center for Transportation Studies, University of Minnesota. Available at: http://www.cts.umn.edu/Publications/ ResearchReports/reportdetail.html?id=1802 [accessed: August 29, 2012].

Mallach, A. and Calavita, N. 2010. United States: From Radical Innovation to Mainstream Housing Policy, in *Inclusionary Housing in International Perspective*, edited by N. Calavita and A. Mallach. Cambridge, MA: Lincoln Institute of Land Policy, 15–77.

Metropolitan Atlanta Rapid Transit Authority (MARTA). 2010. *Policies for Implementing MARTA's TOD Guidelines* [Online: MARTA—Metropolitan Atlanta Rapid Transit Authority]. Available at: http://www.itsmarta.com/ TOD%20Guidelines%202010–11.pdf [accessed: August 31, 2011].

Miami-Dade County (MDC). 1978. *Fixed-Guideway Rapid Transit System-Development Zone, Miami-Dade County Code of Ordinances, Ord. No. 78-74, § 1, 10-17-78, Chapter 33C*. Available at: http://search.municode.com/ html/10620/level2/PTIIICOOR_CH33CFIIDRATRSYEVZO.html [accessed: December 5, 2011].

Nelson, A., Nicholas, J.C. and Julian C. Juergensmeyer. 2009. *Impact Fees: Principles and Practice of Proportionate-Share Development Fees*. Chicago, IL: American Planning Association.

NewsWala. 2013. *World Bank and Hyderabad Metro Rail Ltd (HMR) Conducts a Workshop on "Land value capture for Transit Oriented Development (TOD)"* [Online: NewsWala]. Available at: http://www.newswala.com/Hyderabad-News/World-Bank-and-Hyderabad-Metro-Rail-Ltd-HMR-conducts-a-workshop-on-Land-value-capture-for-Transit-Oriented-Development-TOD-38955.html [accessed: August 22, 2013].

OneBayArea. 2013a. *Frequently Asked Questions* [Online: OneBayArea]. Available at: http://onebayarea.org/about/faq.html [accessed: April 3, 2013].

OneBayArea. 2013b. *Housing and Jobs* [Online: OneBayArea]. Available at: http://www.onebayarea.org/regional-initiatives/plan-bay-area/plan-elements /Housing-and-Jobs.html [accessed: April 3, 2013].

OneBayArea. 2013c. *One Bay Area Grants* [Online: OneBayArea]. Available at: http://www.onebayarea.org/funding-and-grants.html [accessed: April 3, 2013].

Pagliara, F. and Papa, E. 2011. Urban Rail Systems Investments: An Analysis of the Impacts on Property Values and Residents' Location. *Journal of Transport Geography*, 19, 200–211.

Portland Department of Transportation (PDOT). 2006. *Transportation SDC Fact Sheet* [Online: Portland Transport]. Available at: http://portlandtransport.com/ documents/tsdc_fact_sheet.pdf [accessed: April 3, 2013].

Portland Streetcar, Inc. 2010. *Portland Streetcar Capital and Operations Funding* [Online: Portland Streetcar]. Available at: http://www.portlandstreetcar.org/ pdf/%20capital_and_operations_detail_20100908.pdf [accessed: July 17, 2011].

Senate Bill (SB) 375. 2008. *Senate Bill No. 375: Chapter 728* [Online: Official California Legislative Information]. Available at: http://www.leginfo.ca.gov/pub/07–08/bill/sen/sb_0351–0400/sb_375_bill_20080930_chaptered.pdf [accessed: April 3, 2013].

Smith, G.C. 2008. *Use of Fees or Alternatives to Fund Transit*. Legal Research Digest 28, Transit Cooperative Research Program, Washington, DC: Transportation Research Board [Online: Transportation Research Board]. Available at: http://onlinepubs.trb.org/onlinepubs/tcrp/tcrp_lrd_28.pdf [accessed: October 30, 2011].

The United Nations Human Settlements Programme (UN-HABITAT). 2013. *WUF7 Concept Note: Innovative Financing Instruments for Local Authorities* [Online: UN-HABITAT]. Available at: http://www.unhabitat.org/downloads/docs/WUF7_CN_Dialogue_4.pdf [accessed: December 10, 2013].

United States Environmental Protection Agency (EPA). 2013. *Infrastructure Financing Options for Transit-Oriented Development*. Washington, DC: EPA [Online: United States Environmental Protection Agency]. Available at: http://www.epa.gov/smartgrowth/pdf/2013–0122-TOD-infrastructure-financing-report.pdf [accessed: April 03, 2013].

United States Environmental Protection Agency (EPA). 2012. *Transportation and Climate: Basic Information*. Washington, DC: EPA [Online: United States Environmental Protection Agency]. Available at: http://www.epa.gov/otaq/climate/basicinfo.htm [accessed: September 1, 2012].

United States Government Accountability Office (GAO). 2010. *Public Transportation: Federal Role in Value Capture Strategies for Transit Is Limited, but Additional Guidance Could Help Clarify Policies*. Washington, DC: United States Government Accountability Office [Online: U.S. Government Accountability Office]. Available at: http://www.gao.gov/new.items/d10781.pdf [accessed: October 6, 2011].

World Bank. 2013. *Workshop in Nanchang Discusses Land Value Capture for Transit* [Online: World Bank]. Available at: http://www.worldbank.org/en/news/feature/2013/06/12/workshop-in-nanchang-discusses-land-value-capture-for-transit [accessed: August 20, 2013].

Index

enabling environment 159
exemptions 160
horizontal equity 160
institutional capacity 160
revenue 156
revenue yield, stability and growth 160
stakeholder support 159
vertical equity 160, 171

United States Government Accountability
Office (GAO) 12, 79, 199

vertical equity 15, 70, 73, 77, 92, 98, 103,
112, 117, 121, 134, 139, 147–8,
160, 164, 171, 173, 181, 184,
186–7; *see also* Ability-to-Pay
(ATP)

Washington, DC 1, 4, 11, 93, 95, 97, 104
110; *see also* New York Avenue
Metro Station; Washington
Metropolitan Area Transit Agency
(WMATA)
Washington Metro 79; *see also* WMATA
Washington Metropolitan Area Transit
Agency (WMATA) 80, 92–3, 94–8,
109–12, 122–3, 187–8
Wilson Yard Station 135–40, 182–3
case analysis 138
enabling environment 138
horizontal equity 139
institutional capacity 139
revenue yield, stability and growth 139
stakeholder support 139
vertical equity 139

For Product Safety Concerns and Information please contact our
EU representative GPSR@taylorandfrancis.com Taylor & Francis
Verlag GmbH, Kaufingerstraße 24, 80331 München, Germany